HEADS

HEADS

By Alex Kayser

With an afterword by Richard Howard

Abbeville Press • Publishers • New York • London • Paris

Designer: Howard Morris
Editor: Alan Axelrod
Production manager: Dana Cole

Published in the United States of America in 1985 by
Abbeville Press, Inc., New York.

Library of Congress Cataloging-in-Publication Data
Kayser, Alex.
Heads
1. Photography—Portraits. 2. Baldness—Pictorial works. I. Title.
TR681.B35K38 1985 779'.23'0924 85-6007
ISBN 0-89659-524-2

 The text of this book was set in Helvetica. Printed and bound in Japan.

First edition

10 9 8 7 6 5 4 3 2

CONTENTS

The Conversation 9

The Heads 14

The Afterword 122

FOR OTTO STEINERT

God created very few perfect heads. The other ones he gave hair.

—Anonymous

Alex Kayser: A Conversation with Lyn Mandelbaum and Alan Axelrod

LM: This book consists of one photograph, you said?

AK: Yes, 184 times the same picture. Only the faces change. There is a different person in every shot.

LM: Why doesn't anyone have hair?

AK: Some of them have no hair naturally, but most of them shave their heads daily.

AA: What in the world started you off on a project of photographing bald people?

AK: This book isn't about baldness. It has nothing to do with bald people. It has to do with faces, exposed faces. I wanted to eliminate hair in this series in order to deal solely with physiognomy. Hair would have been quite distracting.

LM: It really works. As a viewer, you go directly into the face, and you get lost in its features. This guy is great. Who is he?

AK: He's the vice president of a big steel company, and the one down here is the fourteen-year-old singer of a New Wave band. The people photographed come from just about every walk of life.

LM: This book is all headshots. Amazing. I never saw anything this sharp, this clear before.

AK: I tried to do an honest, straight series, not faking anything, not flattering, but analytic, if you like.

LM: For me, what makes the pictures so attractive *is* their directness. You get totally taken in by the subject. It's almost impossible to escape. But why isn't anybody smiling?

AK: Why isn't Michelangelo's *David* smiling? I tried to do physiognomy studies rather than portraits, which is why I tried to give them all the same neutral expression. Some of my naturally happy models I would ask to stop smiling. Others again I would try to relax. And many would sit down and be just right.

AA: You have enforced such uniformity, headshots framed exactly the same way, shot from the same angle with the same light, all the models without hair. They seem to be identical at first glance, because of their equal abstract quality.

AK: They were designed to work in a group, and not so much as individual pictures. Their identical design was necessary, much as bricks have to be the same size to build a house. If every picture element that you can control is the same, the differences are solely in the faces. That's why the individual physiognomy and character come through so strongly.

AA: How did you find all these people?

AK: Some I saw on television or in the *New York Times*. Others I met in the street, at a club, or restaurant. One day, looking through my window, I noticed this nice guy, he's a sanitation man. He was down there with his huge truck, picking up garbage across the street. My assistant ran down after him to say hello and tell him about our project.

LM: What did he say?

AK: He was delighted with the idea of being photographed and came to the studio a few days later during his lunch break. But most of the people in *Heads* I did not discover myself. My friends and all the other people who frequent my studio during the week always had the greatest ideas and suggestions. They would go: "Oh, you should get my neighbor from the third floor." Or, "My hairdresser has such a beautiful head." And, "You have to get the lawyer of my company." Everybody seemed to know somebody he thought was just right for the series, and I was really amazed to find people so enthusiastic, almost passionate to contribute something to that work. Without them, this book would not be here.

LM: Did you photograph everyone who was sent to you?

AK: Yes. The only requirement was that they have no hair. For the rest, I felt quite comfortable with Warhol's "everything is beautiful" principle. So I worked with everybody who was recommended to me, and one day I ended up having 250 pictures.

LM: Are they all going to be in the book?

AK: I hoped they would be, but then we had to cut the number down to 184 to make the book work.

AA: How did you decide, then, who was going to be in the book?

AK: This was simply a mathematical decision, and not an aesthetic or even personal one. It was hard, though, since these pictures are all the same in any of their qualities. I felt like I wanted to pick and choose with closed eyes.

LM: But, as an artist and photographer, didn't you get bored doing the same kind of shot over and over again?

AK: One would think so, but I could still do more. Originally, I had planned to do a series of twelve, maybe twenty heads. But then the response I got from people, their suggestions and introductions, was so overwhelming that I just went on with it. Also, since I was making groups out of the individual pictures, I would always need another particular face to match the one of Duane, Bill, or Annie. Or I was waiting for another black guy with a big beard. Each of the models brought his or her own aura into the picture. So, somehow, when I put the groups together, these different auras became like different colors when

I'll be damned if I'm not going down in a blaze of color. No gray for me. Lots of color, lots and lots!

—Arthur Turchi

The German magazine *Fotografie*, which devoted a special issue to his photos, was confiscated and banned by the German government in 1983. Zownir was labeled a madman, risked verbal and physical attacks, imprisonment, and psychiatric institutionalization. The *Village Voice* said: "Miron Zownir's photographs become a missile of total warfare against ignorance and hypocrisy."

—Miron Zownir

you paint or different spices when you cook. Depending on how they are put together, each group turns out to have a very specific feeling of its own. I went on and on. Even when this work started to become routine—and the shooting itself took only ten minutes—meeting with this incredible variety of people remained enormously interesting. Some days you had to be up very early to receive a Wall Street broker at 8 A.M. So, over a small breakfast, you would hear some news from the stock market. Then at 9 A.M. you would shoot this yoga teacher, who has to be out by 10, because he is teaching an 11:30 class at Riker's Island prison. At 3 P.M. a rock musician would show up, playing you a cassette of his group's latest concert, commenting on his work. At 4 you would have an inspector from the New York City Health Department, a man who inspects hospitals. He is very kind and modest and at first does not quite know why I would ask him to model for me. Then at 5 P.M. the actor Harve Presnell, already with some make-up on for tonight's show (or for me?), would tell me about what it was like playing Daddy Warbucks in Broadway's *Annie* 1,600 times. Finally, at 8, this New York City fireman would come, accompanied by his brother—who had hair—and their two wives. Drinking tea and wine, and, of course, we were talking about fires. So I told them my fire story too.

LM: Which one was that?

AK: The one in Germany. At 3 A.M. screams of my neighbor out in the street woke me up: "Aaalex! Aaalex! Feuer!" and then I discovered that the whole hallway was one big hell. After my girlfriend climbed down the famous knotted sheets, the electric guitars were thrown out into the dark and picked up by neighbors in the cornfield below. They were scream-

continued on page 33

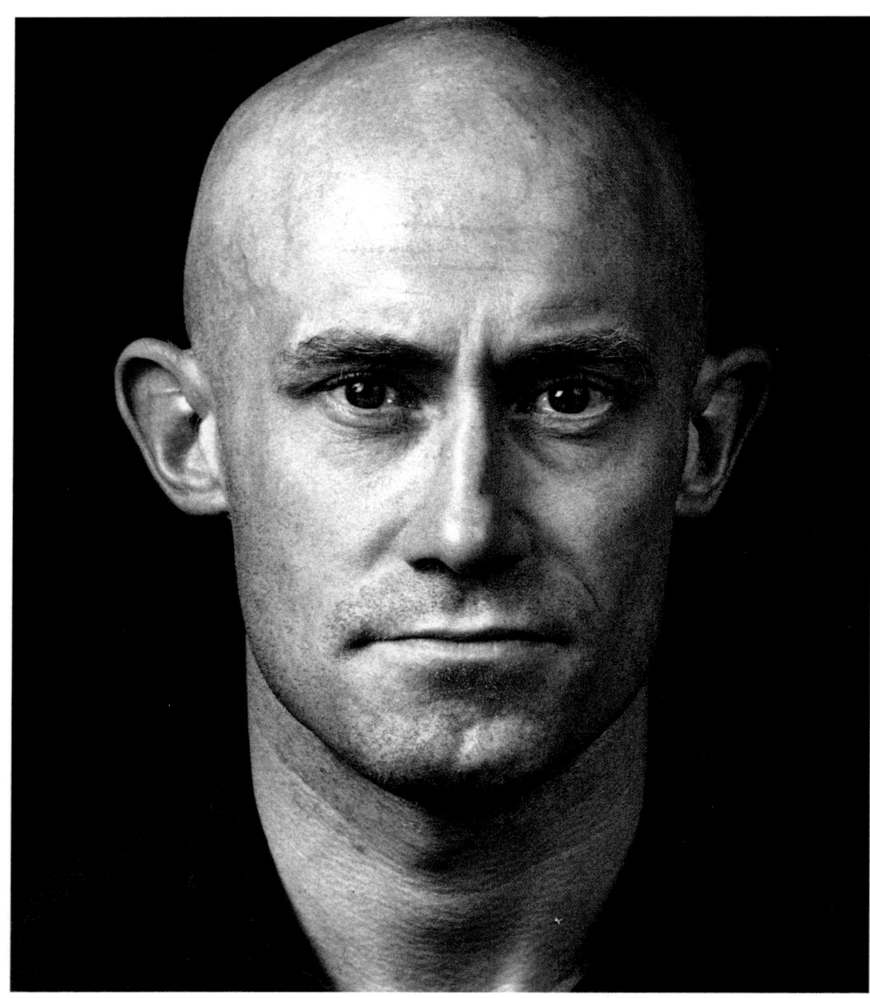

Ron Walker, New York City: photographer and architect, I. M. Pei Associates

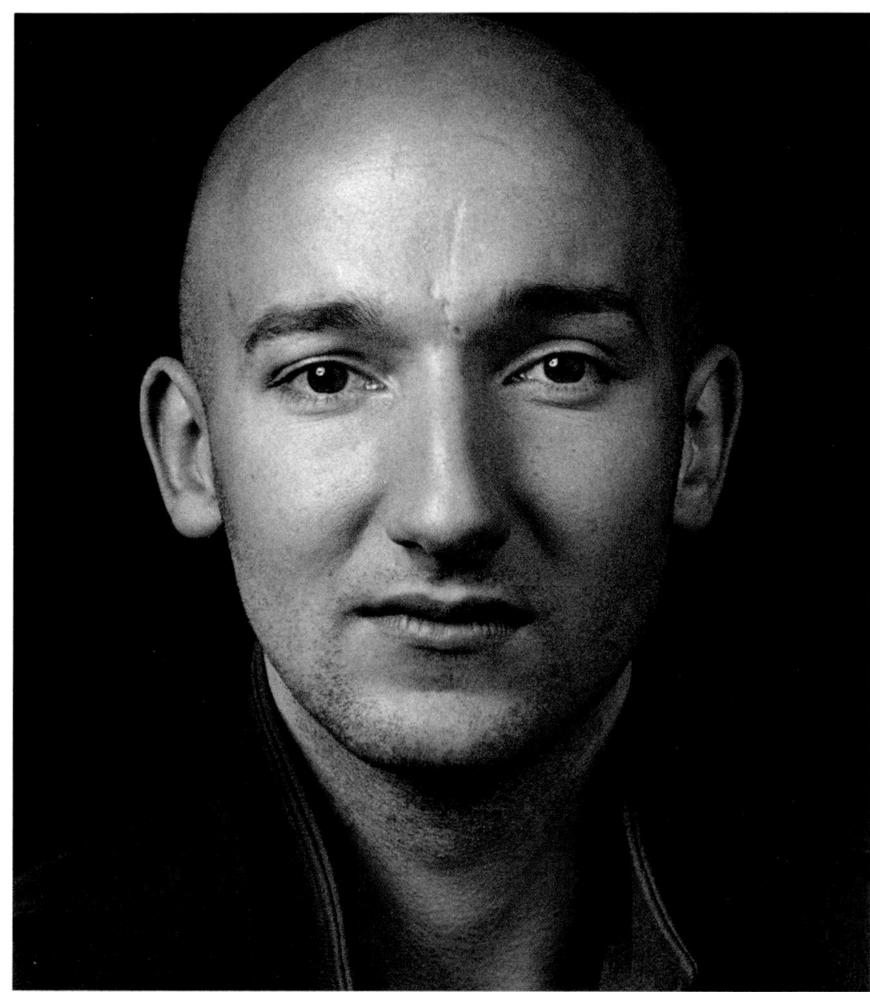

Stephen Jones, London: hat designer

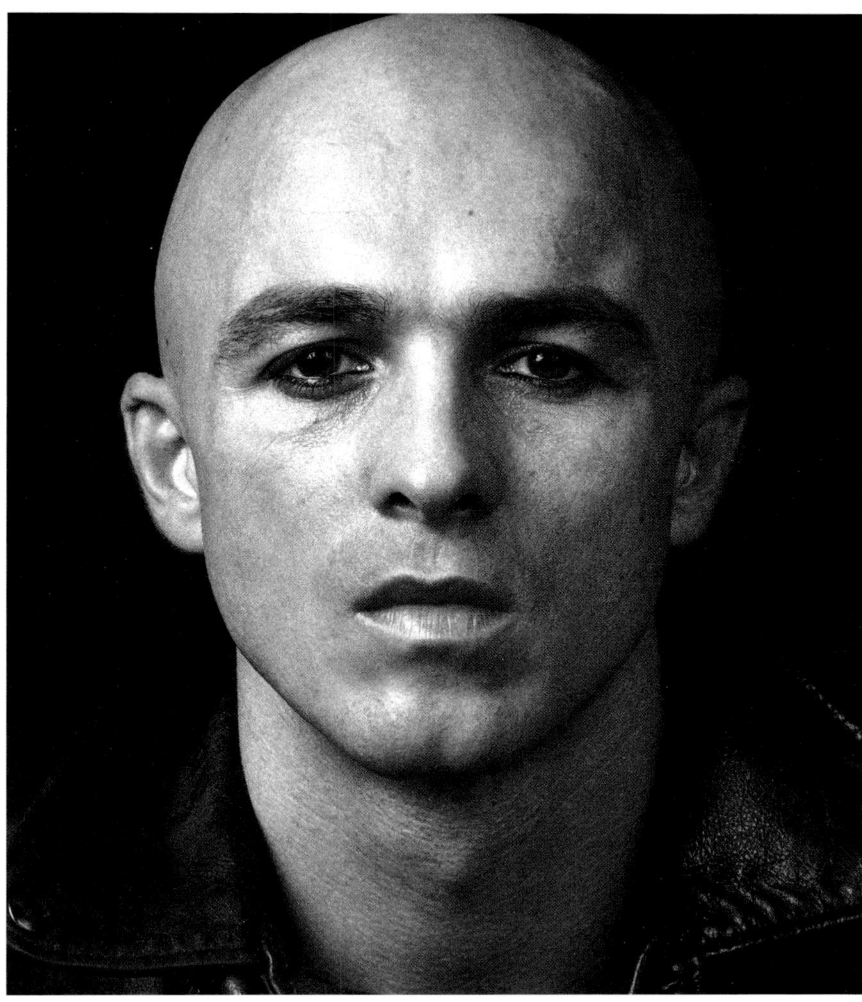

Miron Zownir, New York City: "poet of radical photography"

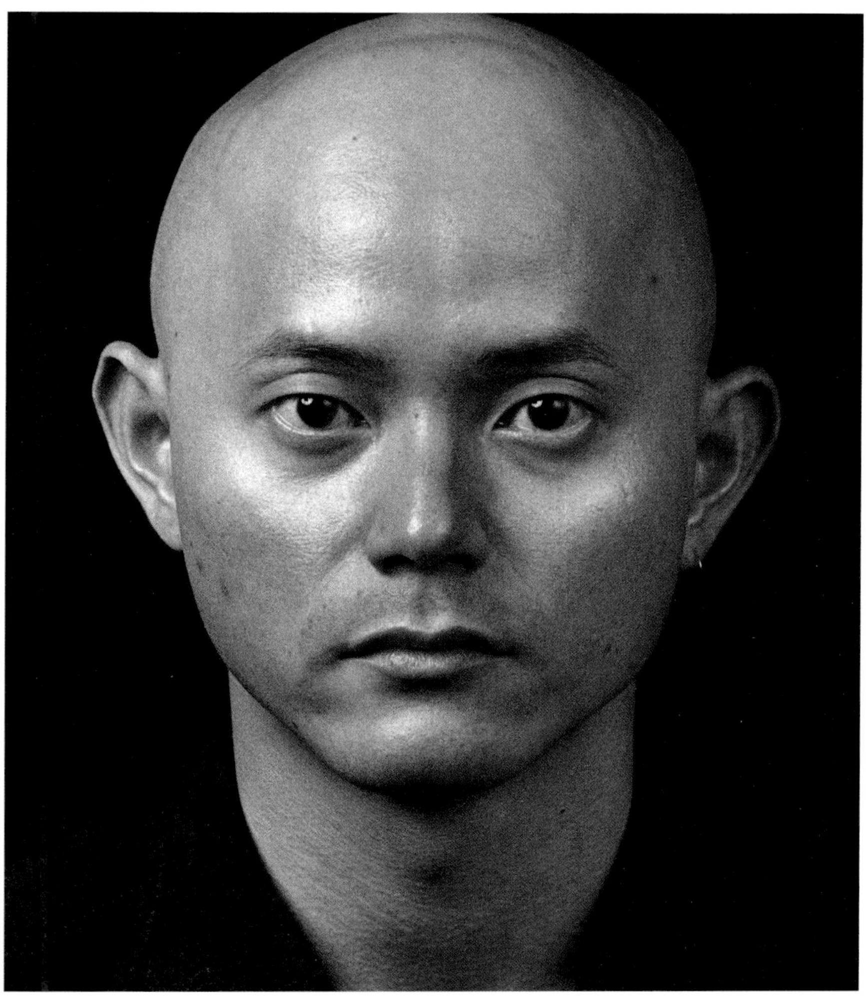

Chosei Funahara, New York City: actor, appeared in the film, *I'm Alright My Friend*; musician, cofounder of shock-rock band, The Plasmatics

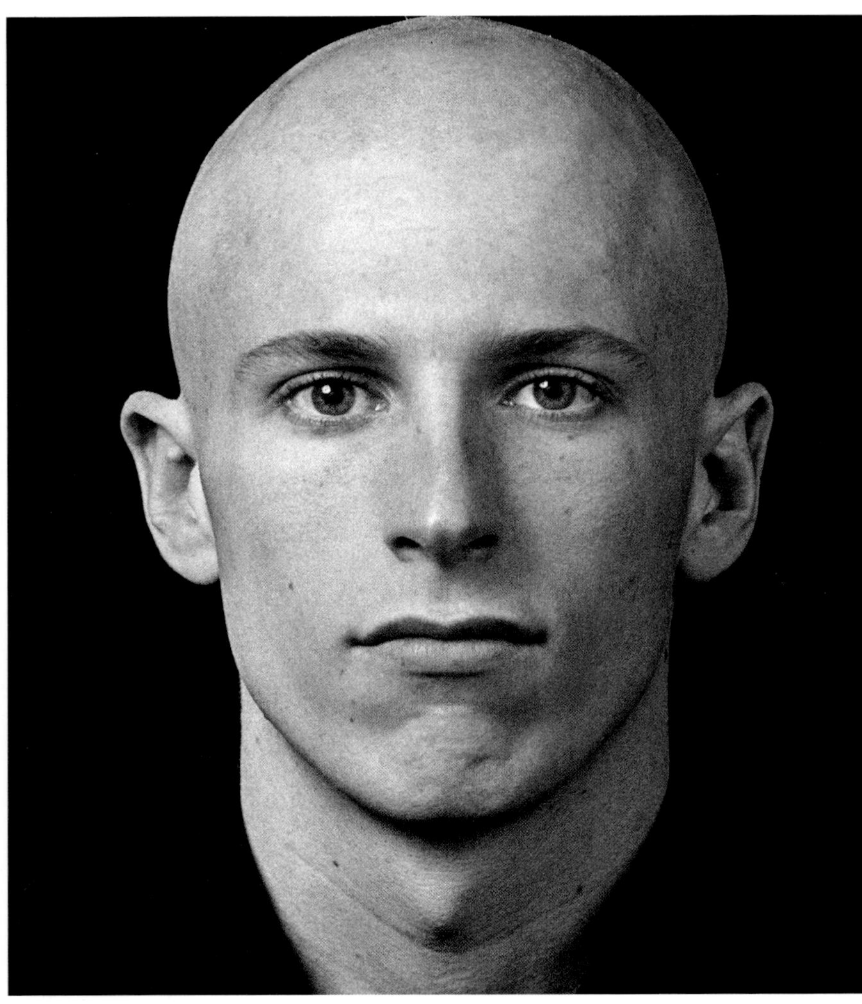

Carlo Saraceni, New York City: architect and interior designer

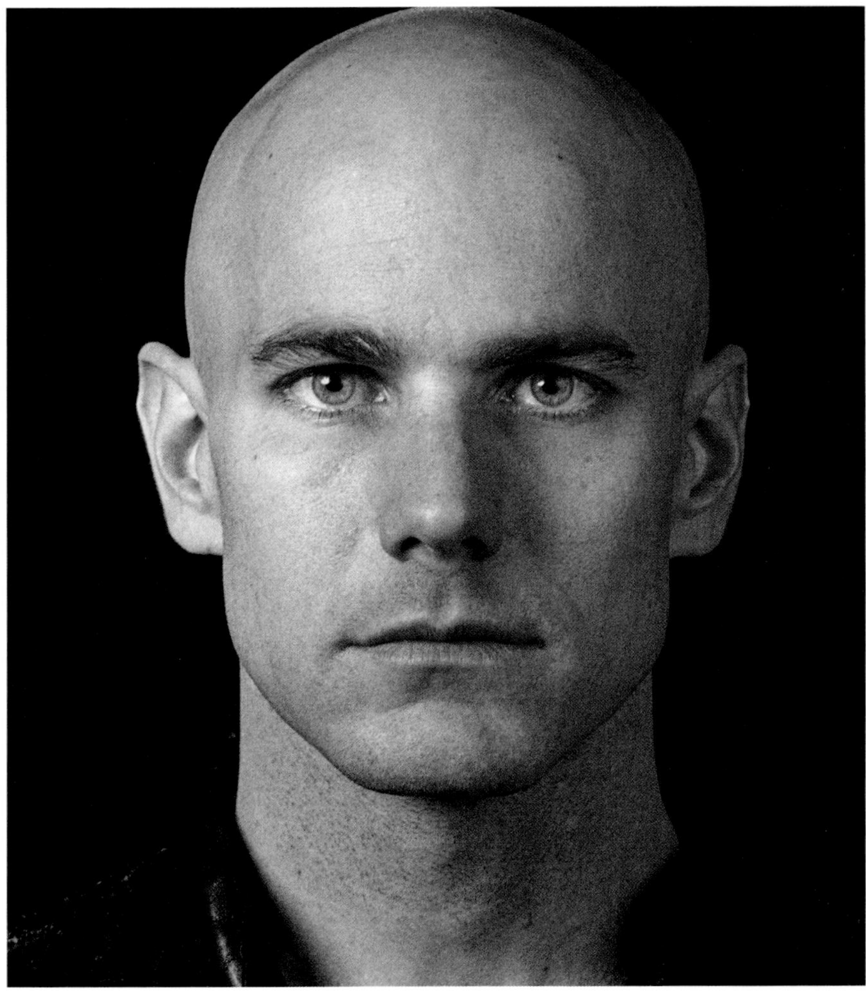

Ivan X, New York City: rock 'n' roll musician

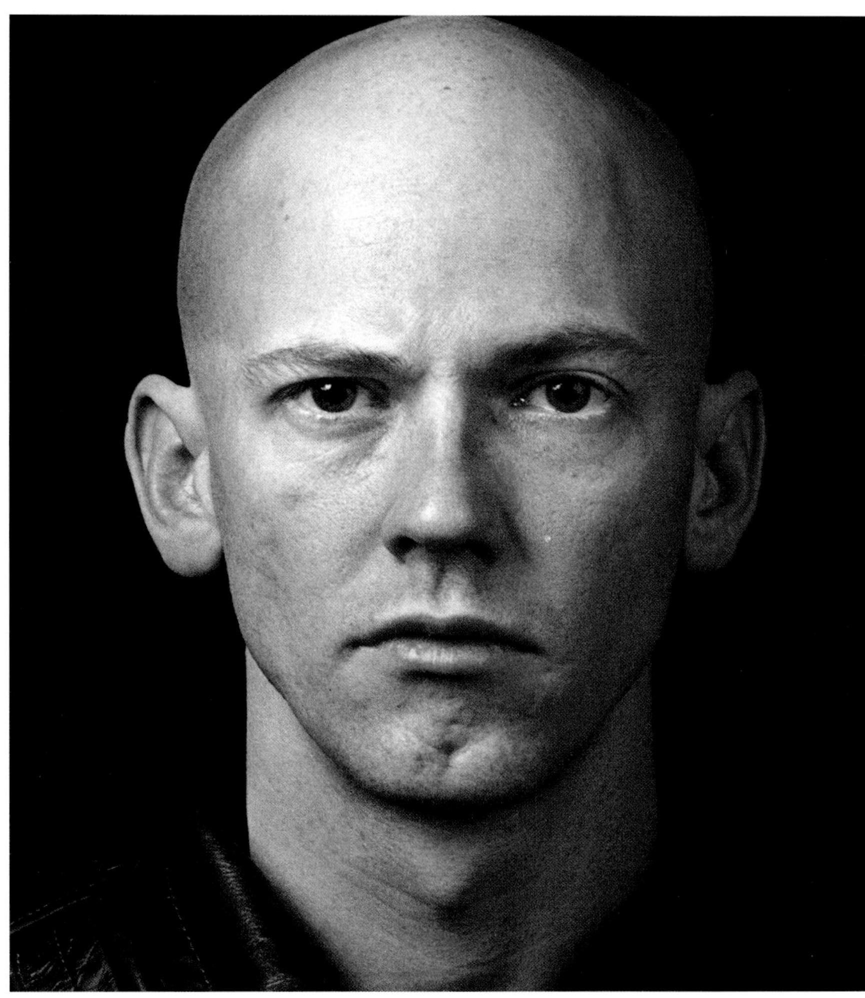

Rodney Watts, New York City

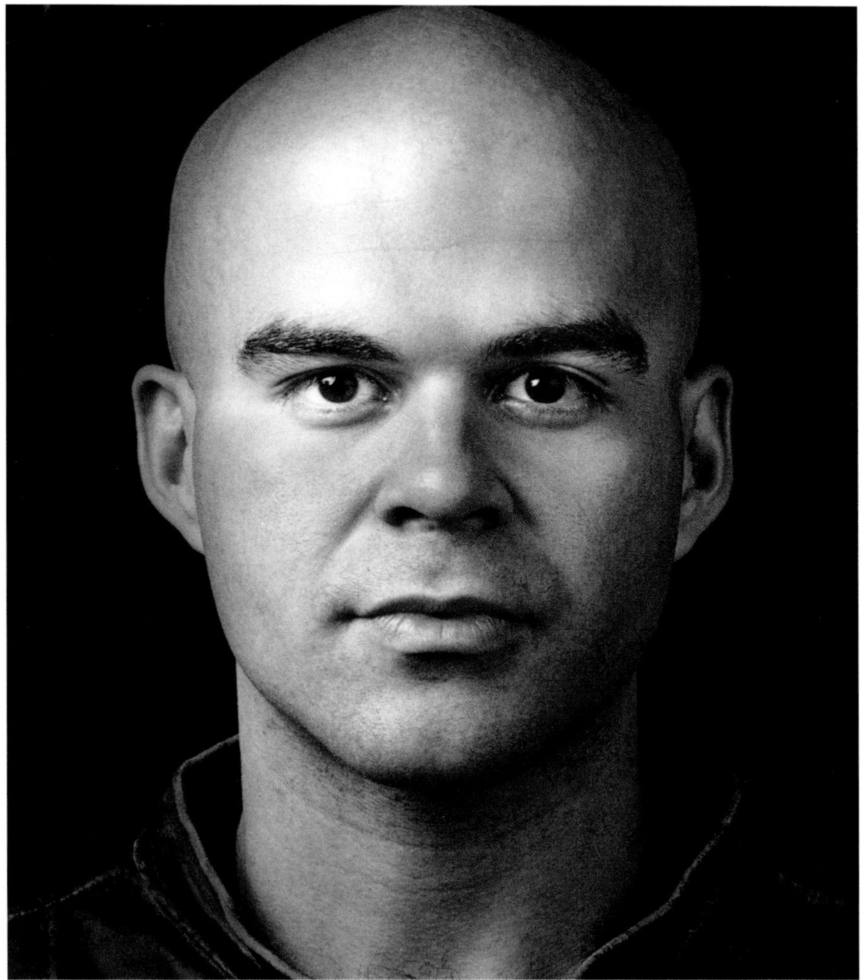

Louis Gonzales, New York City: student of historical conservation

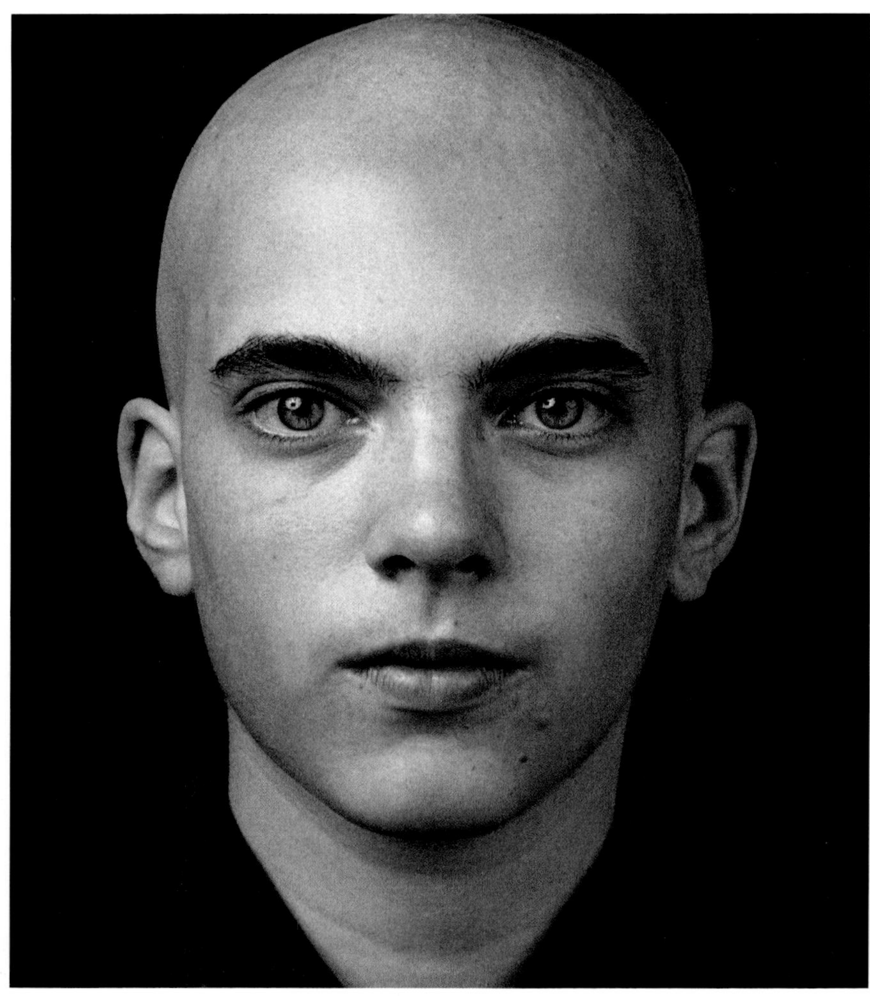

Rachelle Garniez, New York City: editor for *Gem* newspaper; cofounder (with Ray Kelly) of Ha-Ha Video Dating Service

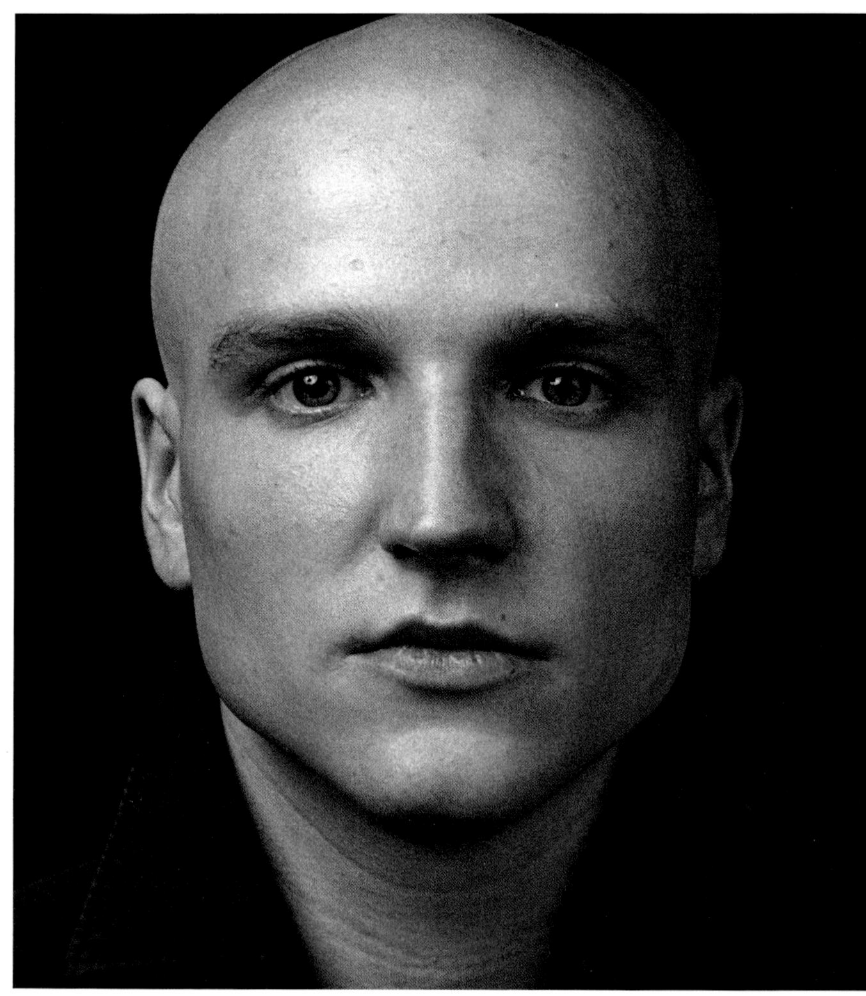

Mario Gawrys, Berlin: window and fashion designer

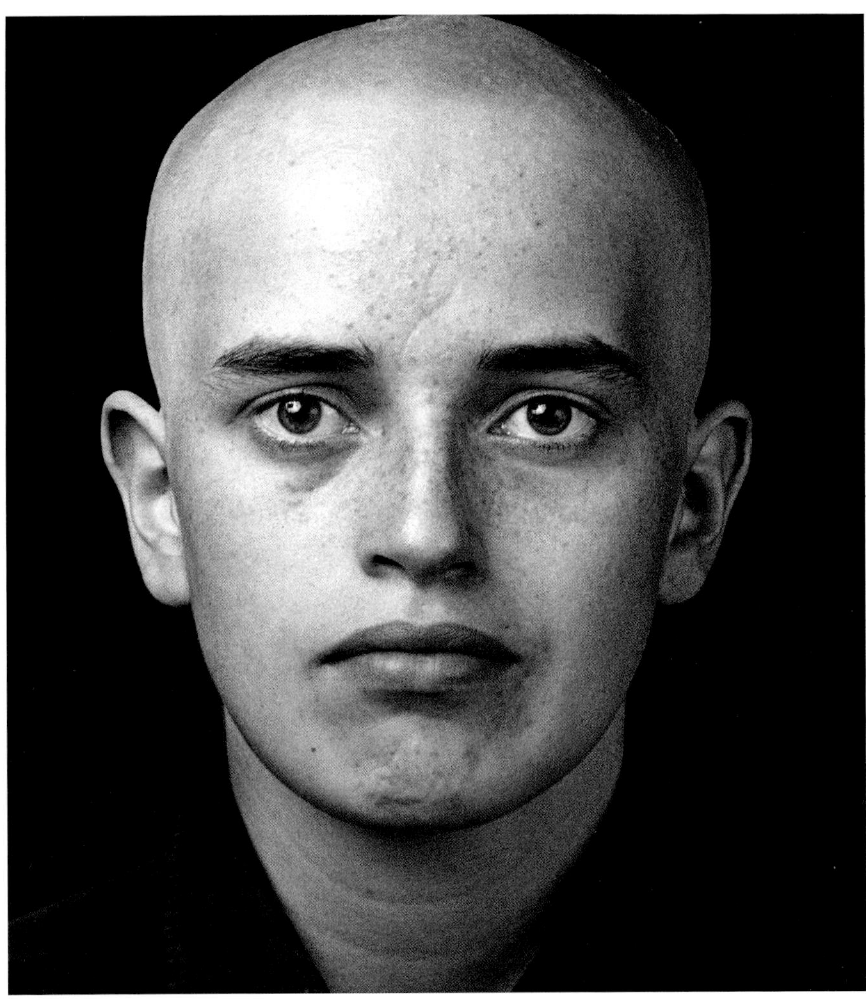

Silke Ecks, New York City: artist

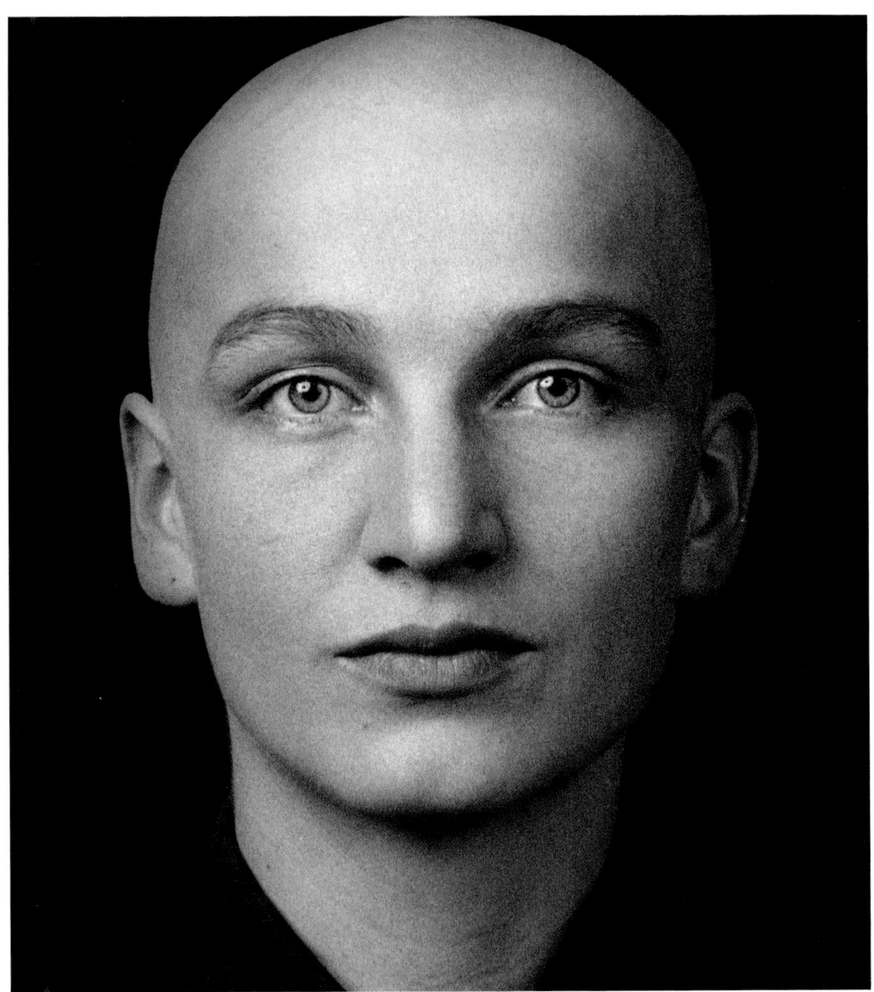

Anna Klinckhammer, Düsseldorf: sculptor

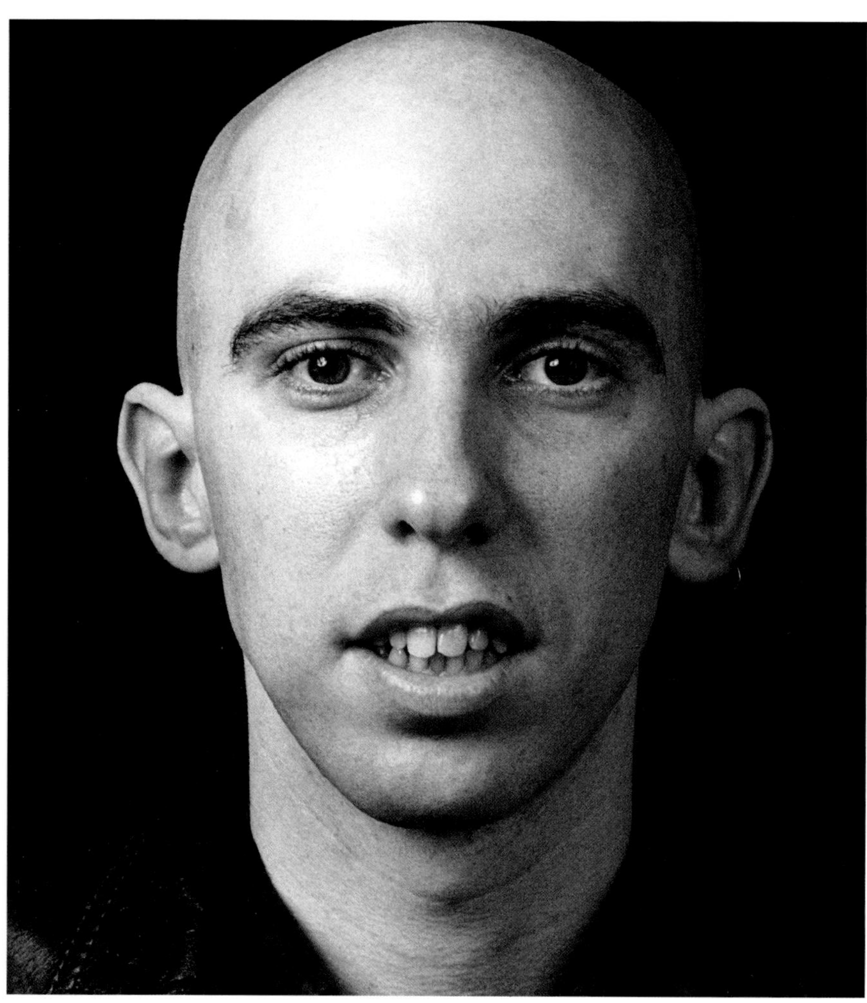

Gary Sunshine, Florida: musician in The Screaming Sneakers

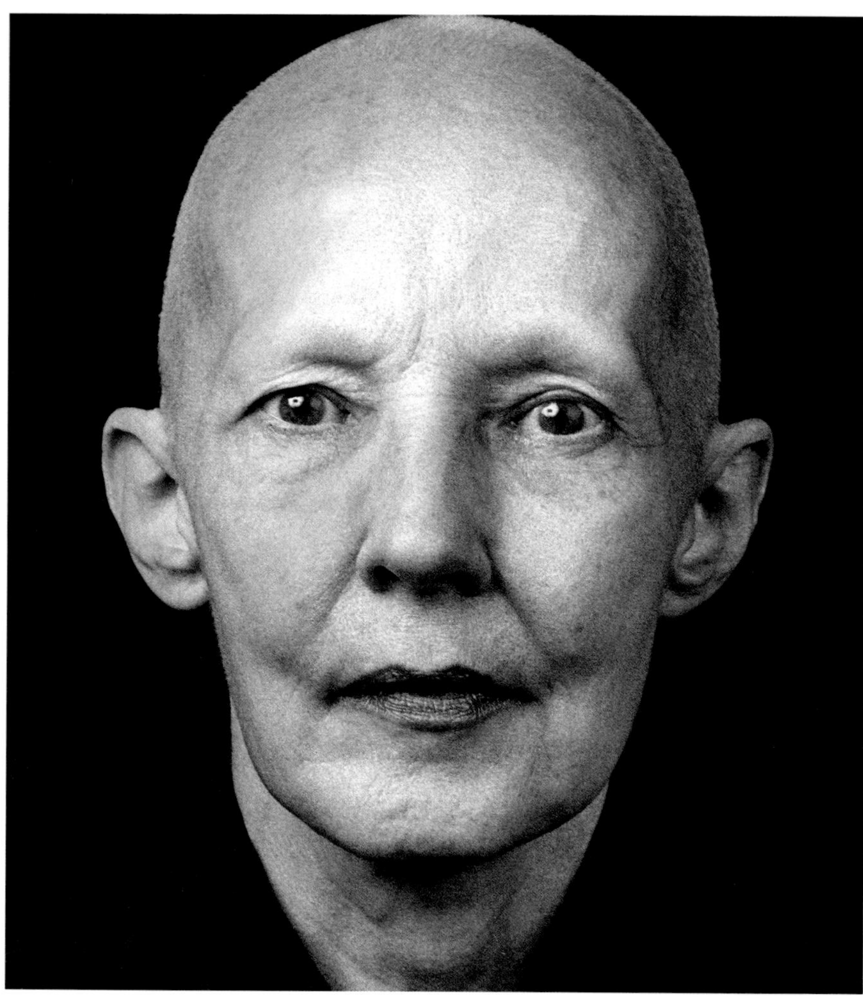

Mae Alexander, New York City: administrative assistant

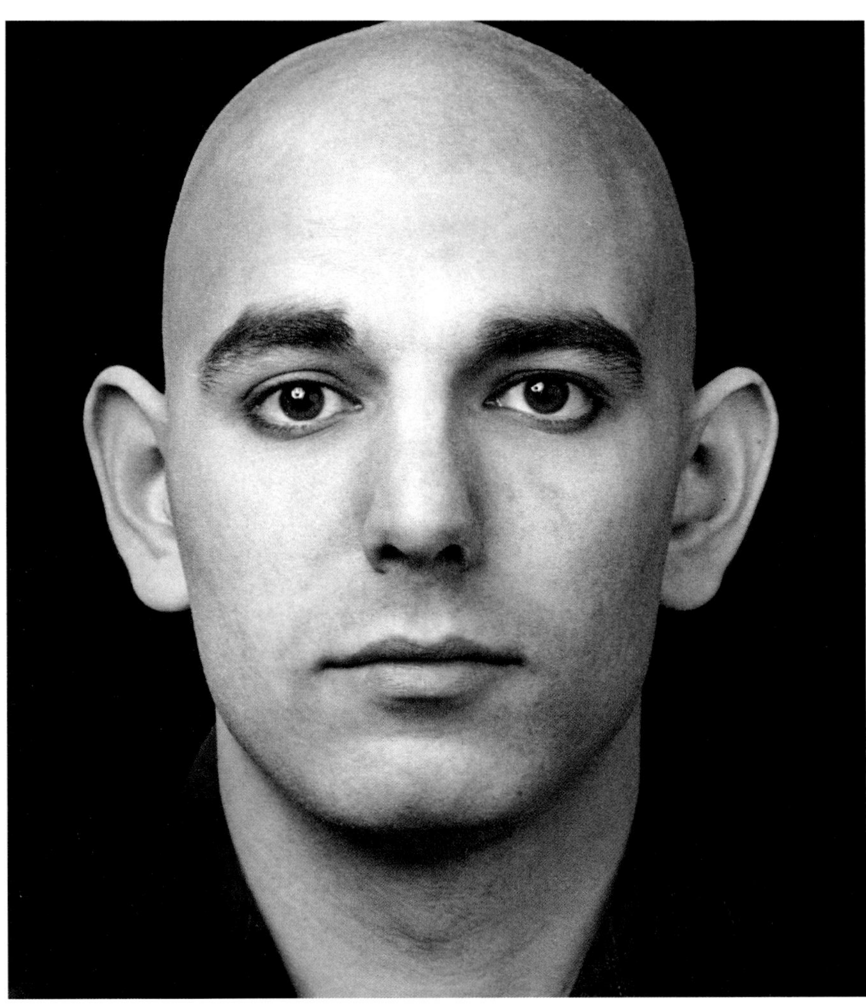

Stephen Jashjian, New York City: artist and performer

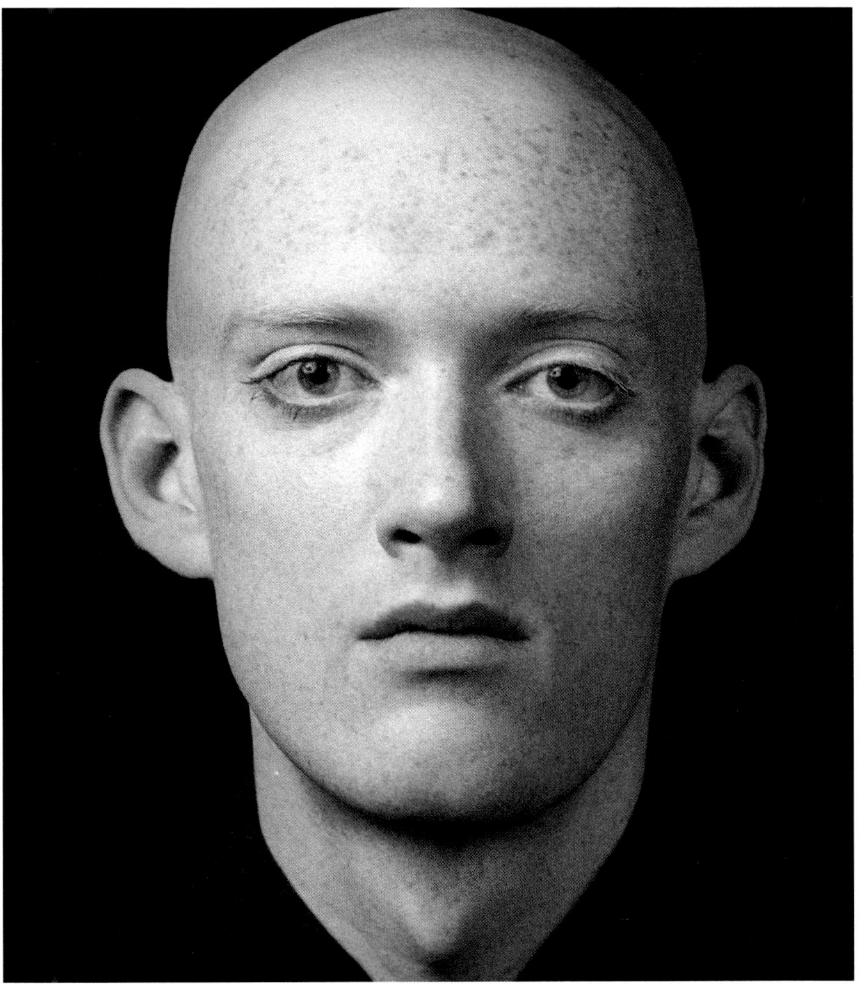

Dean Johnson, New York City: poet and performance artist; works at various Lower-East-Side nightclubs, including Pyramid and Save the Robots

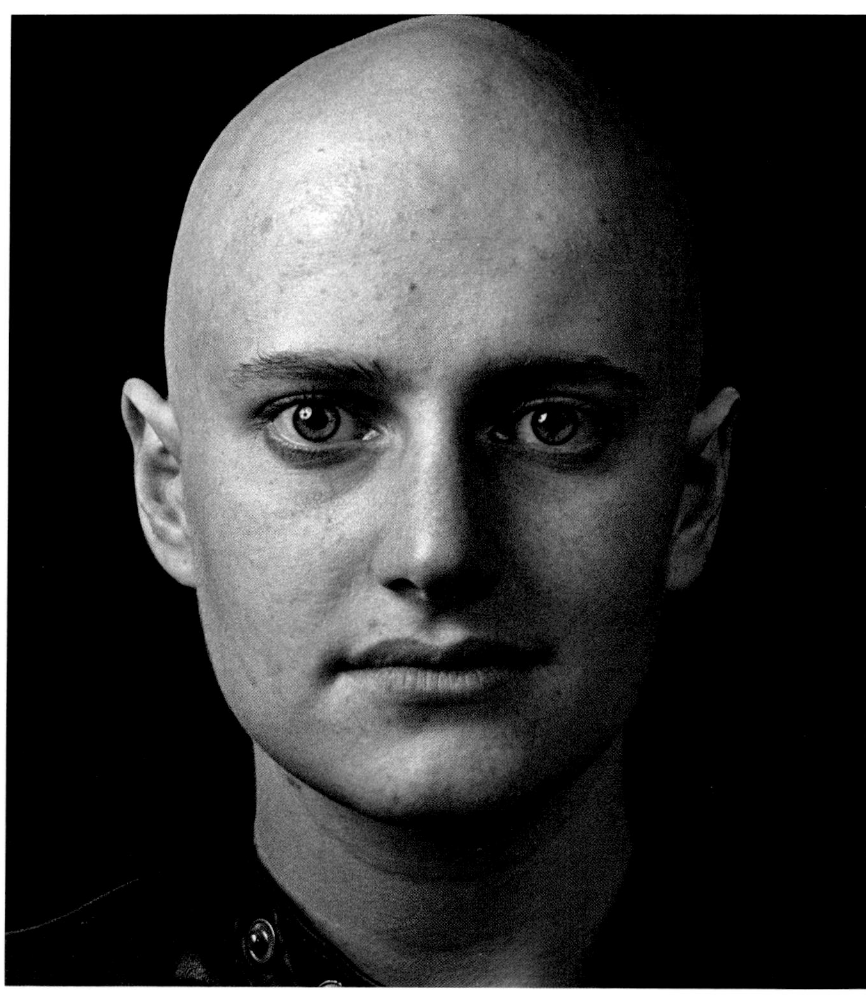

Kate Isler, Basel: art student and multimedia performer

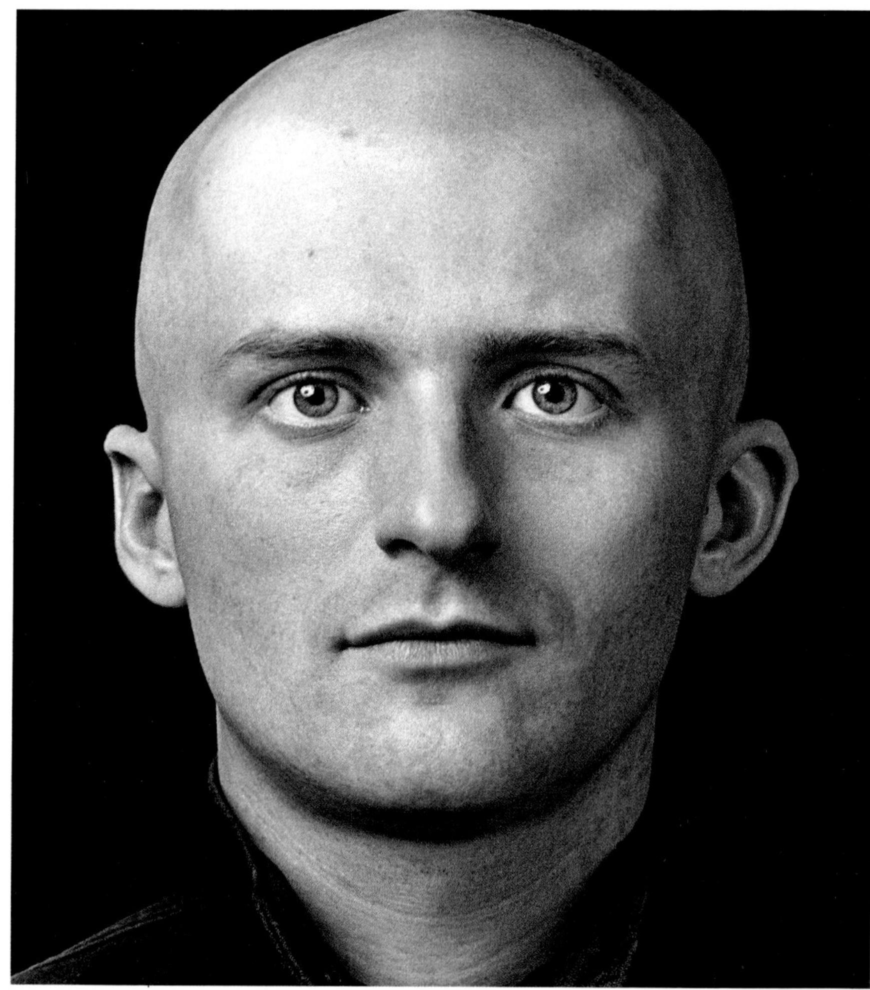

Luca Pizzorno, New York City: photographer

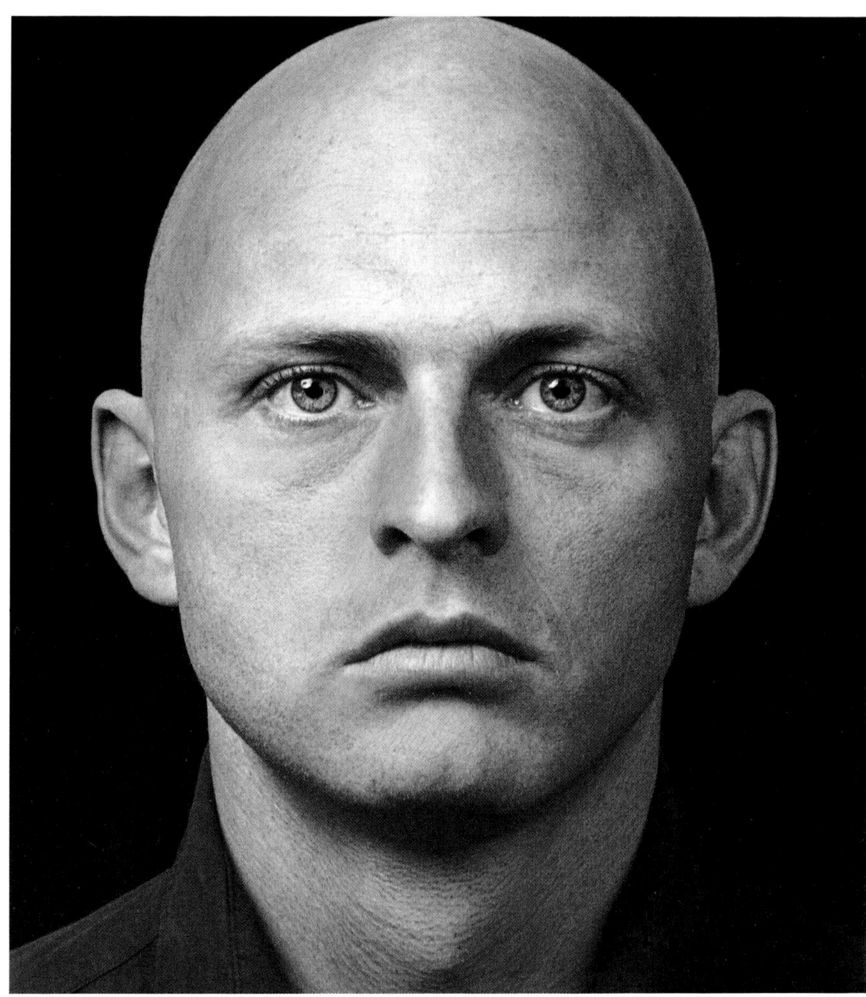

Lance McMahan, New York City: illustrator

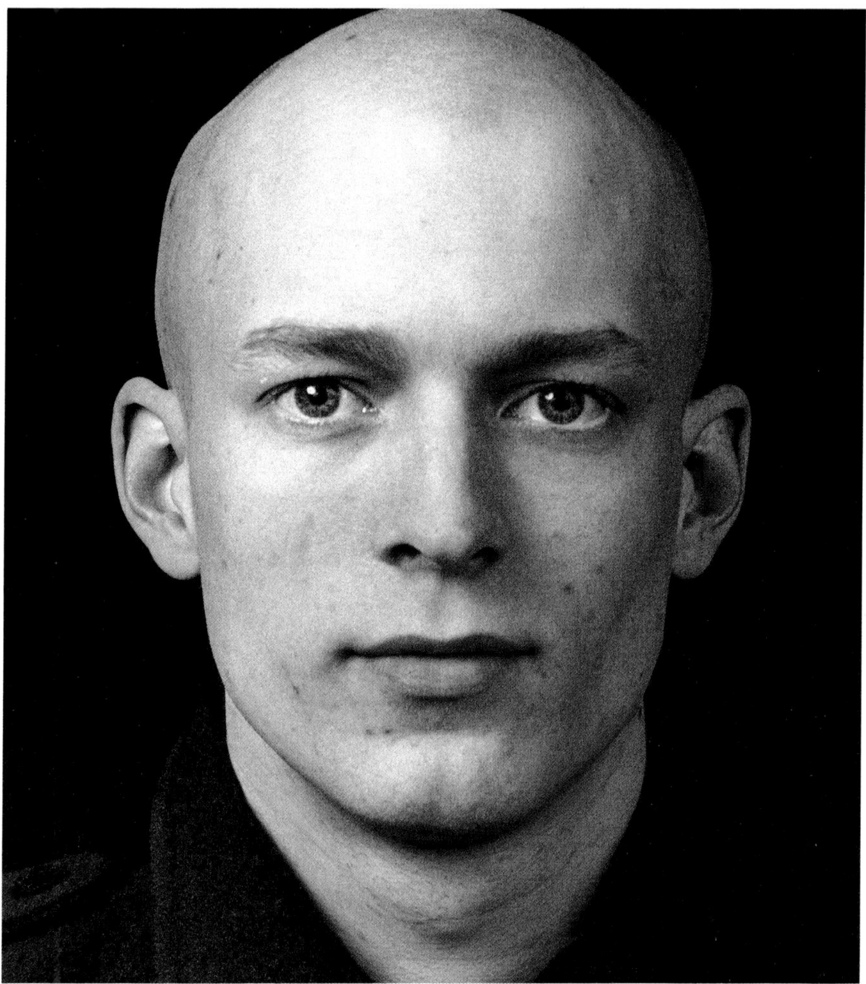

Craig Coleman, New York City: Lower-East-Side artist, exhibits at New Math Gallery

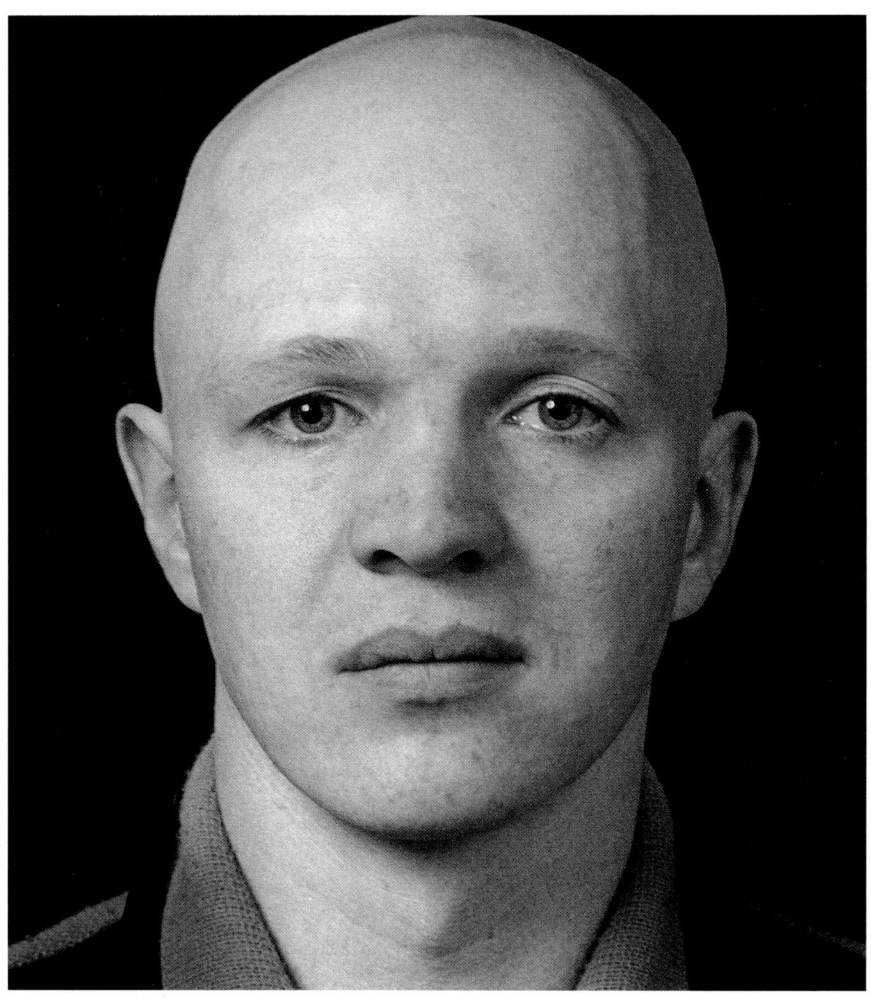

Wilson Amayen, New York City

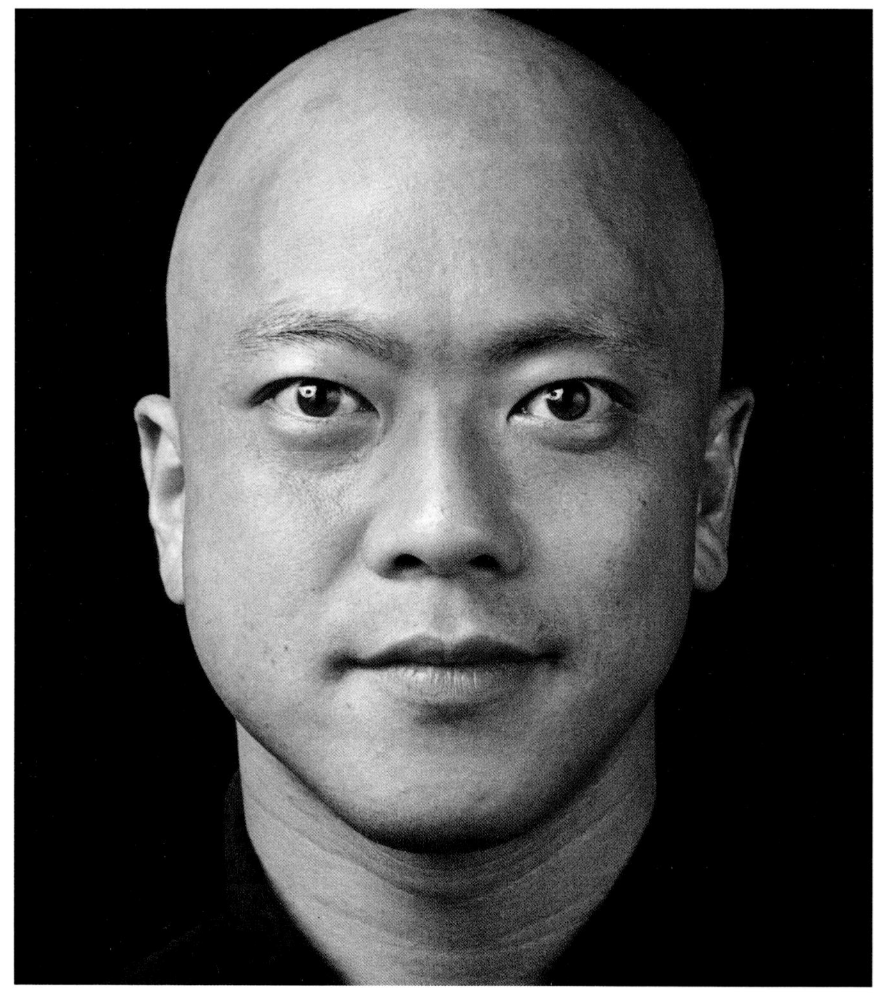

Massa Tsuda, New York City: peace movement worker

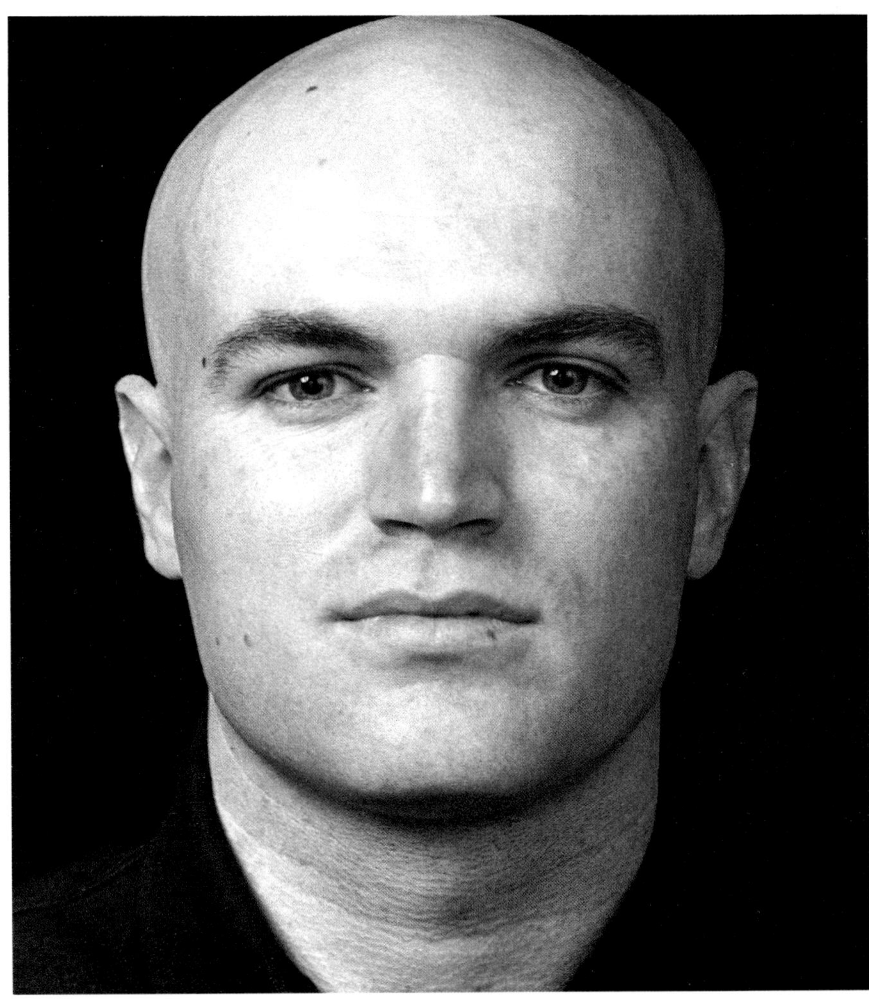

Charles J. Ryan, New York City: fireman, Staten Island

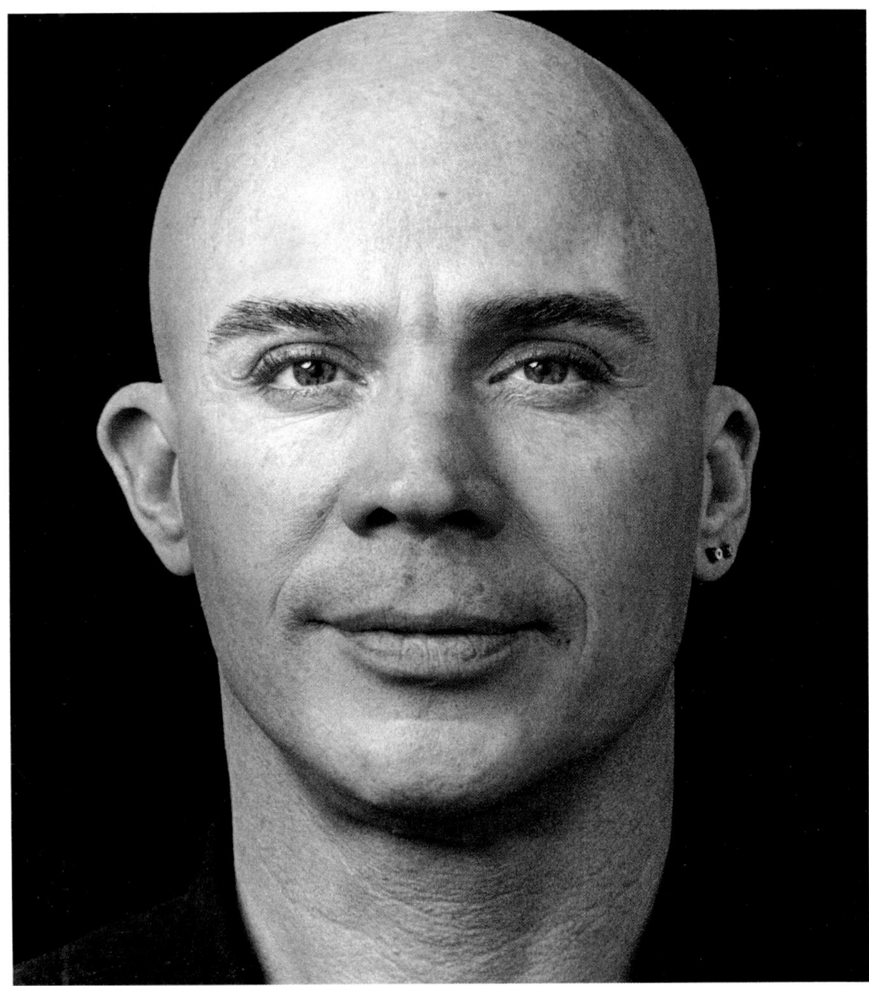

Tucco Perez, New York City: entertainer

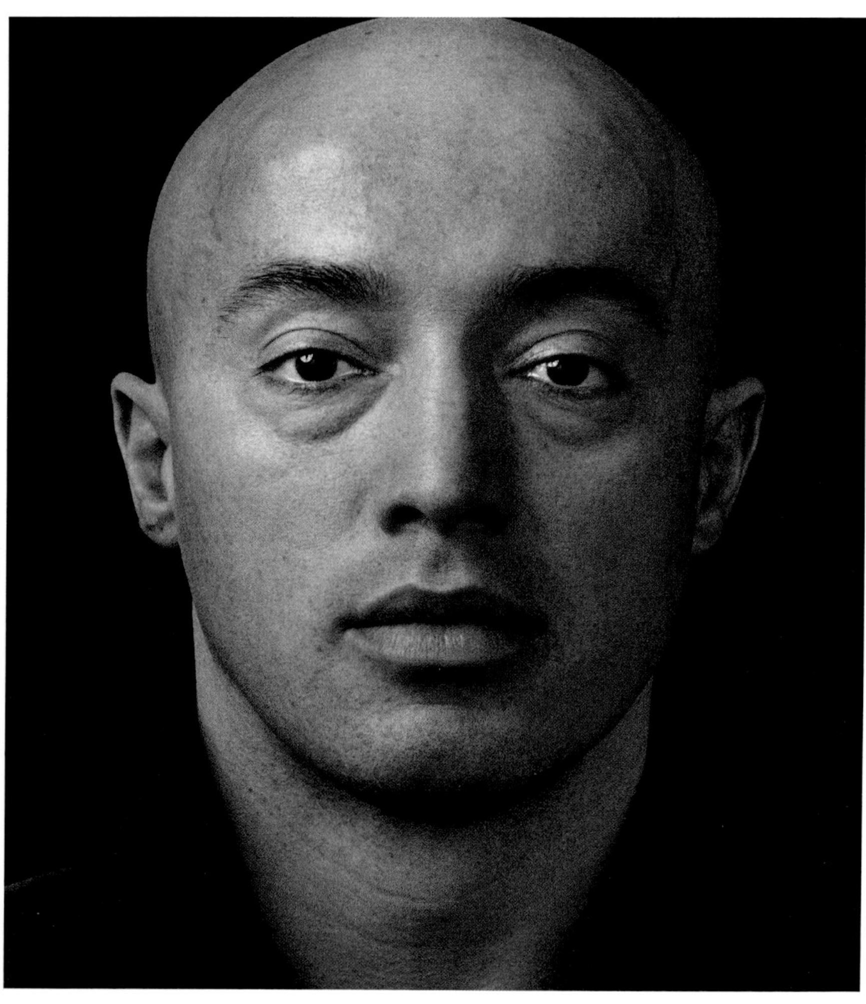

Juan Antonio, New York City: dancer, choreographer, and director, *Les Ballets Jazz* and others

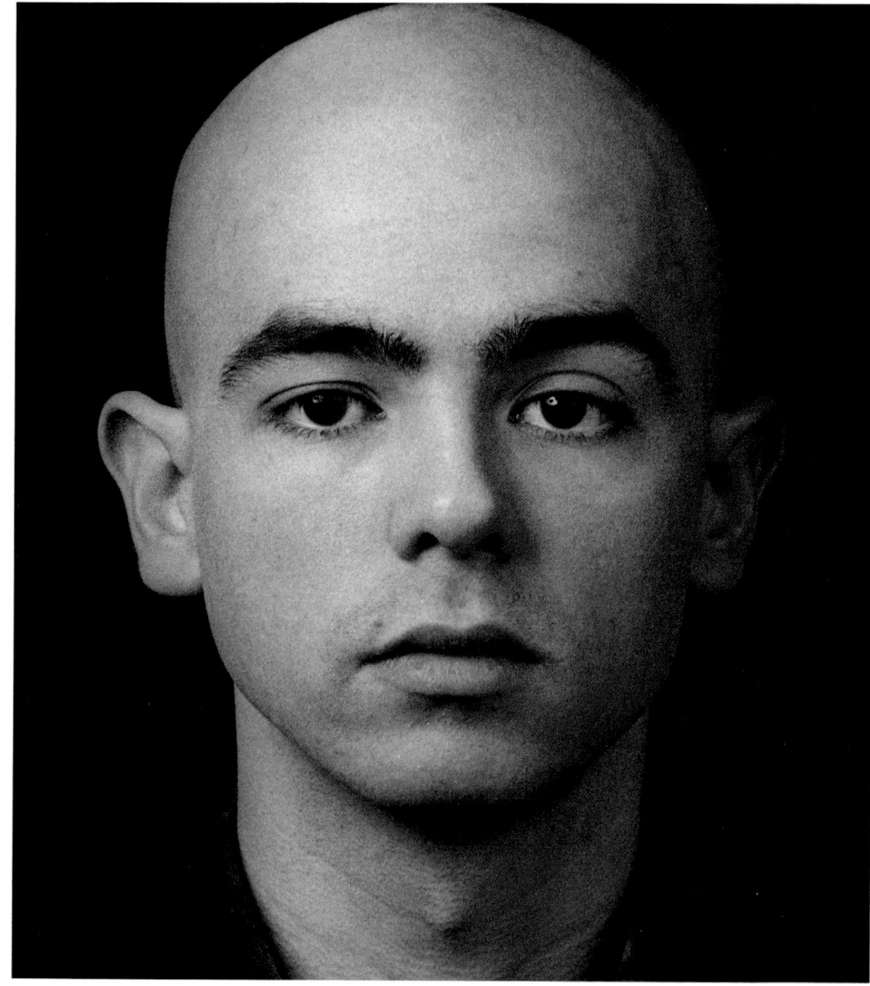

Marc Contratto, New York City: art student, Parsons School of Design; works in nightclubs

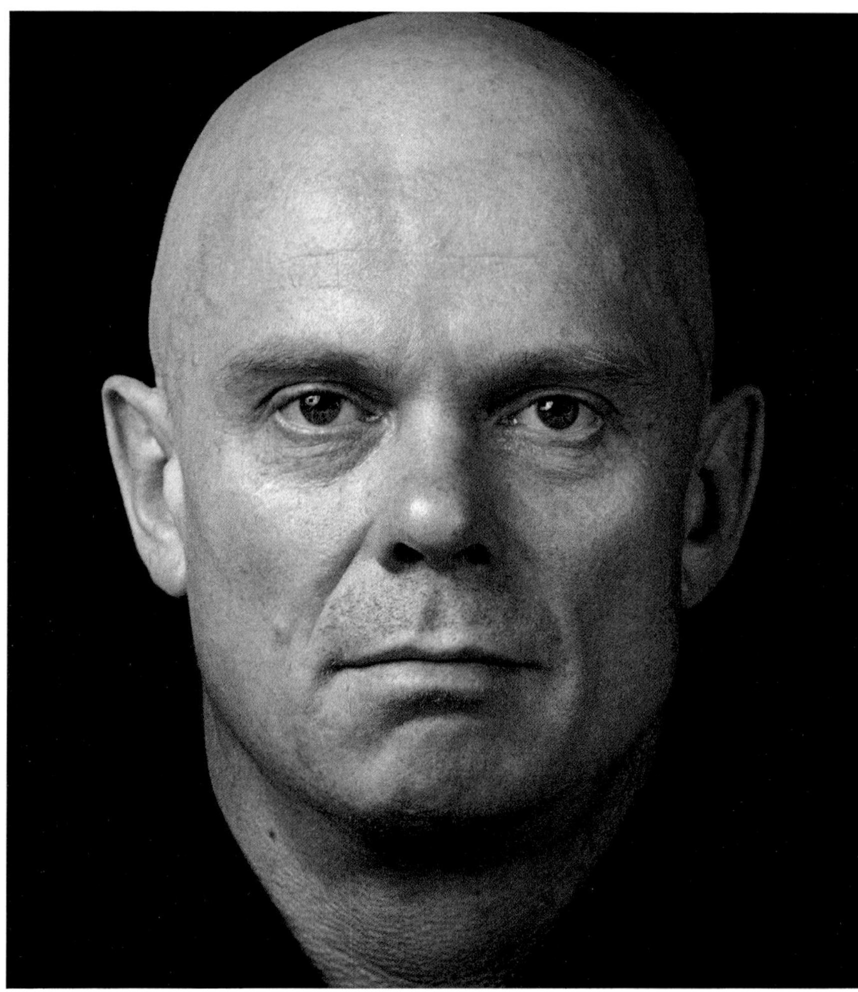

Ray Kelly, New York City: editor, *Gem* newspaper; cofounder (with Rachelle Garniez) of Ha-Ha Video Dating Service

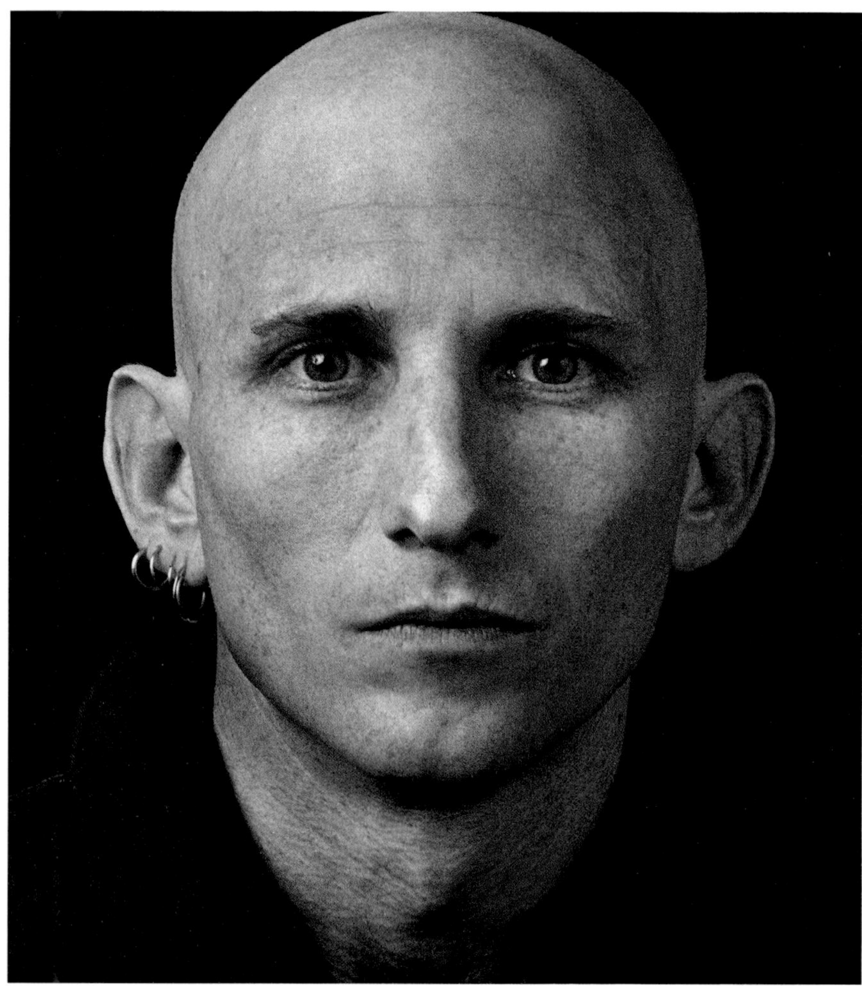

Zev, New York City: experimental percussionist

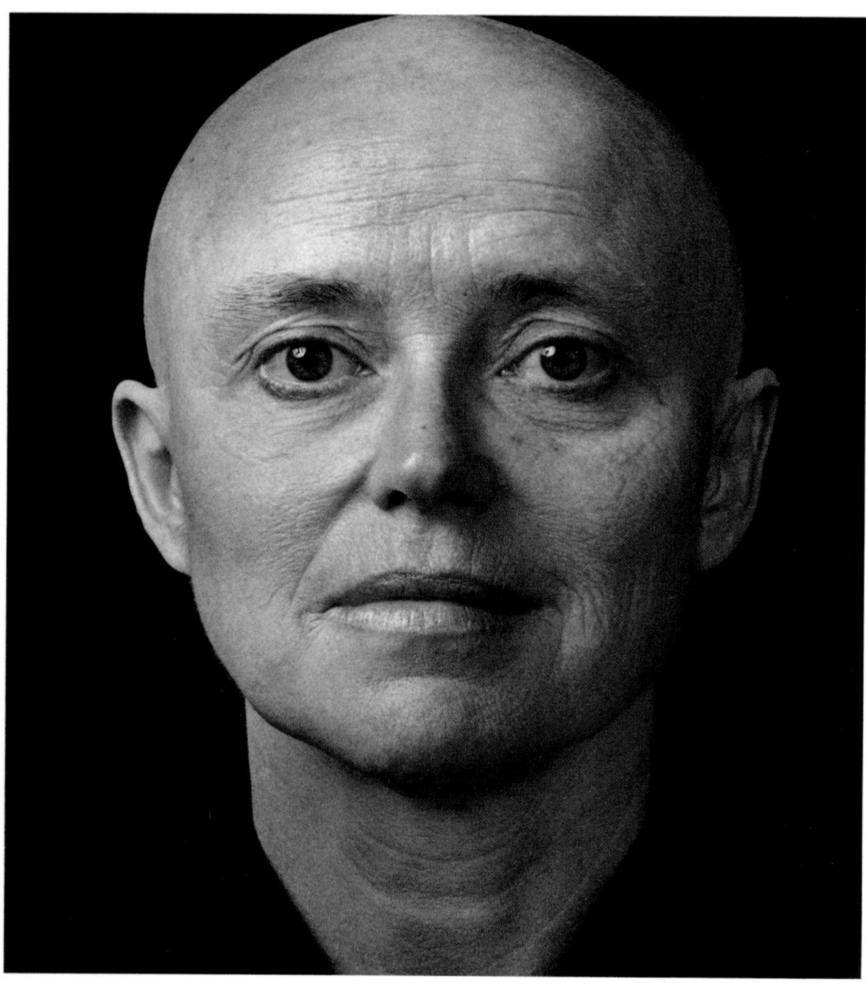

Jaan Haag, Muktananda Ashram, India: former director of the American Film Institute; resigned to join Muktananda Ashram

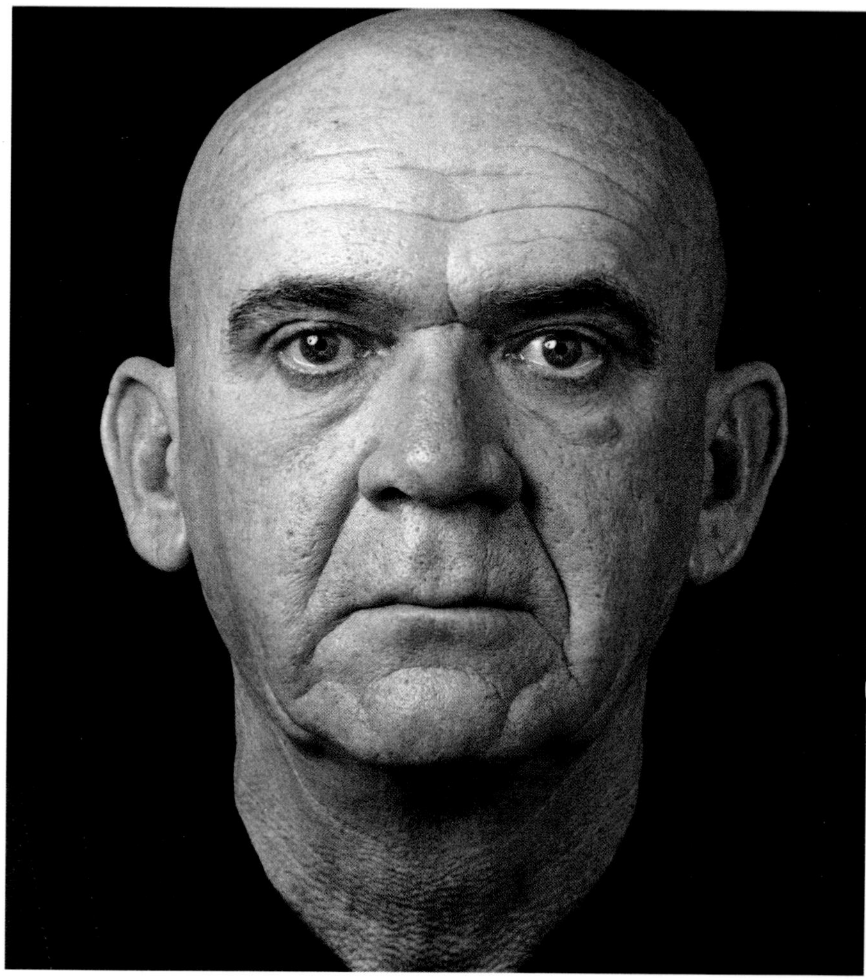

Adrian Kellard, Westchester County, New York: policeman and head of Westchester County Police Department Photography Division

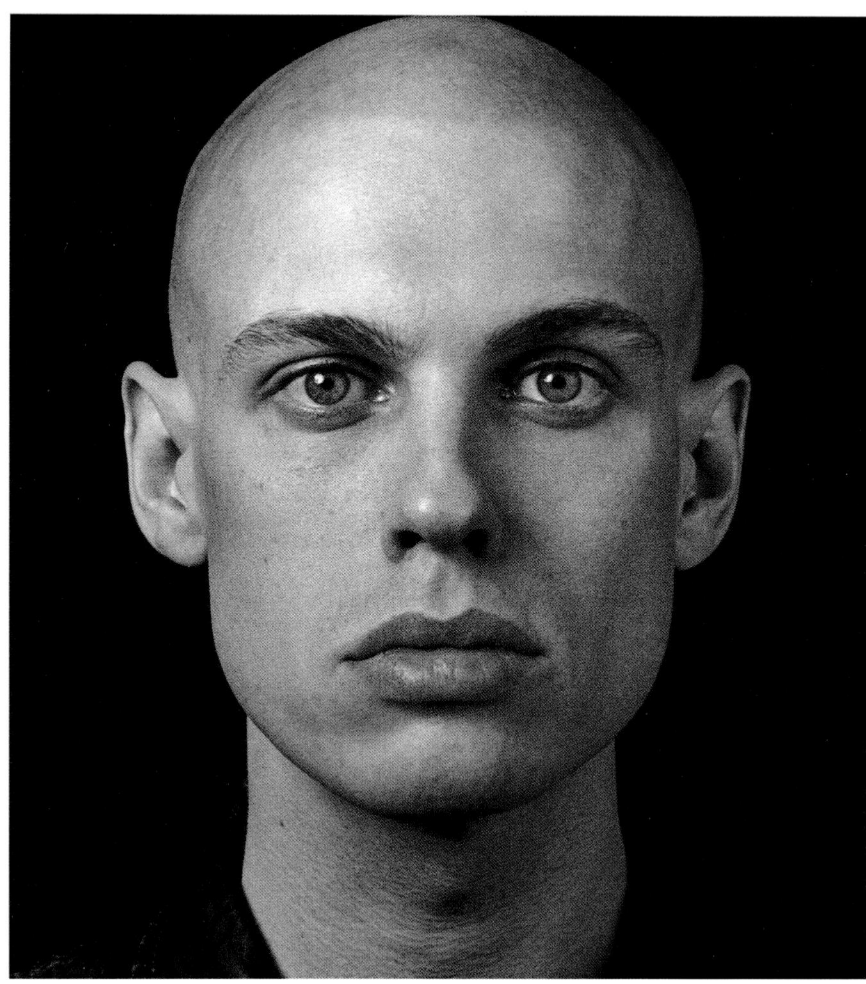

Richard Sohl, New York City: pianist and keyboard player, performed with Patti Smith, Iggy Pop, Nina Hagen, and others

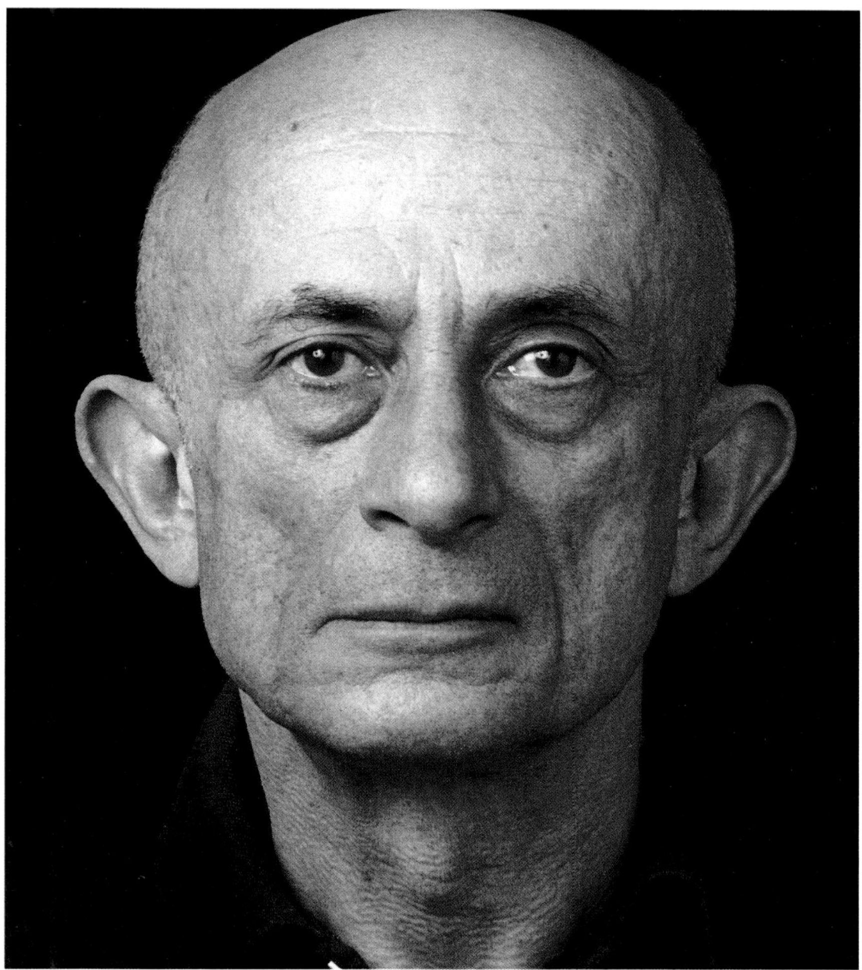

Leon Golub, New York City: artist

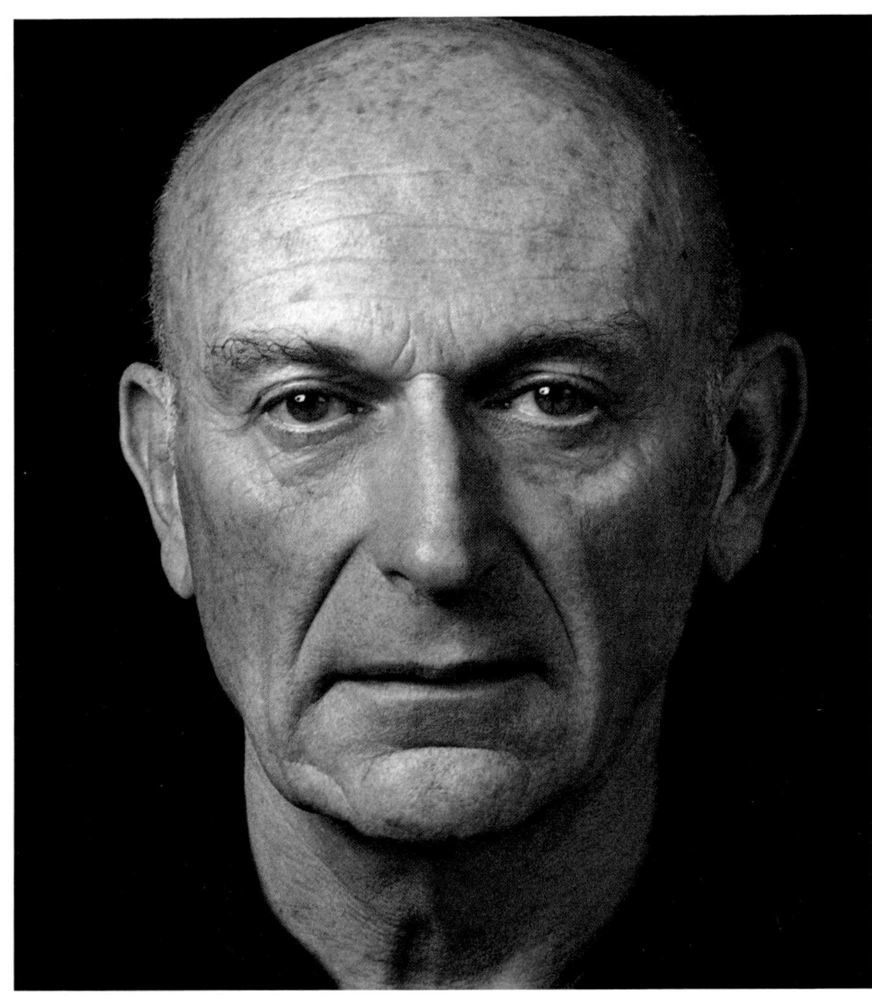

Benno Premsela, Amsterdam: architect

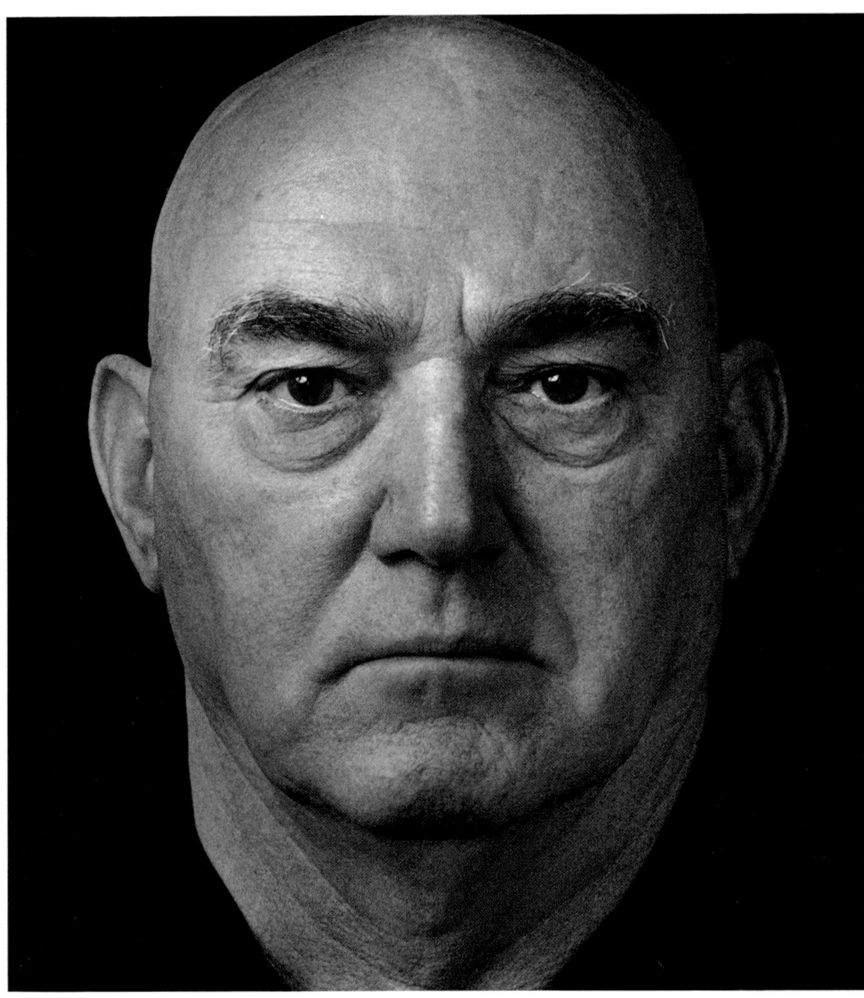

Jim Spera, Long Island, New York: bus driver

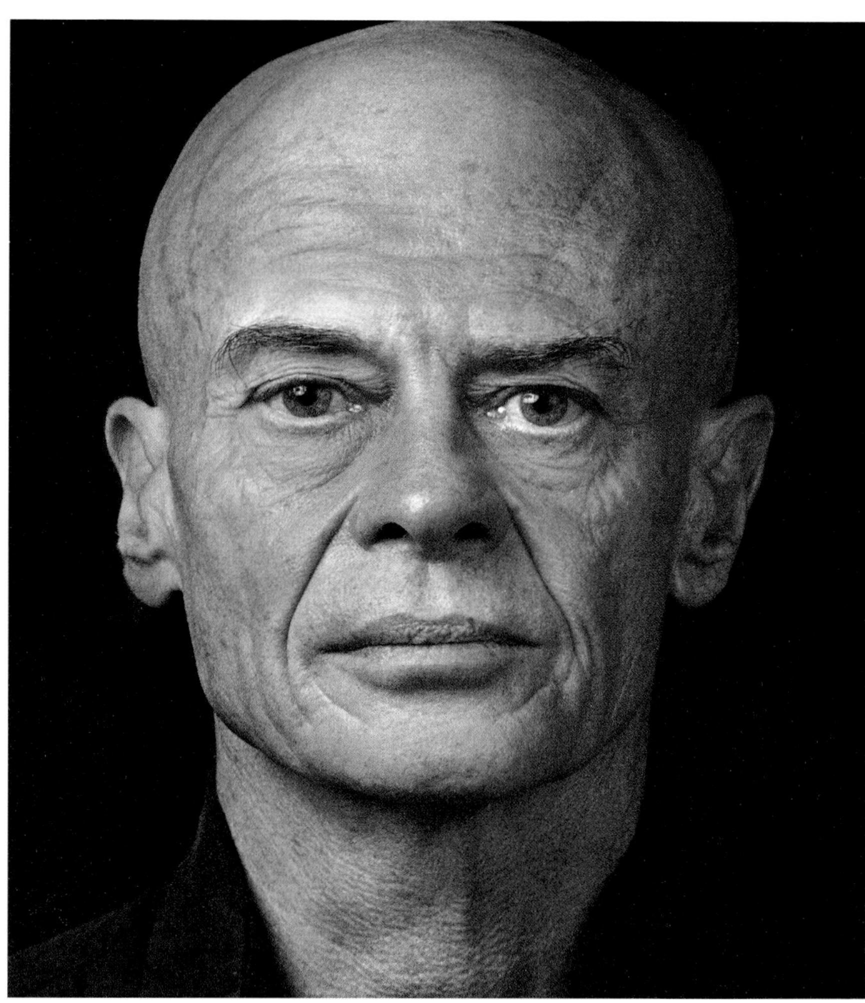

Norman Friedman, New York City: works in data processing

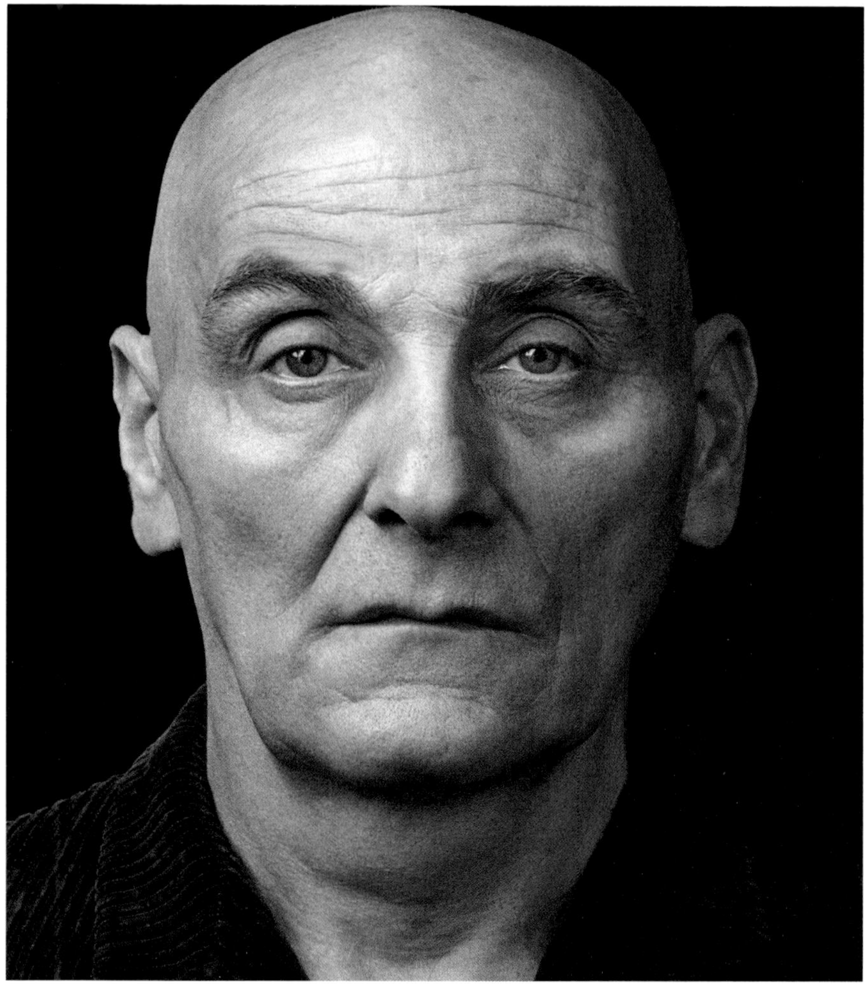

Duke Figliuzzi, New York City: deceased; assistant to Marisol, the artist; owner of a California gold mine

On February 6, 1983, the first night of a snow storm in New York, while finishing up a workday at Burghard's, a SoHo avant-garde fashion boutique, Araken Oliveira was robbed at gunpoint. During the robbery transaction, the gunman fired his revolver directly into Araken's mouth, whereupon Araken physically spat out the bullet. Authorities later found the bullet on the floor near where Araken's body had collapsed. Immediately following the shooting, the "junky-type robber" fled the boutique, taking with him two large bags of leather clothes and jewelry.

After spitting out the bullet, Araken was rushed to St. Vincent's Hospital in New York. He was hospitalized for only two days and, miraculously, needed no stitches. Also, no facial damage occurred when he fell to the floor following the shot in the mouth. In fact, no one can see any visual damage to Araken or his face. He looks not one bit different from the picture in this book, taken just a couple of days prior to the shooting.

Upon positive identification, the robber was apprehended by the police, tried by jury, and sentenced to sixteen years in prison.

—Araken Ribeiro de Oliveira

continued from page 13

ing: "Jump! Jump!" Then it came to my mind: my negatives—the last ten years' work! Already so stoned from the hot smoke, with eyes not hurting anymore but blind, I finally found the two heavy boxes containing mostly sheets of processed Tri-x, and off they went through my top-floor window. The next thing I remember was the oxygen mask and then being washed in a huge bathtub at this German hospital by two male nurses, a handsome one and one not so pretty.

LM: You lost a lot in those flames, didn't you?

AK: Well, lots of prints, video tapes, stupid little antique collections, many books, and all my clothes. It was crazy, but soon it felt like a big release, and I could cancel that shipping container to my new studio in New York.

AA: You mentioned electric guitars. Were you a musician?

AK: Yes, as a teenager in the late sixties. First we formed a group, then bought the instruments, and then learned how to play them, and soon we did gigs in the clubs of Switzerland and southern Germany.

AA: Has the music influenced your photography?

AK: Whenever there was a chance I would do portraits of the same people I listened to, like Little Richard, Mick Jagger, Chubby Checker, but also Devine or Dead Kennedys. The music and club scene seemed so rich here in New York at the beginning of the eighties that I was out every night to hear live music and to flash SX-70 portraits backstage. Every member of a band was photographed individually, front flash, against the same background: the dressing-room graffiti walls, or pieces of colored fabric. Then the pictures were put together to form a strip or a pattern. Some of the works were quite large, like when I photographed Count Basie and his orchestra, Frank Zappa, James Brown, or Sun Ra. The great thing about Polaroid, of course, was that you could do the whole thing right then and there; so, quite often, the musicians would want to help with their group's piece, and we would all kneel around the pics on the floor, designing a grid—the SX-70 puzzle. This series also had more to do with recording types and styles than with photography.

LM: How big is that series?

AK: About 300 groups. Lots of the young local bands, but also people like Ray Charles, B.B. King, Talking Heads, and so on. We called it "The New York City Rock Series" and it was shot in places like Max's Kansas City, Madison Square Garden, CBGB, The Palladium, Danceteria, the Ritz, or the Savoy.

LM: Did the audiences interest you at all?

AK: Oh, I kept seeing all these cool-looking boys, or were they girls?

LM: Ah, that's the androgynous series . . .

AK: Yeah, it was fascinating to run into people and be uncertain about their sex. So I did "Men and Women," a series of very straight headshots, very simple. One strobe umbrella—a gray seamless—people with no make-up and no smile. It was surprising how well the series worked for the viewer, who would go from one picture to the next and, after about one or two dozen, would stop at a face and ask: "Is this a boy or a girl?" Then, having once raised that question, the person would turn back in the series and also question the sex of the subjects he or she had looked at just minutes before.

AA: What was so interesting about the androgyny?

AK: It created abstraction. Eliminating one element, sexual identity, makes you focus on the subjects as people only, not as men or women. Or it abstracts sexuality from what you are seeing and makes you think about it abstractly and self-consciously, so that it seems something amazing instead of ordinary and everyday. Abstraction is only a tool, a way of making you see instead of overlook. It's a means of describing character, and *Heads* takes formal abstraction even further than "Men and Women" did. In that series, there was hair. In *Heads*, without hair, one gets straight into the face. Nothing distracts from the topography of the features.

LM: In your *Heads* layout I see only groups of four, but here you are showing me a series of six prints.

AK: The original series has from four to seven pictures in a group, 16 x 20 prints, which is a little over life size. For the book, though, we had to design equal groups of four, to get the best presentation on a spread.

AA: The groups look very solid, almost like families. How did you decide who goes with whom?

AK: Grouping them into small series turned out to be quite a delicate undertaking. It's almost like dealing with people in real life, and it felt like putting a dinner party together. If you invite Vincent, you'd like to invite Richard, but then let's have Paul some other time. Often you find out only after the party who should have sat next to whom. Visually, this works the same way, and again it feels all of a sudden like a very responsible job. It's like getting people married—except, once the book was printed, it would be too late for a divorce. So, often you would put a group together, and then the next day you would take it apart again. But it would make you feel so good, once a group would last, when you still liked it after a week or months. It also happened that new models attacked or even destroyed groups that were already intact. I would see a print of Mark, who we shot yesterday, and all of a sudden feel he has to go with Lawrence, but Lawrence is already in a group.

continued on page 55

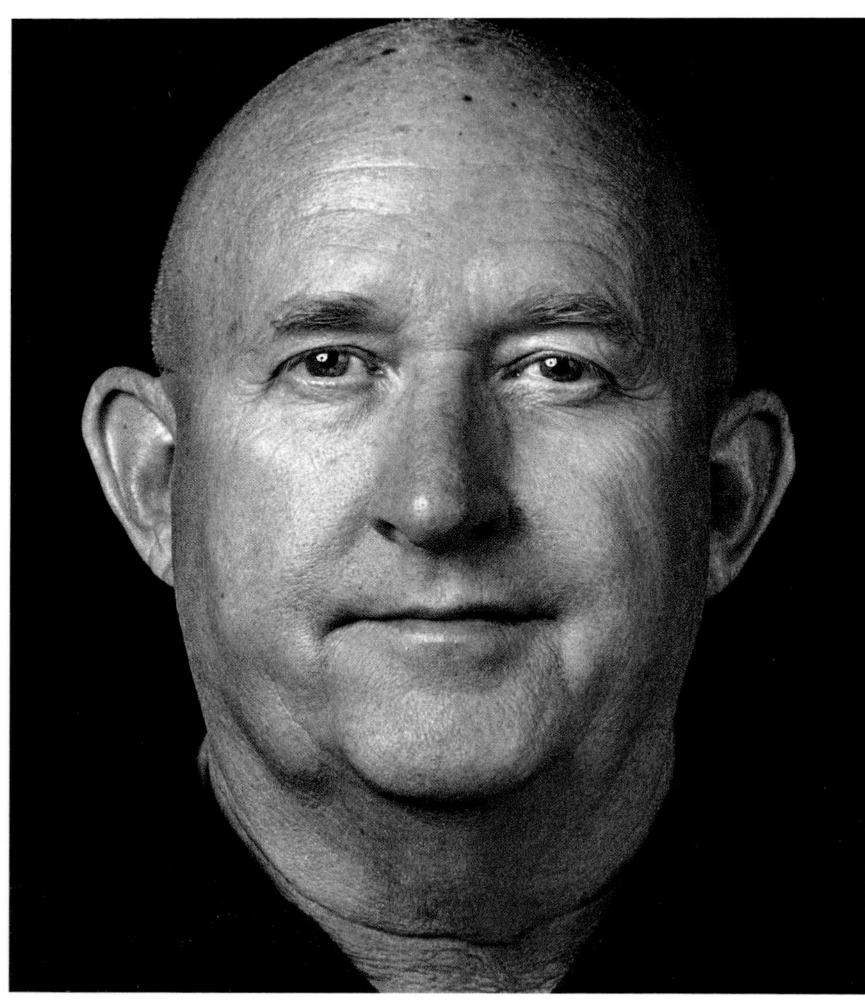

Charles Lamback, Jacksonville, North Carolina: retired master gunnery sergeant, United States Marine Corps

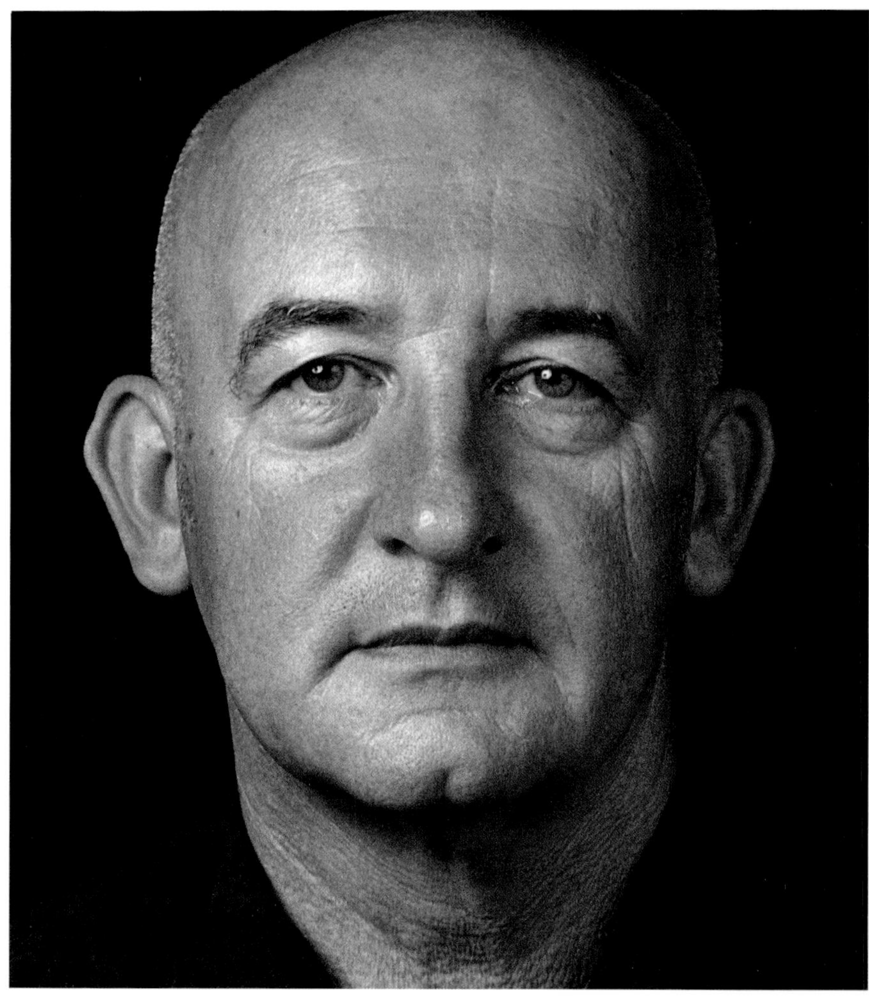

Mark Adams, Tega Cay, South Carolina: tire retreader

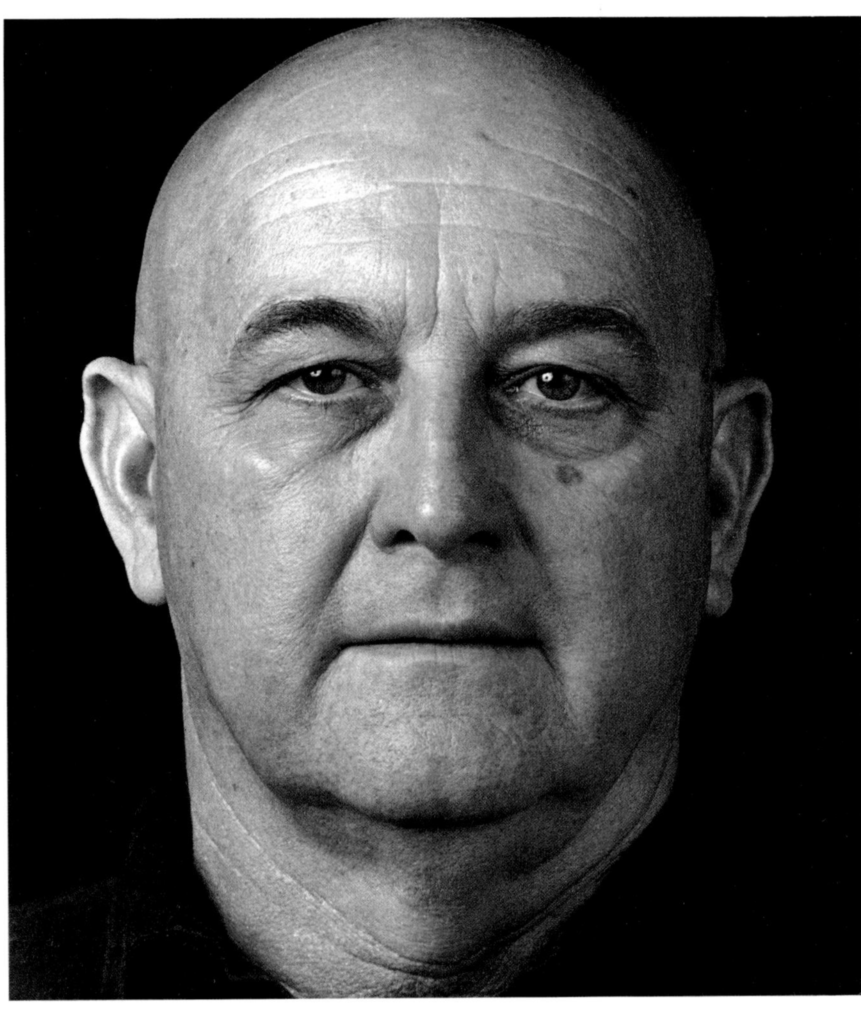

Bill White, Raleigh, North Carolina: tour superintendent, United States Postal Service

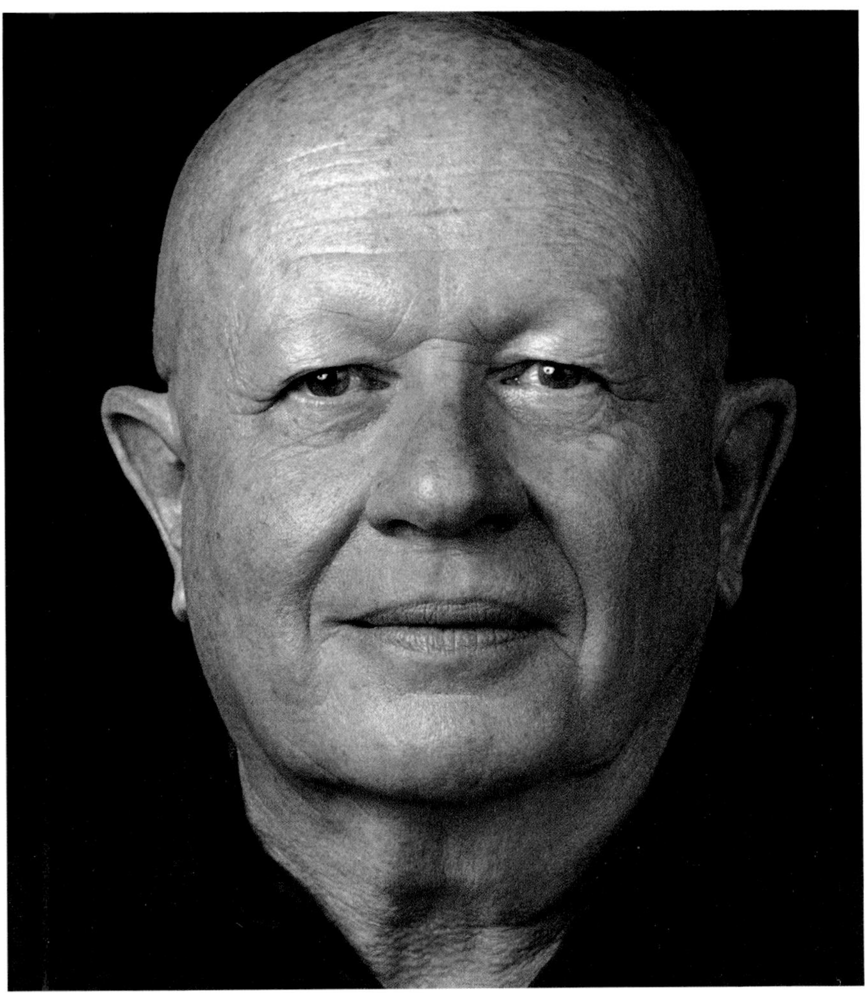

James H. Gunn, New Bern, North Carolina: semiretired public relations promoter and newspaper columnist; writes Canadian history books

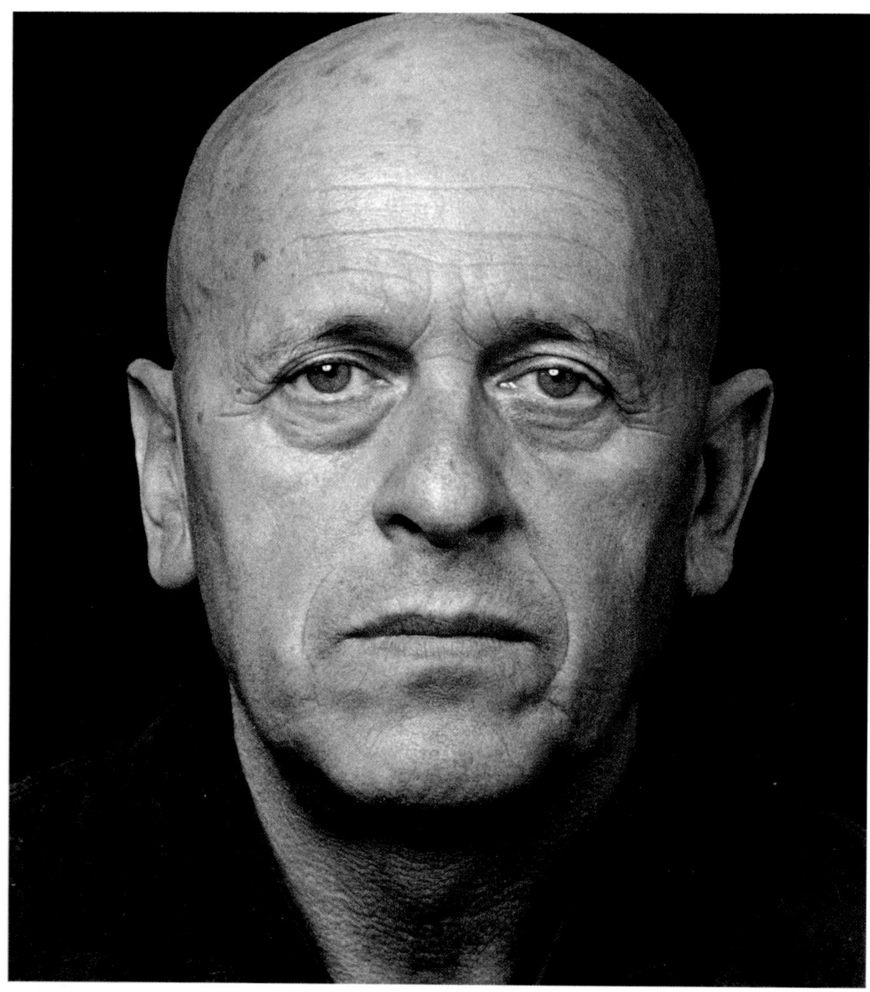

Mario Comensoli, Zurich: painter

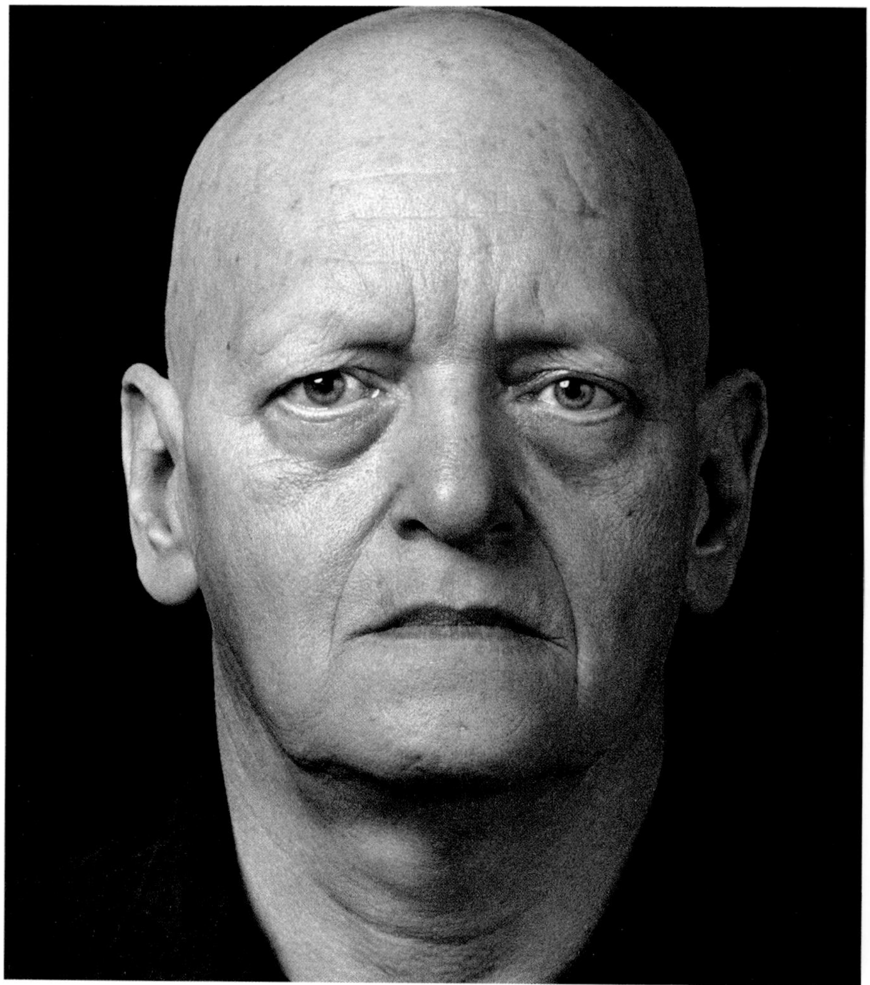

Anonymous

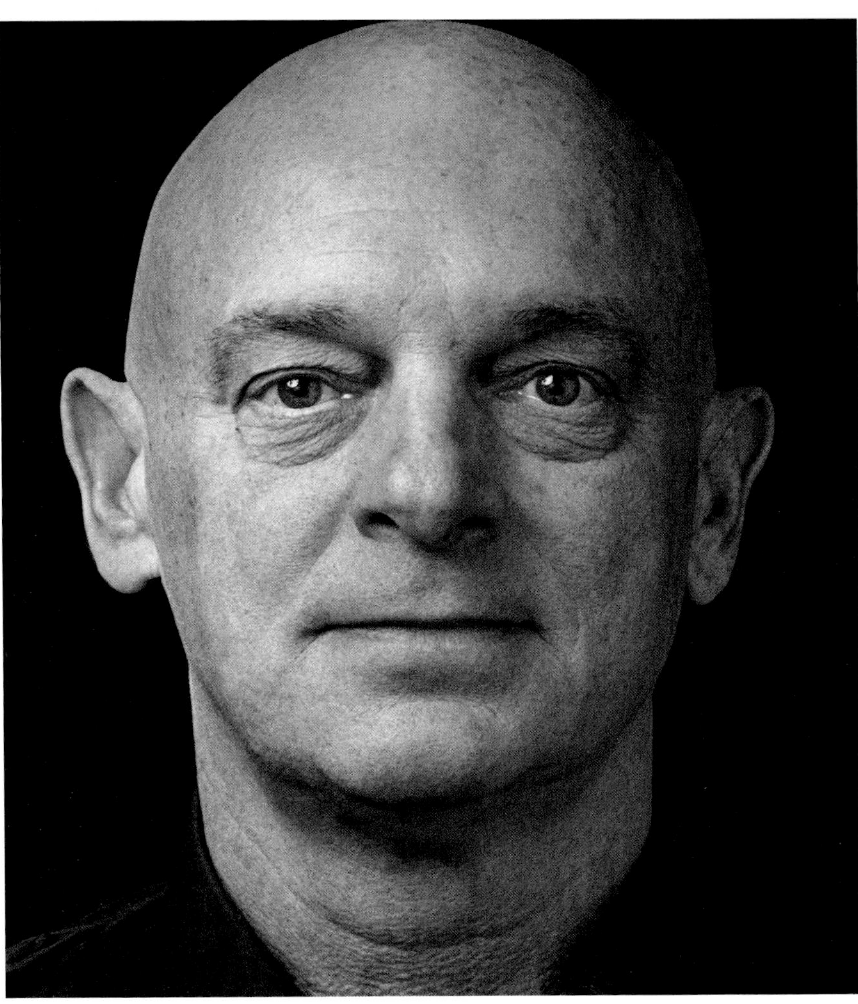

Gerald Carrus, New York City: president, Infinity Broadcasting

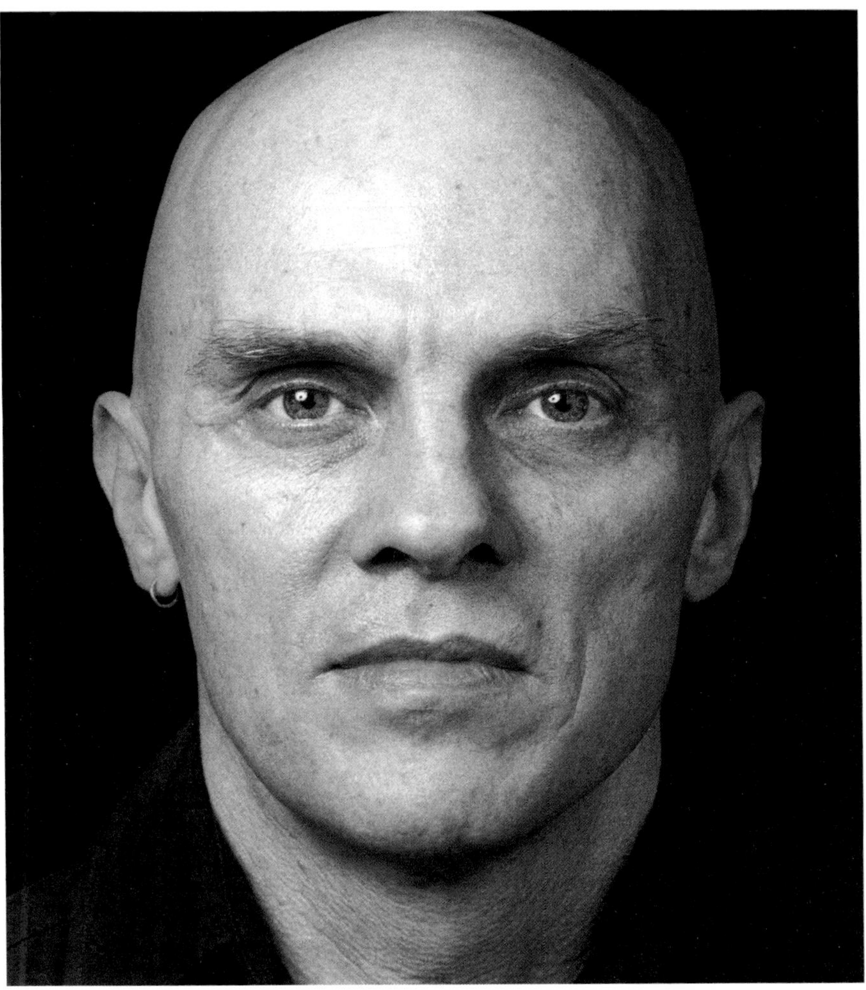

Henry Shaver, New York City: poet; receptionist for an interior design firm

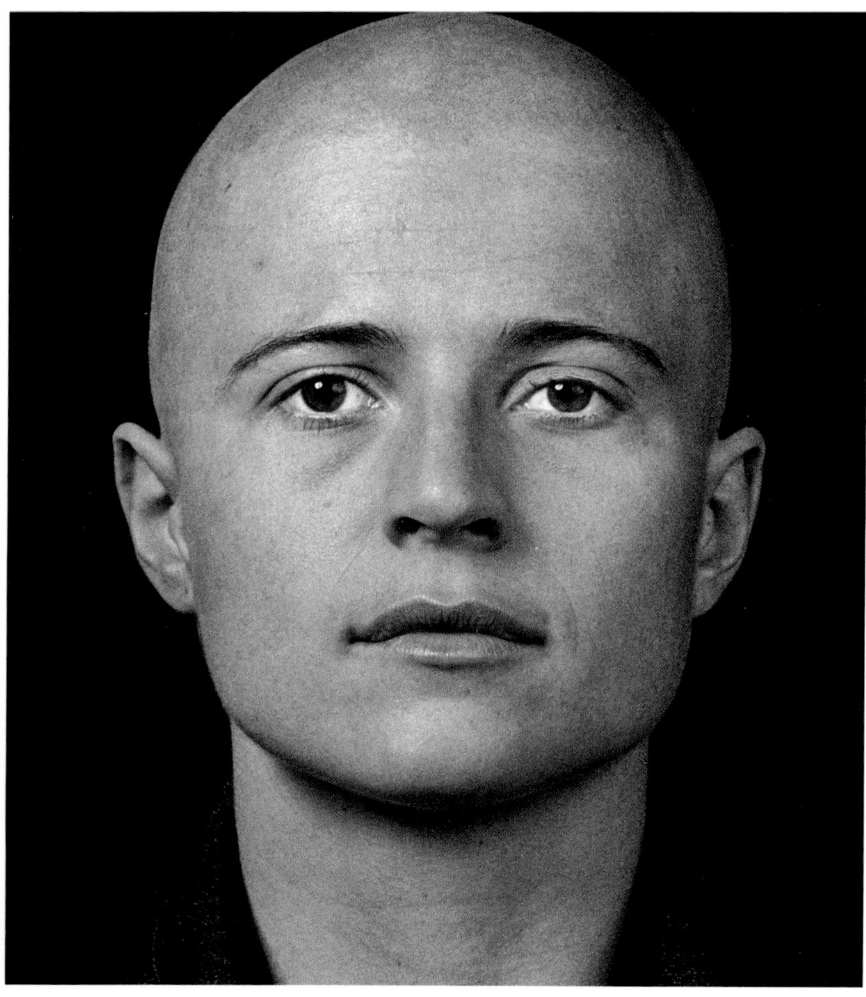

Isabelle Schnyder, New York City: photographer

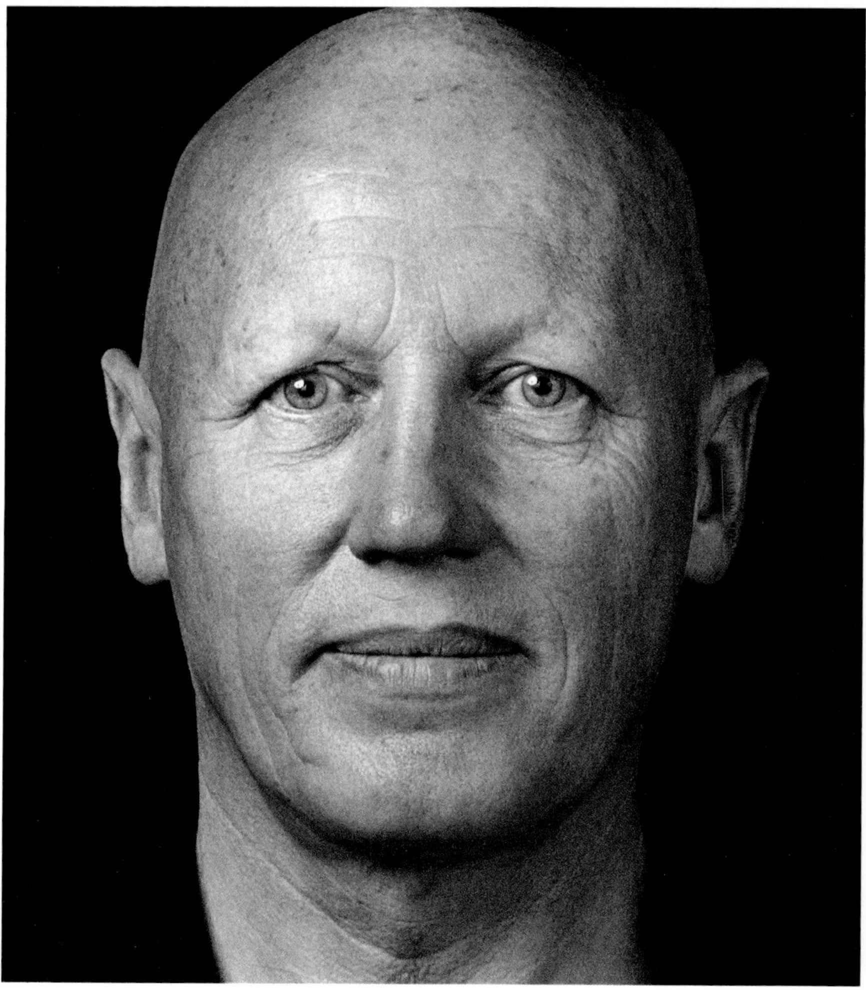

Prof. Dr. Jur. Ingo von Ruckteschell, New York City: Chief, Personnel Unit, United Nations; recruits experts for projects in developing nations

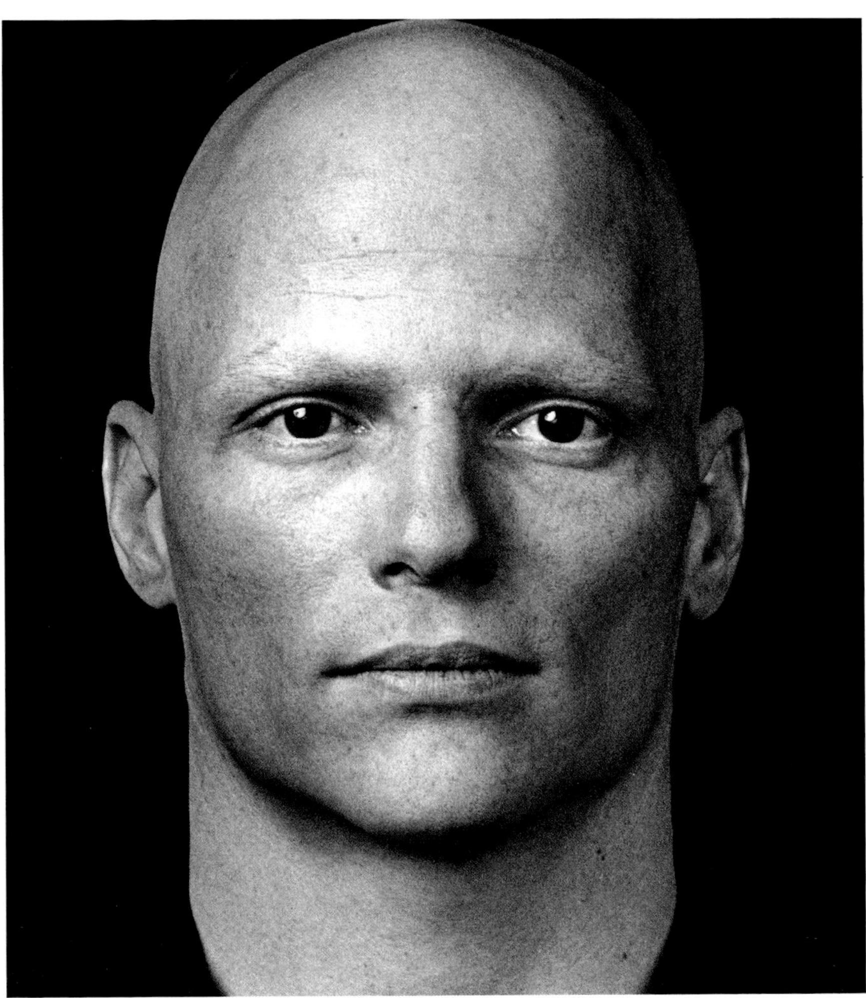

Andrew Skalko, New York City: deceased

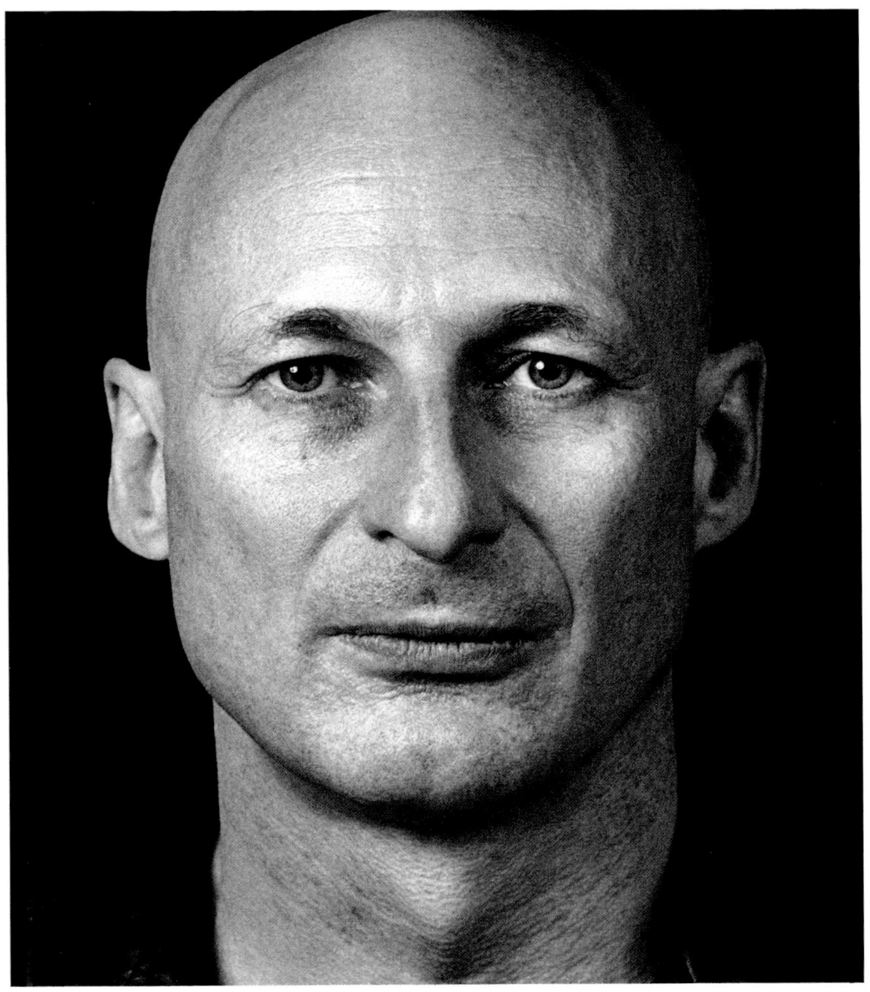

Richard Bonker, New York City: free-lance mathematician for large corporations

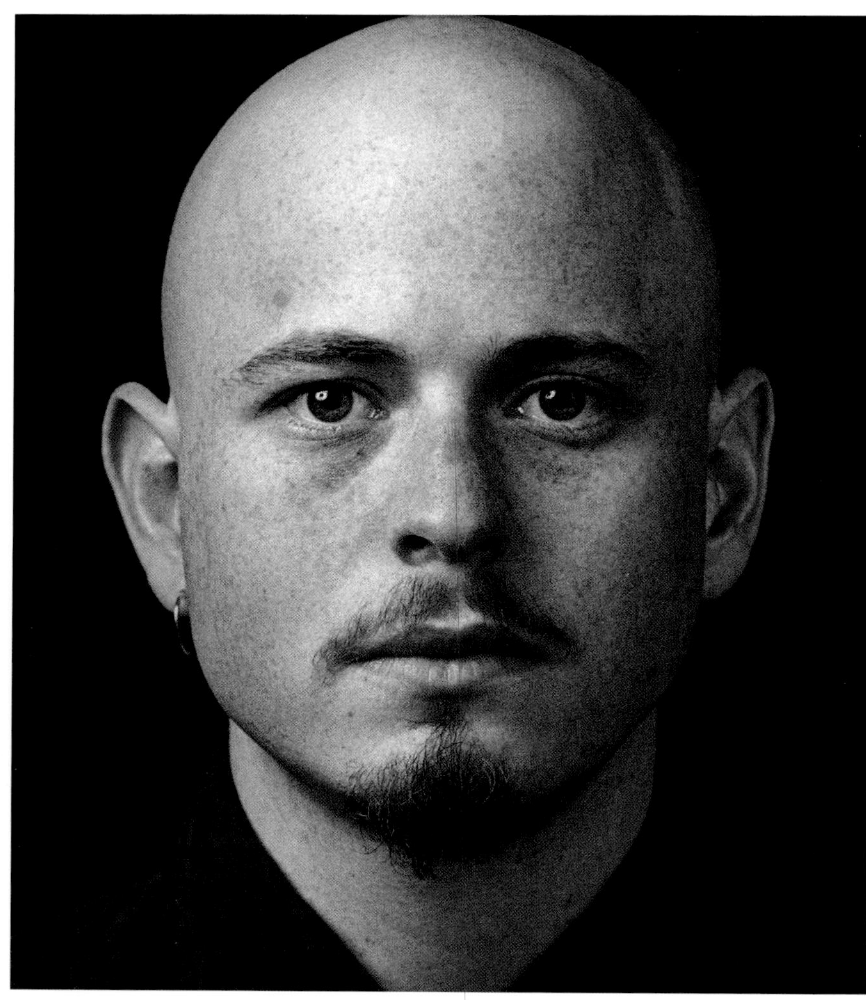

Richard Norman, New York City: Good Humor ice cream salesman

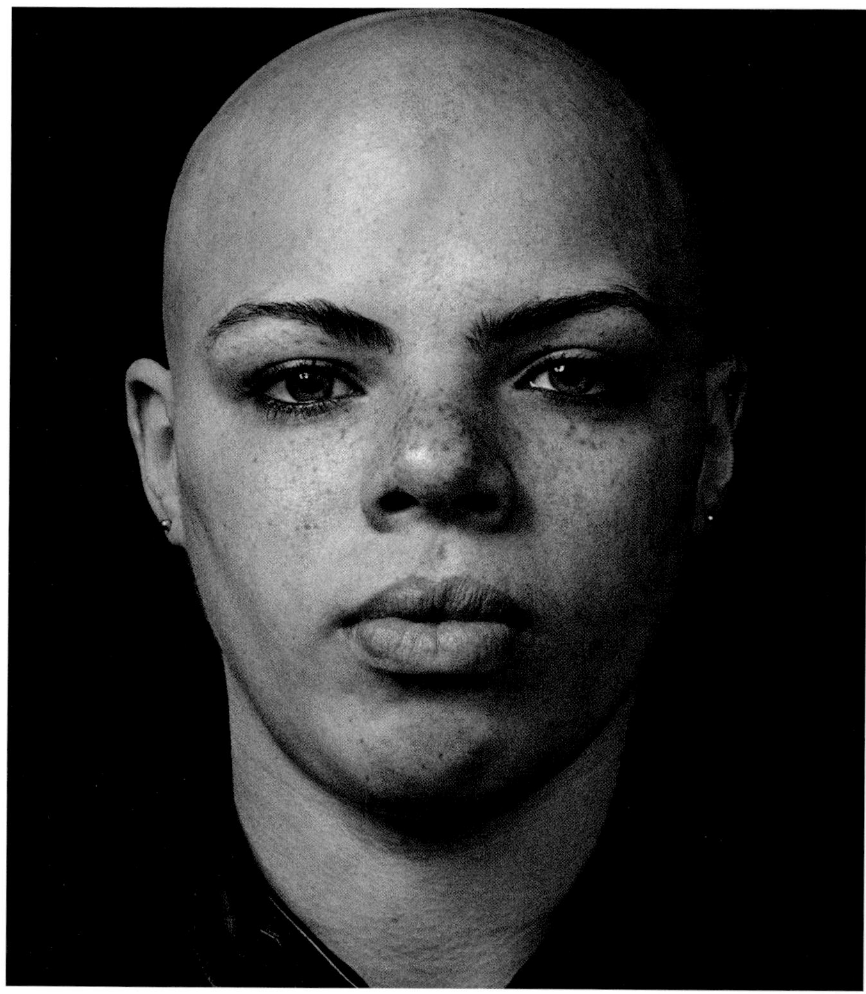

Felicia Kyle Alexander, New York City: singer and songwriter

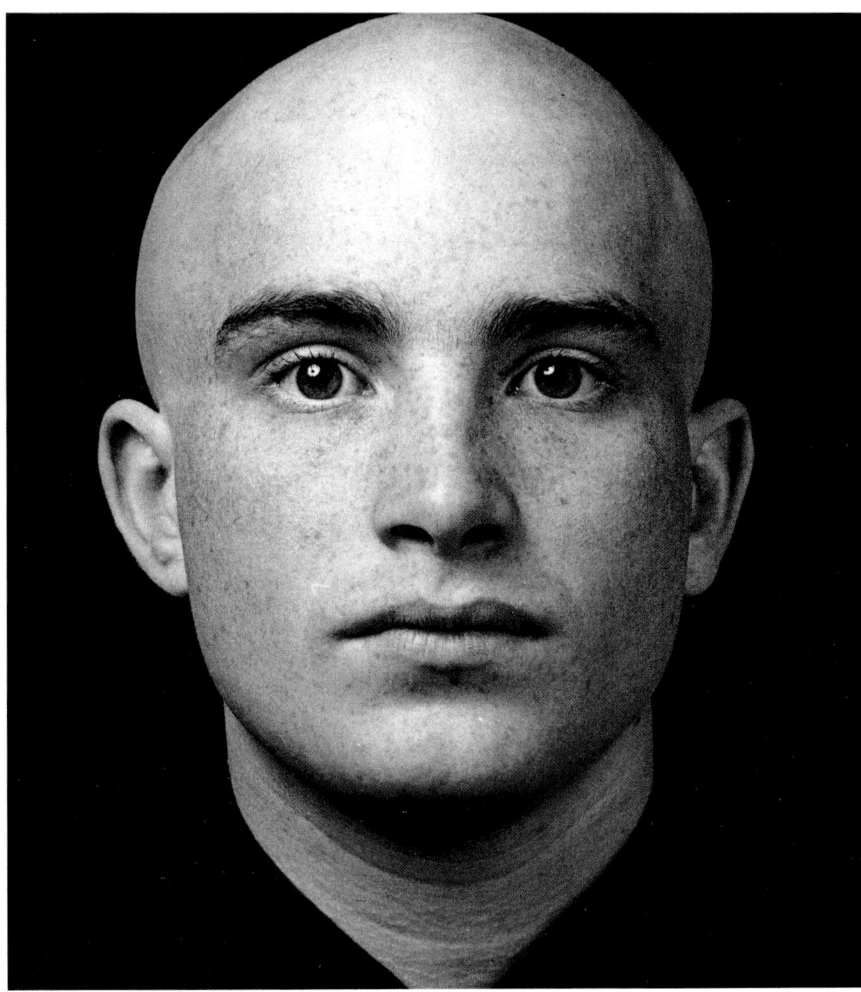

Frank Sulzer, New York City: painter

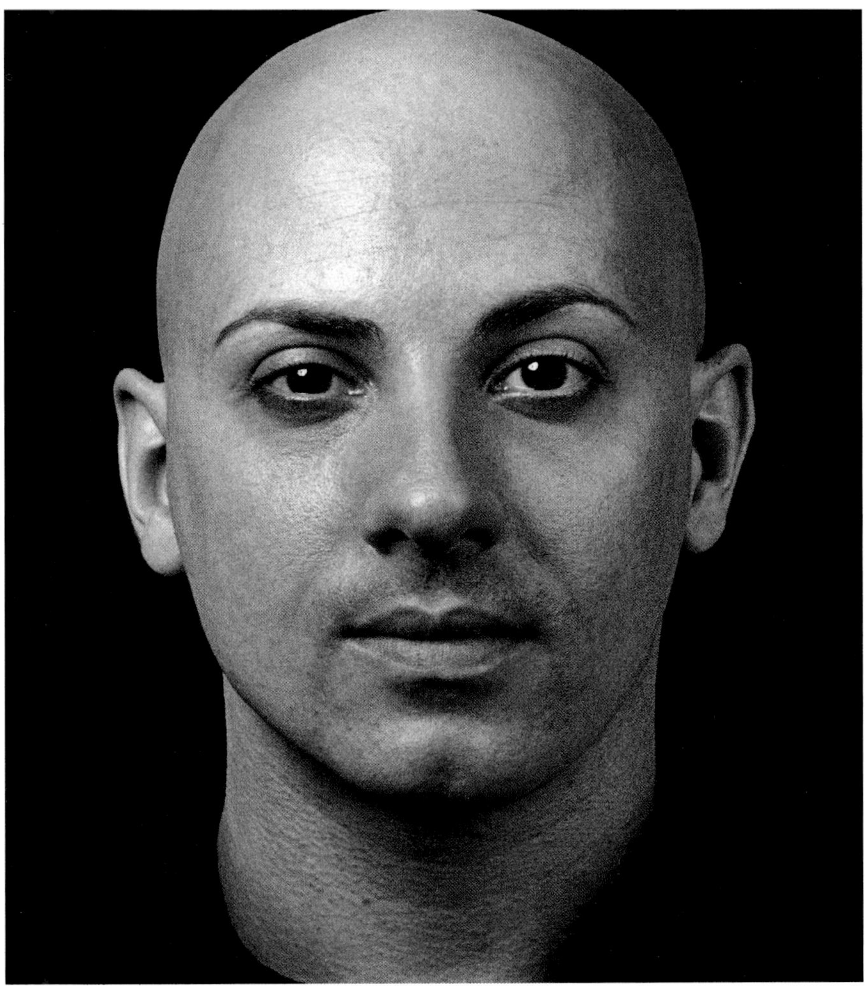

Arthur Turchi, New York City: hairstylist, make-up artist, and performer

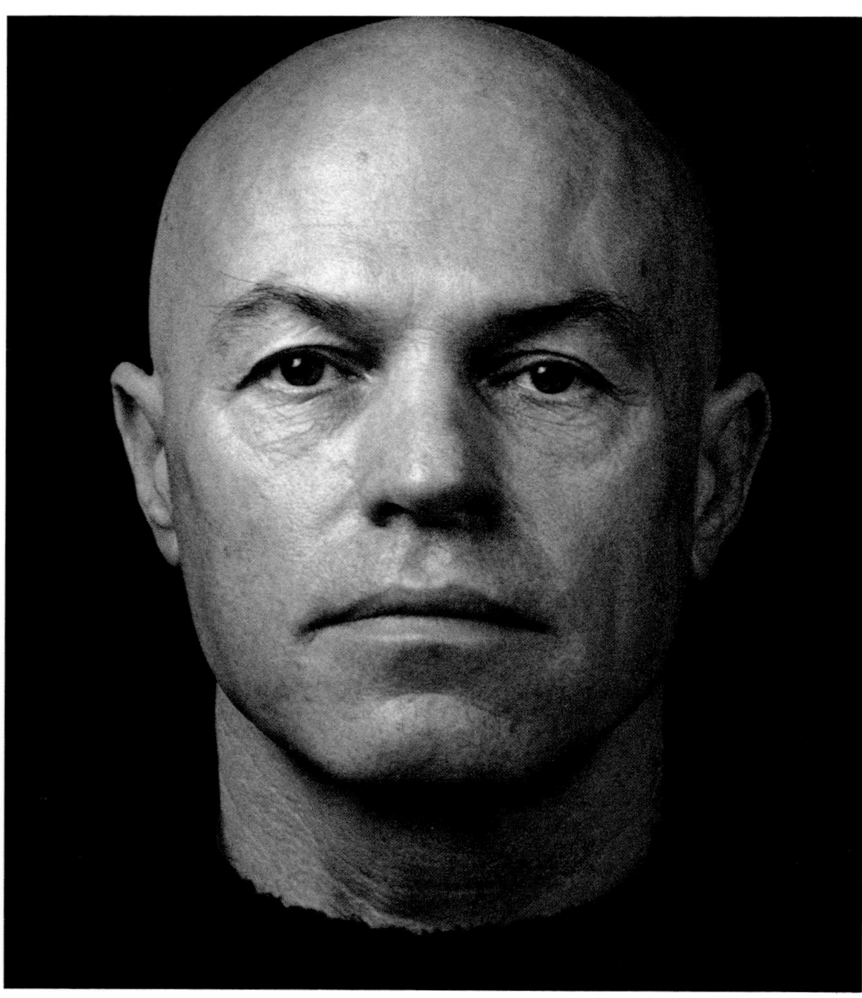

Peter Le Blanc, New York City: painter

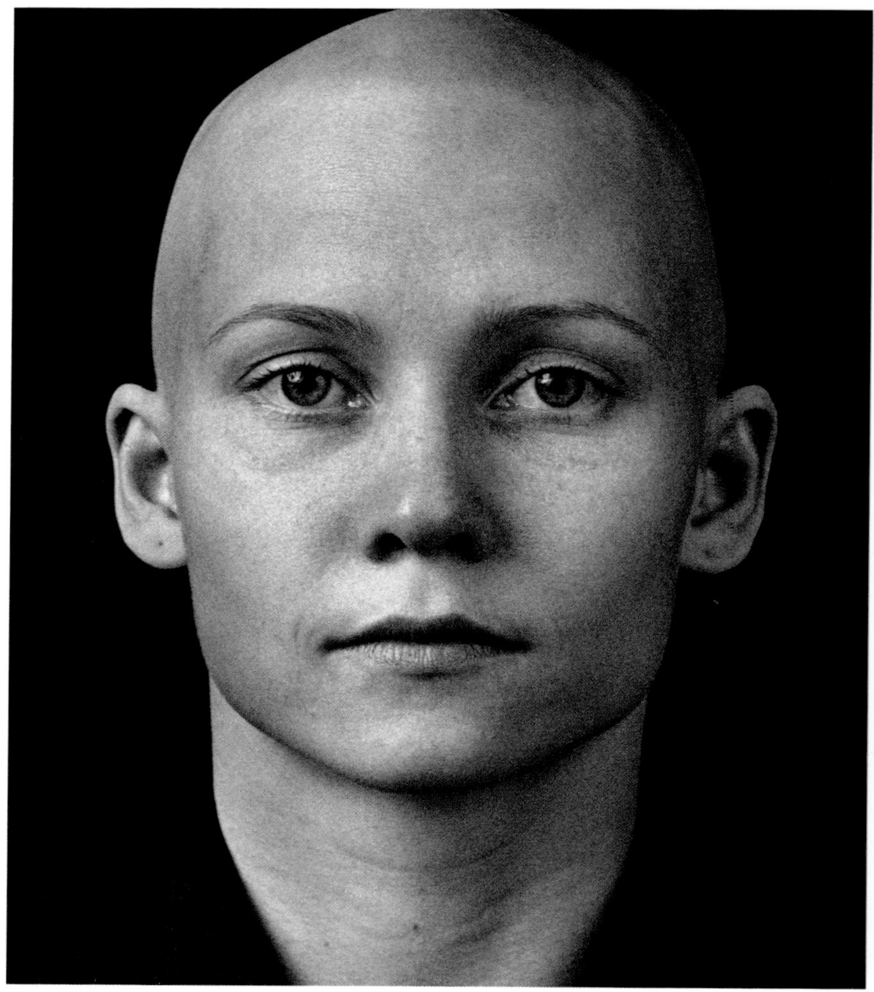

Marika Blossfeldt, Berlin: dancer

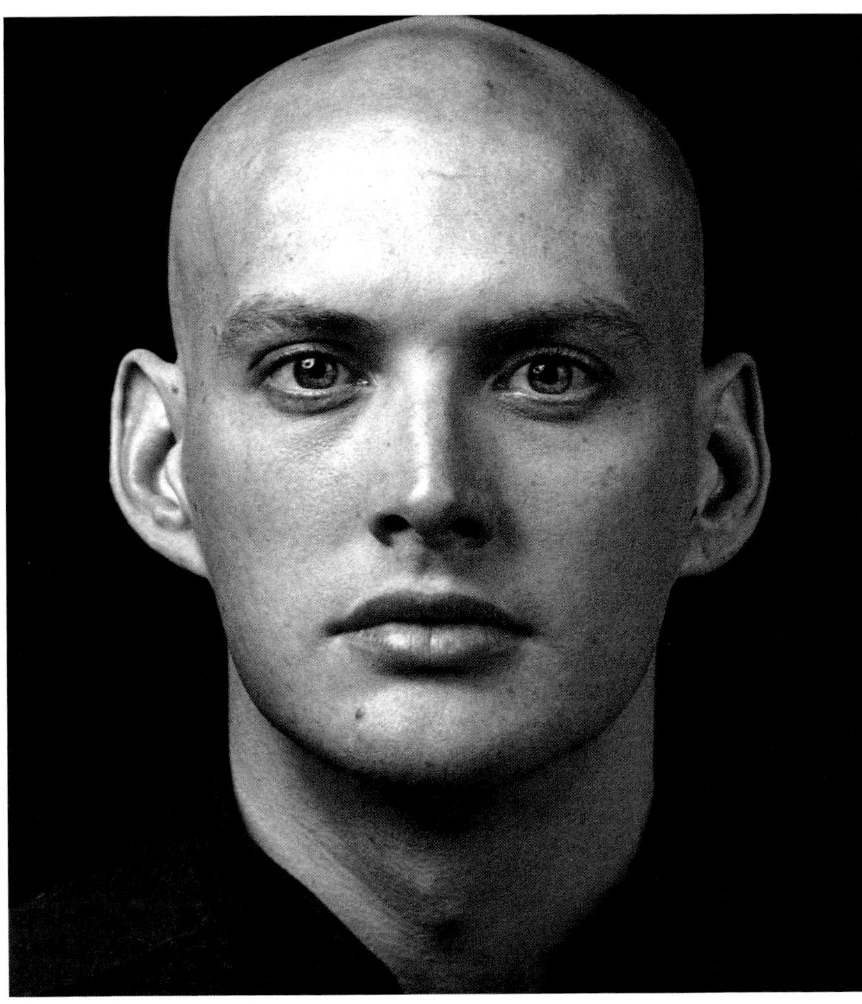

Berns Fry, New York City: fashion representative, Barney's

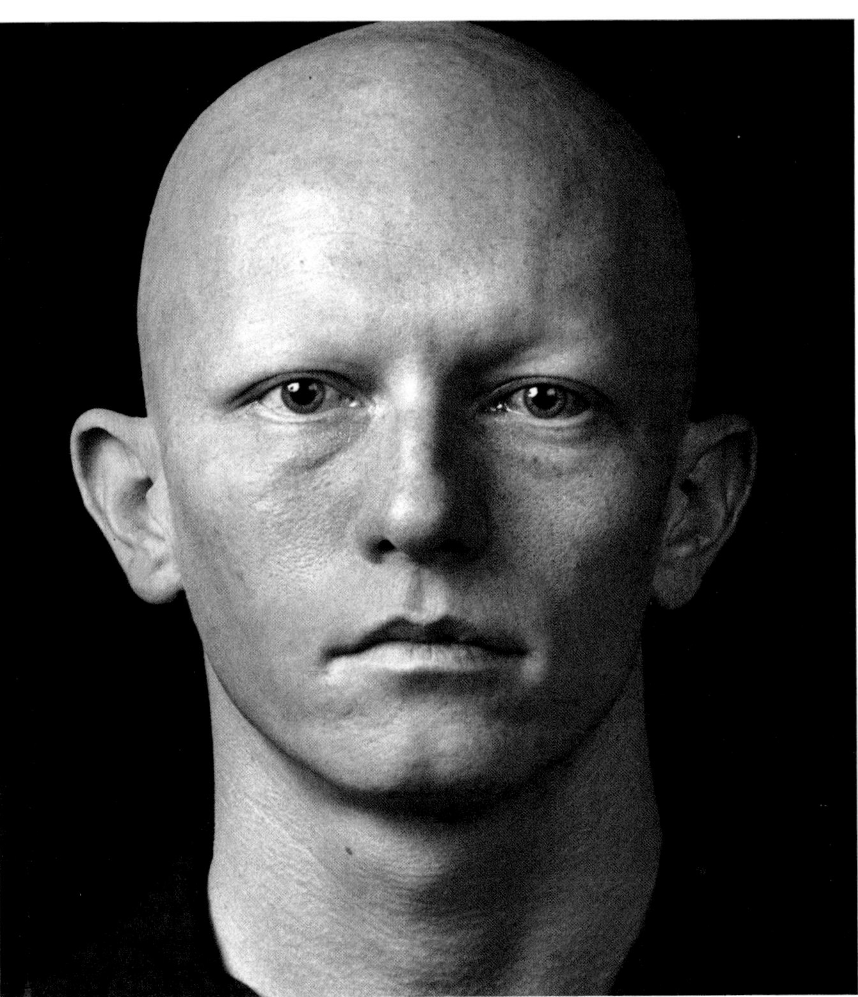

Robert Sherman, New York City: performer and professional masseur

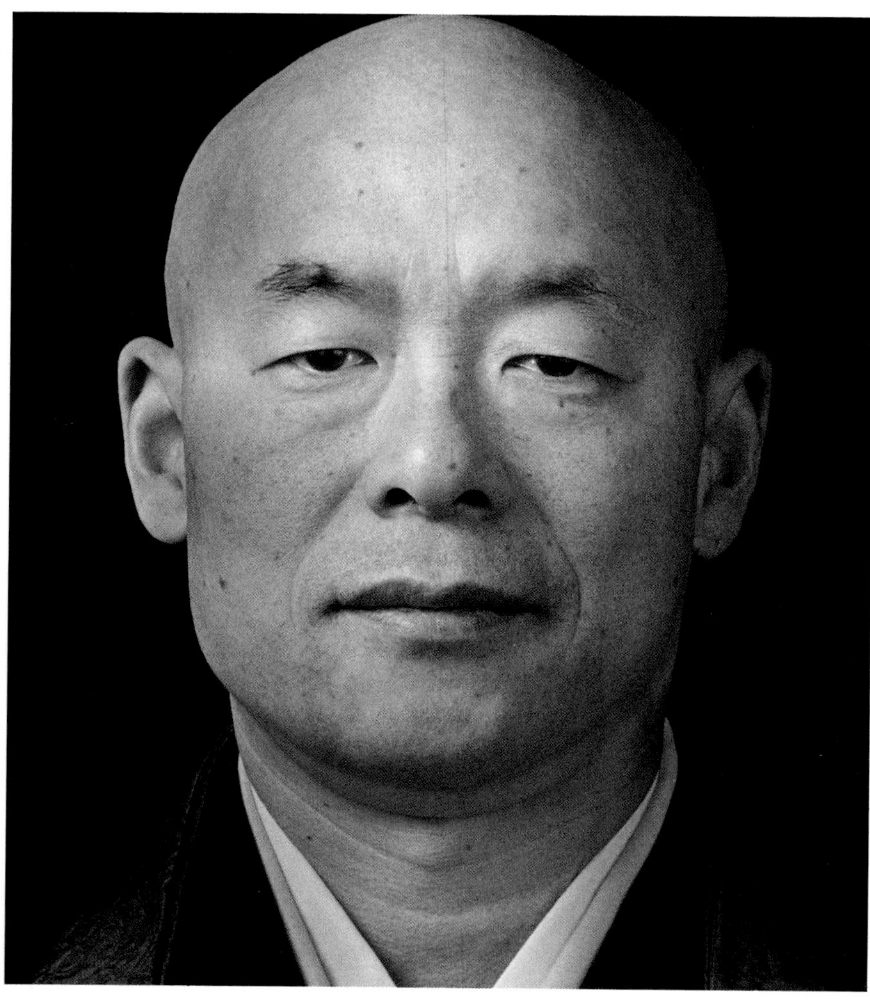

Eido T. Shimano (Roshi Tai San), New York City: Zen Buddhist priest, the Zen Studies Society

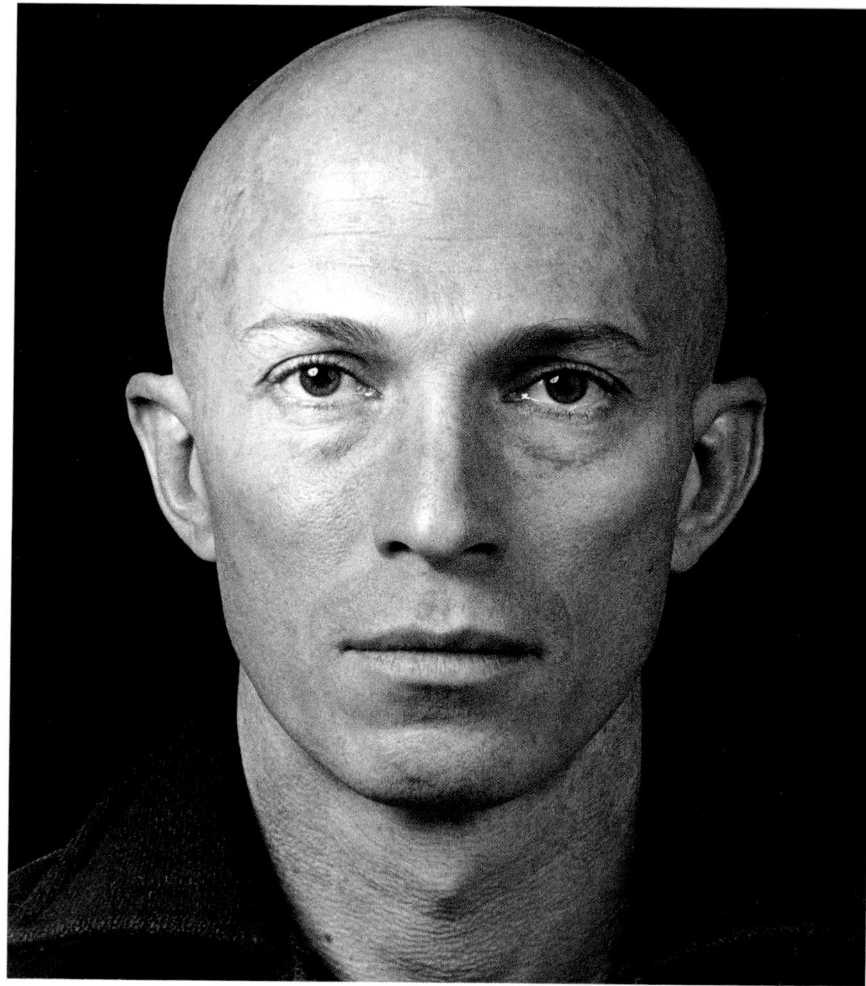

Stephen English, New York City: artist's model, School of Visual Arts

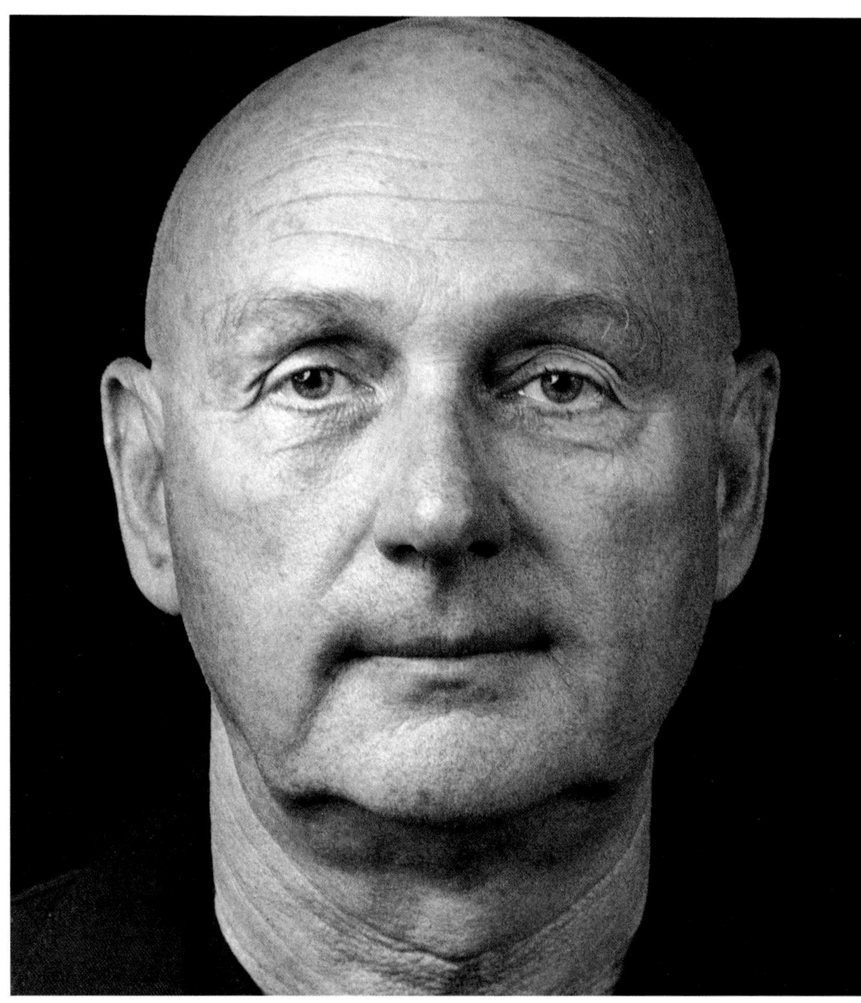

John Lukaszuk, New York City: investigator, New York City Health Department

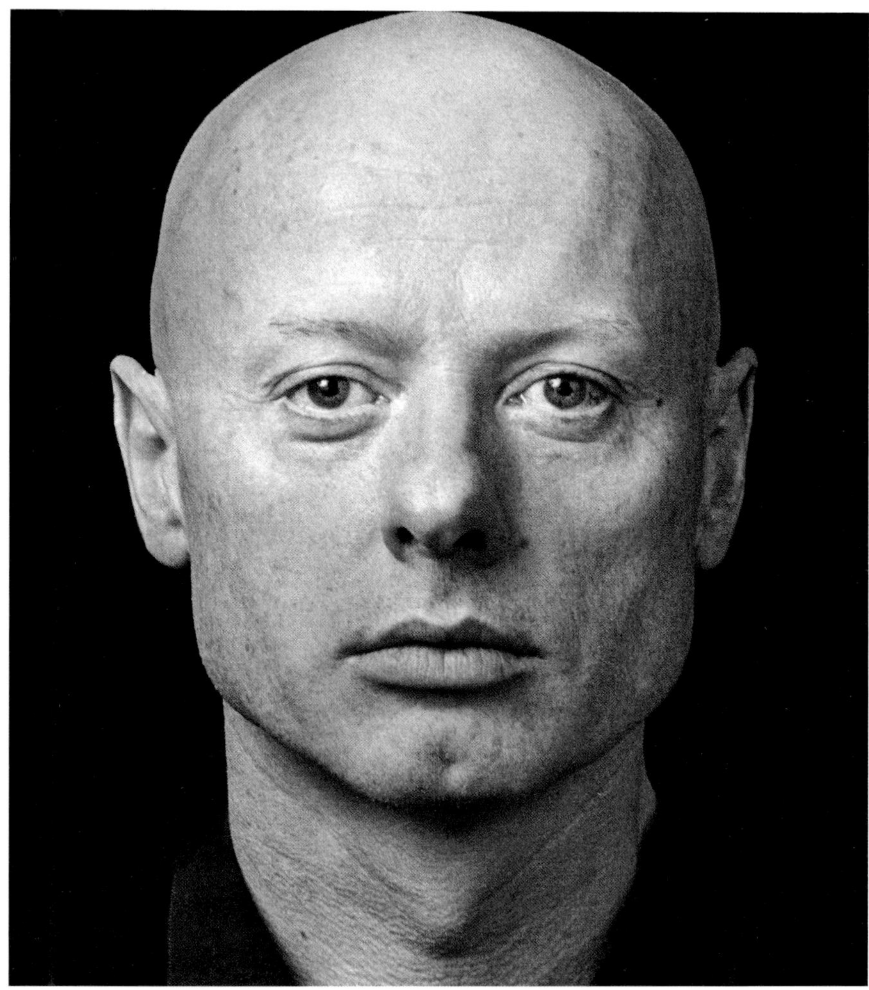

Klaus Knaup, New York City: German photographer

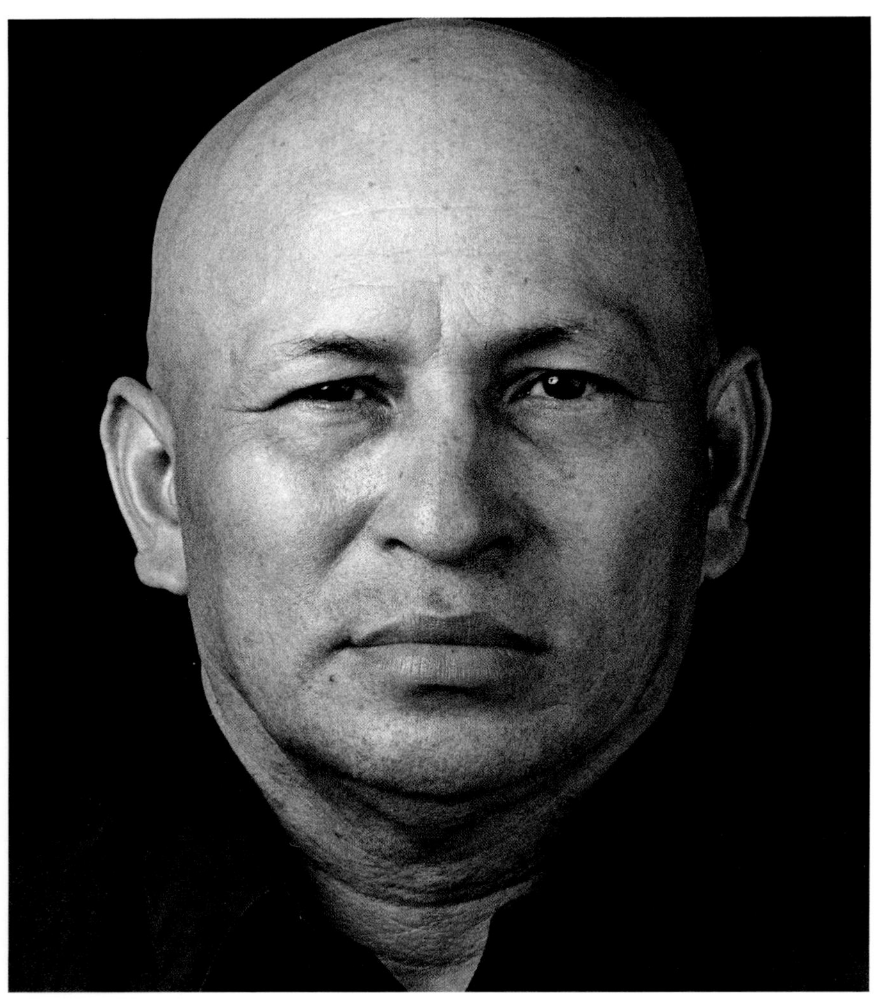

Cesar A. Uguillas, New York City: salesman, Canal Street flea market

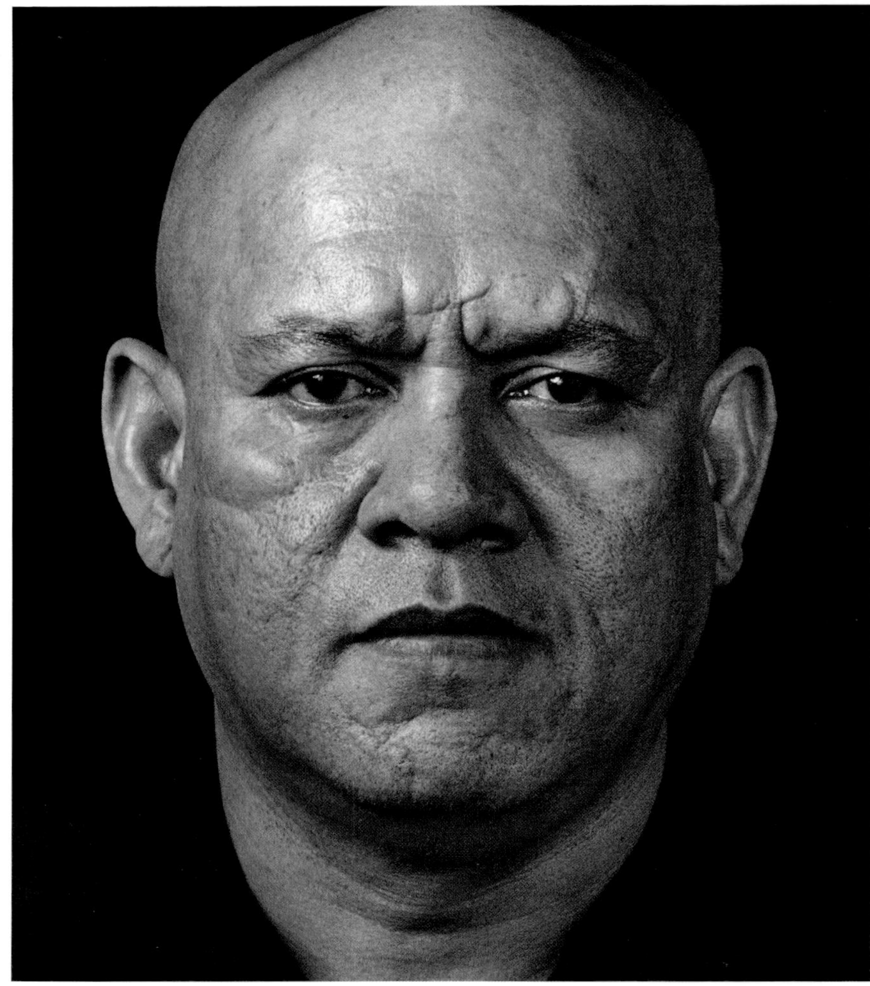

Bill W. Karena Kaukeano, New York City: thanatologist

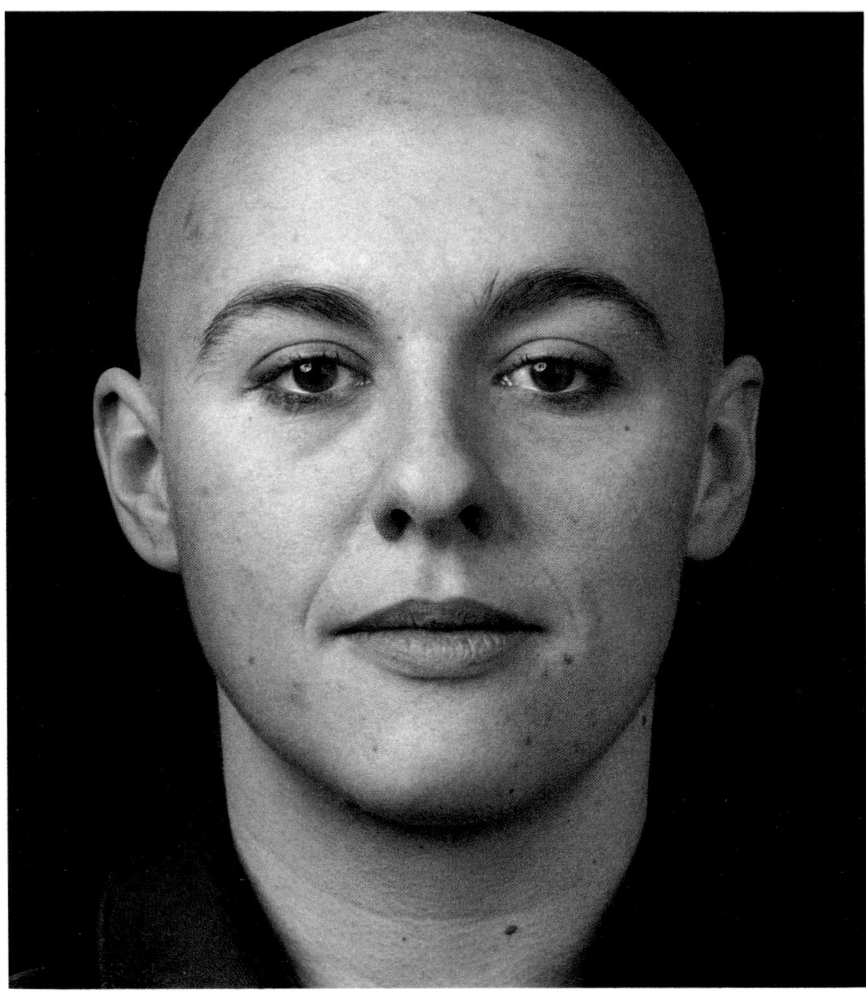

Denise Geiser, Basel: actress

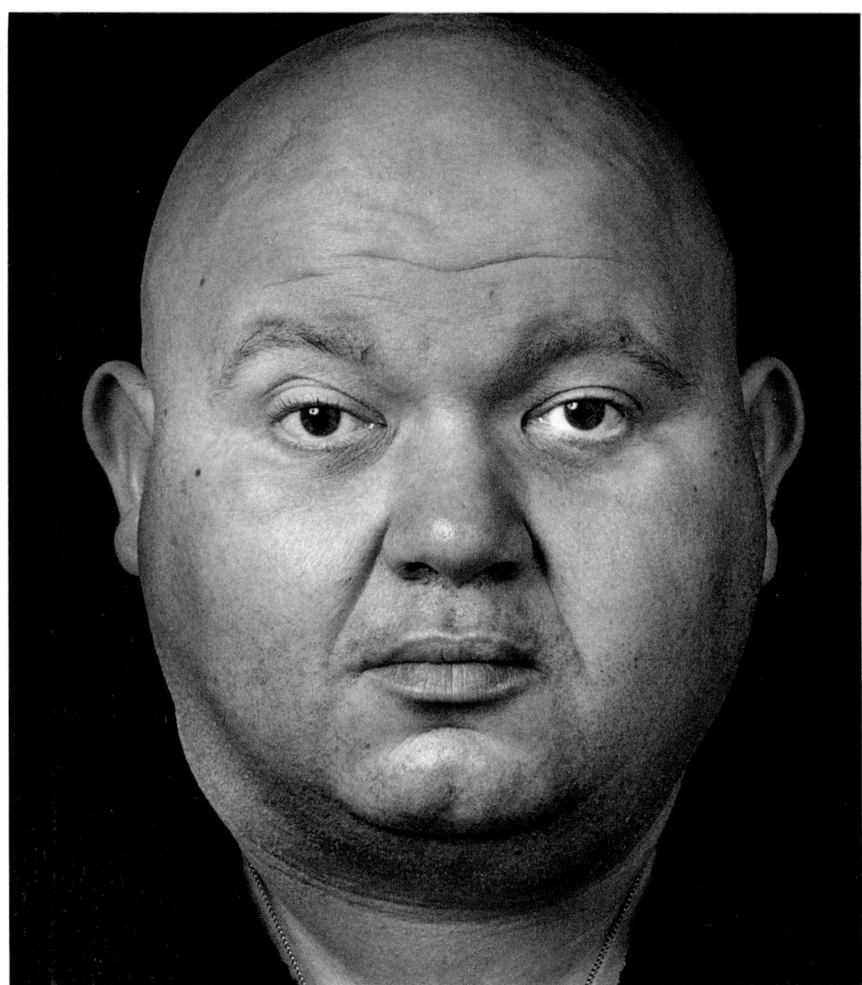

Leonard Tepper, New York City: entertainer for Buddha-Gram

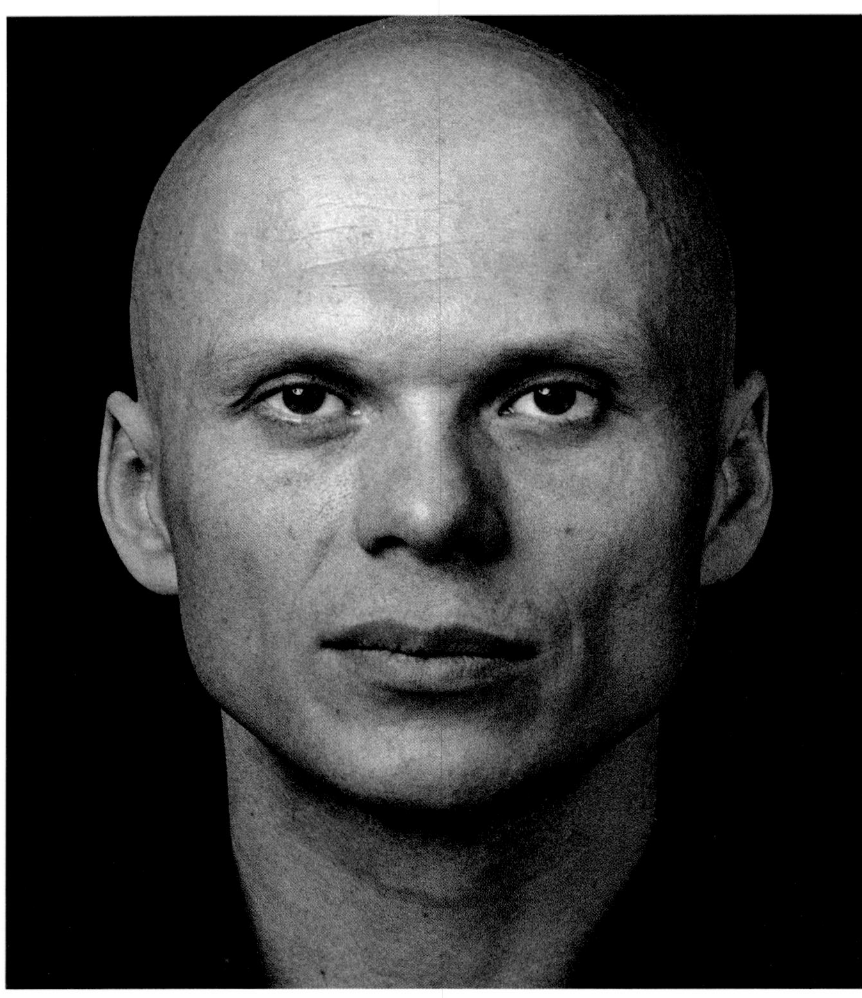

Pavel Libovichy, New York City: former art dealer; makes videos in South America

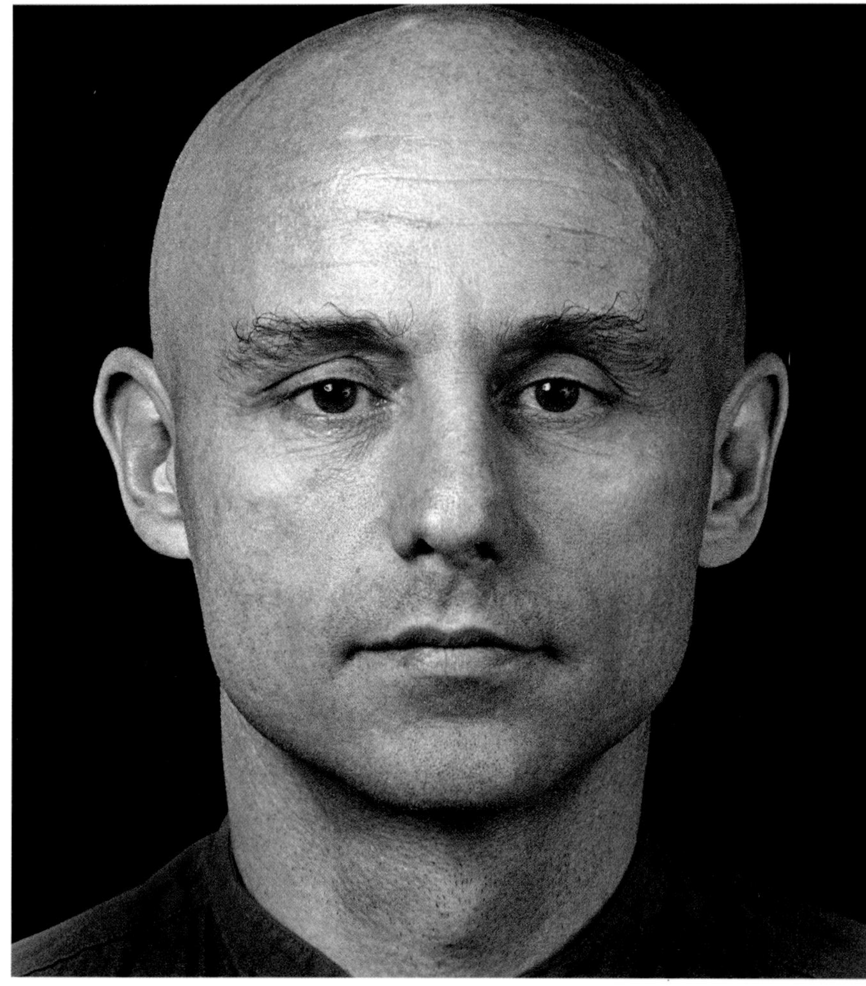

Paolo Serra, New York City: real estate investor; co-owner, Serra di Felice Gallery

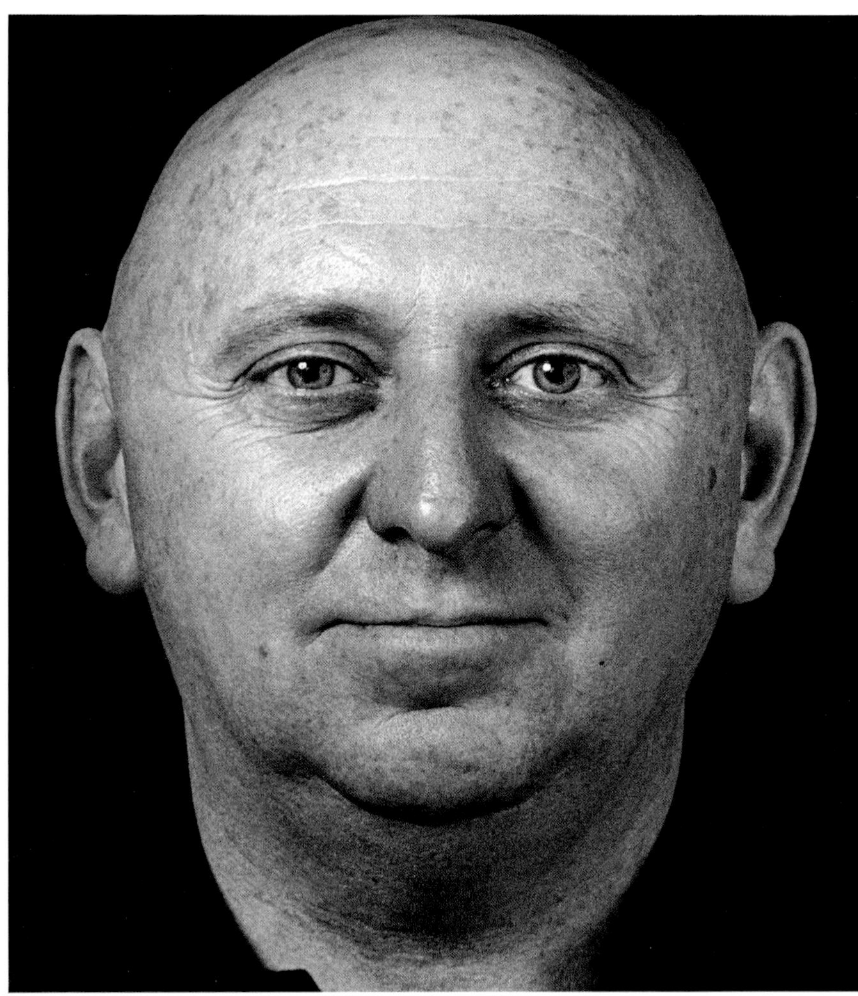

Ray Frier, New York City: works in public relations and marketing research

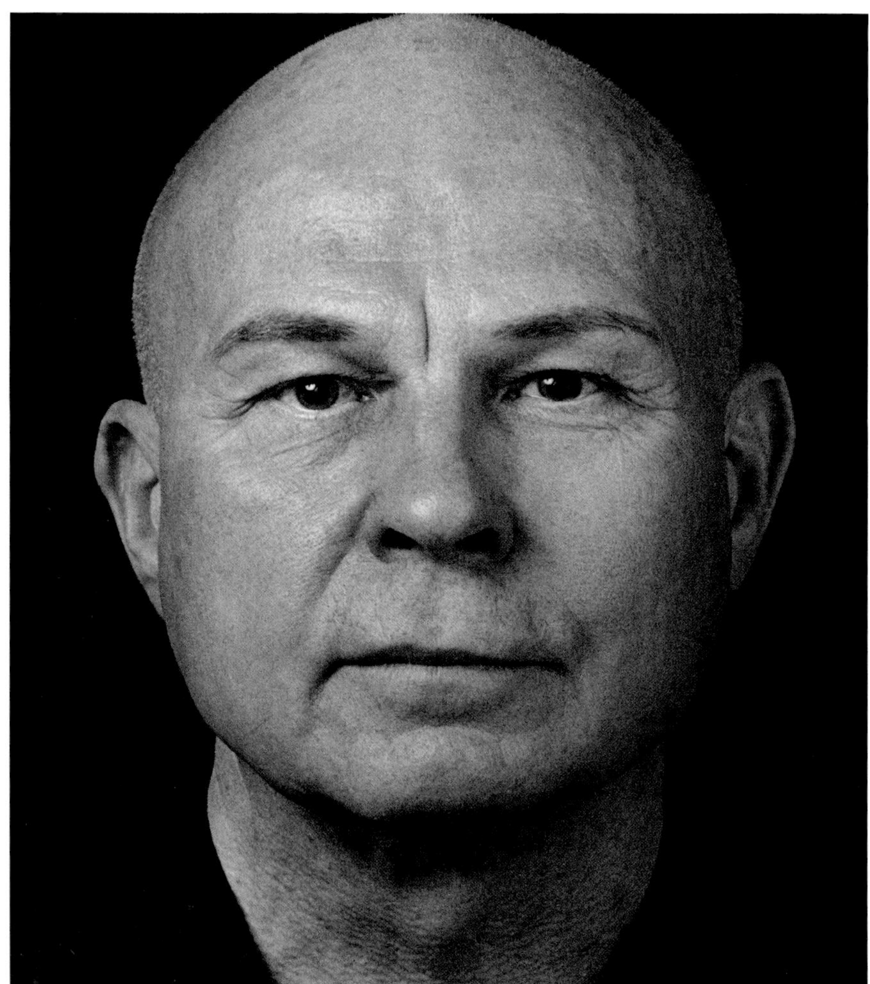

William Burdick, New York City: dancer and dance instructor

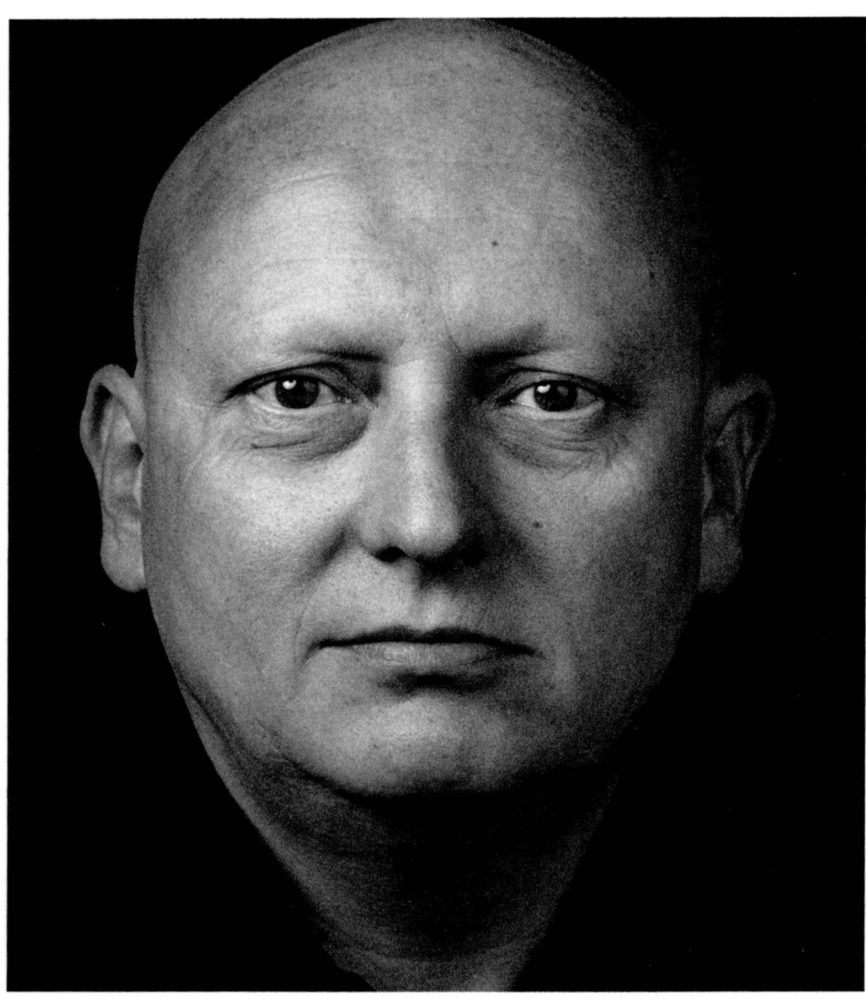

John Wolffe, London: musical promoter

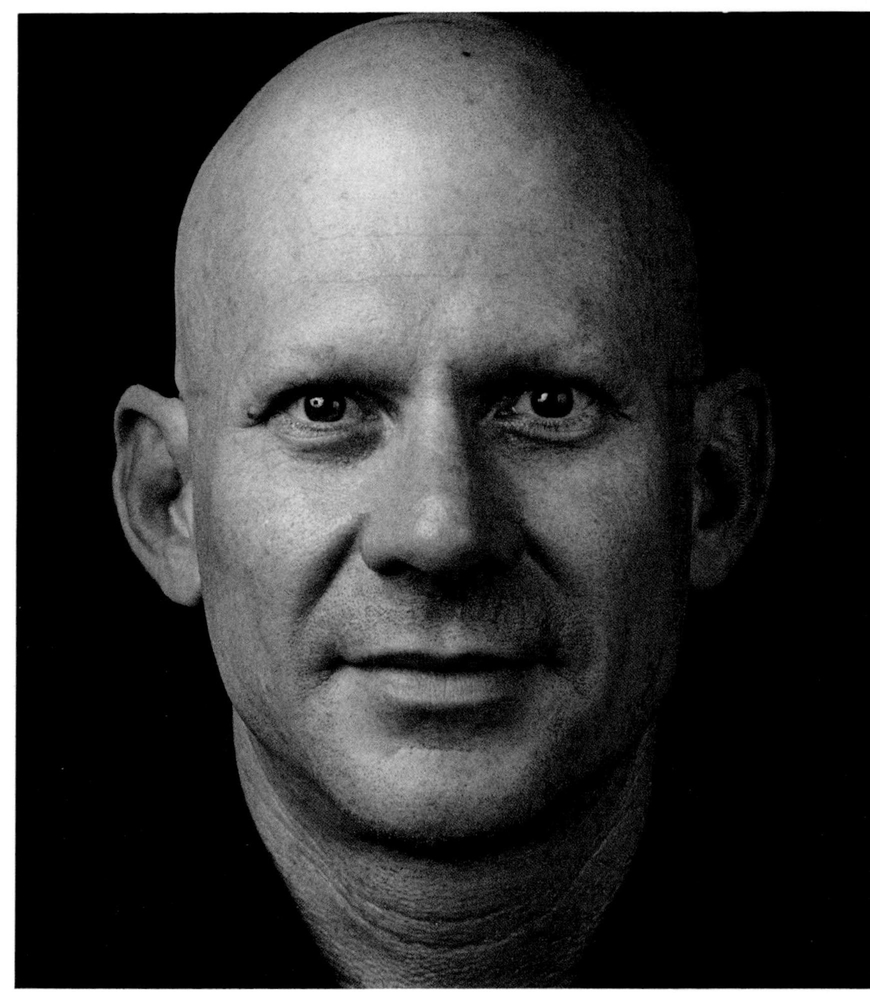

Peter Kowald, New York City: musician, Peter Kowald Trio

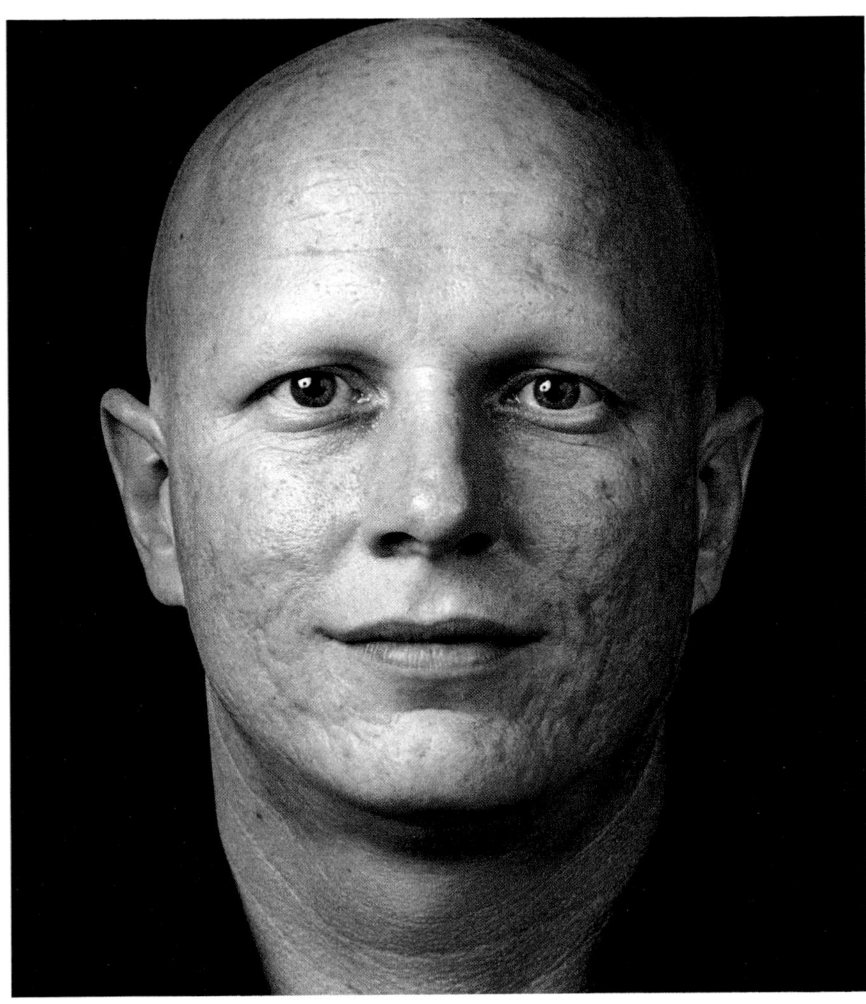

Alexander Torrance, Morehead City, North Carolina: pilot, United States Marine Corps

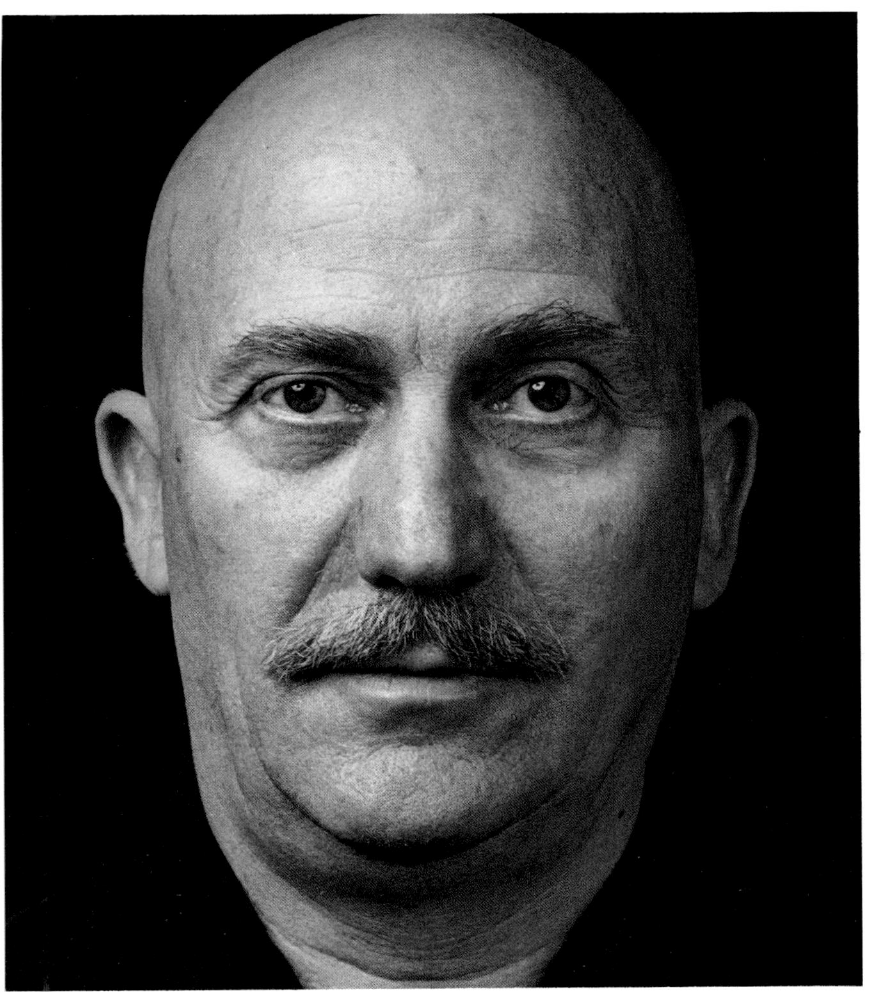

Victor Del Mastro, New York City: engineer, Grand Hyatt Hotel

We struggle to go to utopia. This itself is an unrealistic, most impractical burden. The practice of Zen Buddhism leads us to realize that there is no answer to *why*, no answer to *what*, no utopia someplace hidden. When these external searches have been completely abandoned, then we see that "this very place is the Lotus Land of purity, this very body is the body of the Buddha," as Hakuin Zenji says in *The Song of Zazen*. In this way, Zen Buddhism teaches us to grow and to realize true peace of mind.

—Eido T. Shimano

President Reagan looked up and wanted to know why some of his aides were shaking my hand. Somebody told him that I was a guy on T.V. The President said, "Oh, I've seen you too. Let's get a picture together. We're members of the same union." He promised that his office would send me a copy. It never did, but I don't really mind. I didn't vote for him anyway.

—Gordon Ray Press

continued from page 35

Its like in real life. The whole grouping was done purely by intuition, by considering the visual aspects. I work more with my stomach than with my brain. A few heads appeared to be very magnetic toward each other visually, because of the shape of the skull, the eyes, nose, or lips, and so on; others because of their common warmth of expression, their coolness, or even their complementary differences.

AA: Your earlier book, *Artist's Portraits*,* is very different from *Heads*, much looser, closer to what one might expect from portrait photography.

AK: *Artist's Portraits* is much more narrative, as maybe my whole life was more hand-colored at that time over there when I lived in Germany. I was traveling constantly and went to see all kinds of artists, at least the ones I knew through their work. The meetings took place at their homes, studios, or sometimes I shot them during a walk, a fast-food lunch, or during a ride in a cab. The environment, as it related to the subject, was always a strong element; it was part of the portrait. In each session, outside on location or at somebody's house, you would not only get to know a person, but also a new place, a new meal, different furniture and architecture, new books and art, and lots of signs of different lifestyles. So you would create a totally different picture idea for every person you'd photograph—influenced also by chance events. *Heads* is exactly the opposite. The creative part of the work is mainly in the concept. After that, you just become a collector and practice good craftsmanship. The challenge of photographing people in my studio was incredible. All of a sudden, you had to find the essence of a person almost exclusively through conversation, sitting on the same couple of chairs with each person, or on the sofa, having tea or a glass of wine. The studio: an environment

*New York: Harry N. Abrams, Inc., 1981.

unknown to the person being photographed and too familiar to inspire you as the photographer.

LM: Can any portrait be realistic?

AK: An old question. Interestingly enough, I have discovered that portraiture is most realistic when, for example, one might photograph a leading figure in politics or big business, whose peers and colleagues praise the portrait as nice and quite flattering, while, at the same time, his critics or political enemies find it great because of its ironic or sarcastic quality.

AA: How much of a portrait comes from you as the artist, and how much comes from the person photographed?

AK: I can imagine a papparazzo catching a good shot, a strong portrait revealing a part of someone's personality. But achieving this is probably as rare as good sex between a rapist and his victim. The reason for failure is the lack of let's-do-it-together. In order to create a portrait you rely on the cooperation of your subject. As in a business, love, or even casual relationship, there has to be a certain amount of equal exchange between the people involved. The source of an accurate portrait is the communication that occurs before and during the actual sitting. And that's where the whole fun is, too. To get to know a person and try to translate his or her essence into a visual form. It would be interesting to put together an exhibition, let's say about Picasso: all the portraits ever taken of him by other artists or photographers. He loved to be photographed, so it would be an immense show. One could possibly separate the accurate portraits from the superficial ones, but would one be able to "read" the relationship between Picasso and the individual who photographed him? If one portrait had to be picked as the best, which one would be chosen by his peers and fans, and which one by his old friends? And why?

LM: Can you imagine two good, but totally different, portraits of a person: number one would not be at all like number two, but you'd like them both, because they each deal with very different aspects of the subject?

AK: Let's take an example: Mozart. My visual experience of him was shaped when I was a teenager in Switzerland. I was familiar with Joseph Lange's eighteenth-century portrait in oil, which was for me very much in harmony with the Mozart music. This harmony would probably still exist for me if I hadn't checked out the Hollywood version of our classical master. Trying to take Milos Forman seriously, it still took me almost an hour to loosen up my nice, fixed image and become friendly with his hero's giggle. My whole W. Amadeus M. slightly dissolved, and it was like seeing the Sex Pistols' Sid Vicious or Johnny Rotten translated back into the eighteenth century.

LM: Did anybody ever shave their head for you, to be photographed by you?

AK: Yes, but these were very rare exceptions. This art student from Germany, a beautiful girl I got to know just a few weeks earlier, showed up one day to surprise me with a brand new clean head. Oh, and then there was this designer from Zurich, and from him I got a real assignment to take his portrait that way, bald. "I really need this experience," he said, and went to the barber shop across the street. And once in a while we gave that barber business, because someone would show up who hadn't shaved in the past few days.

AA: Did you ever have your head shaved?

AK: Oh yes, when I was nineteen, after going through a few Mohawk creations, I shaved it a couple of times. I remember it felt like the face wouldn't end when you'd go with a cold, wet washcloth over your head

continued on page 77

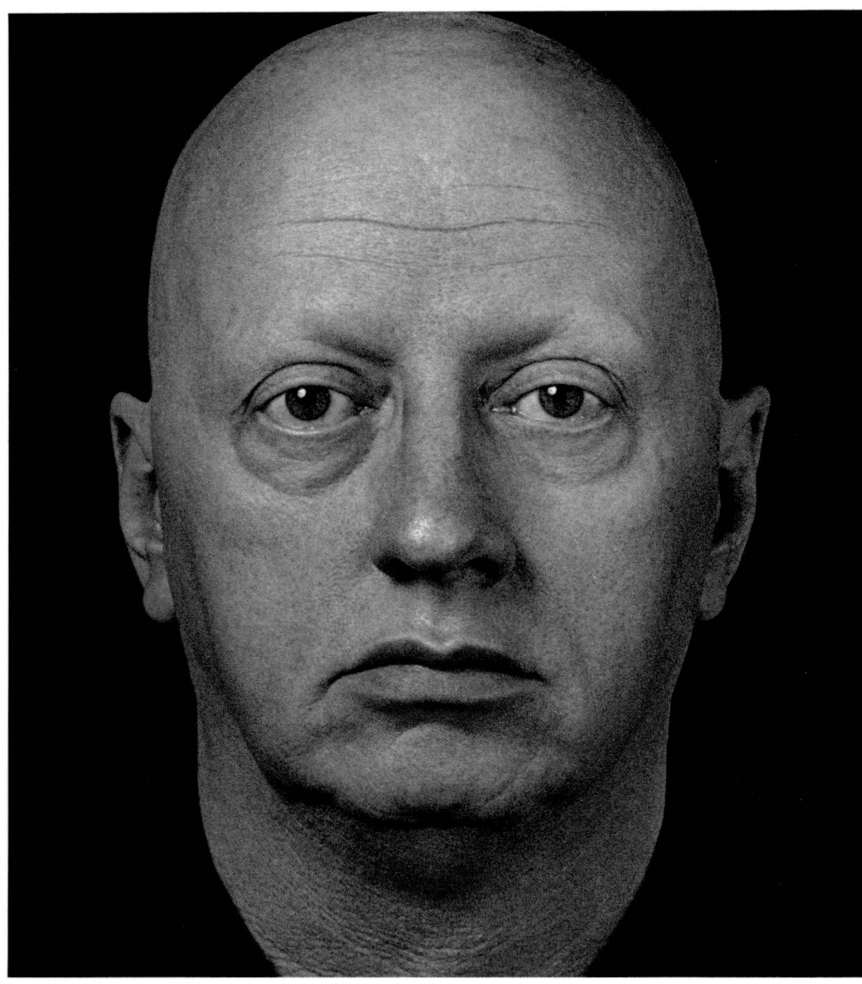

Huyh Foy, New York City: owner, Best Limousine Service

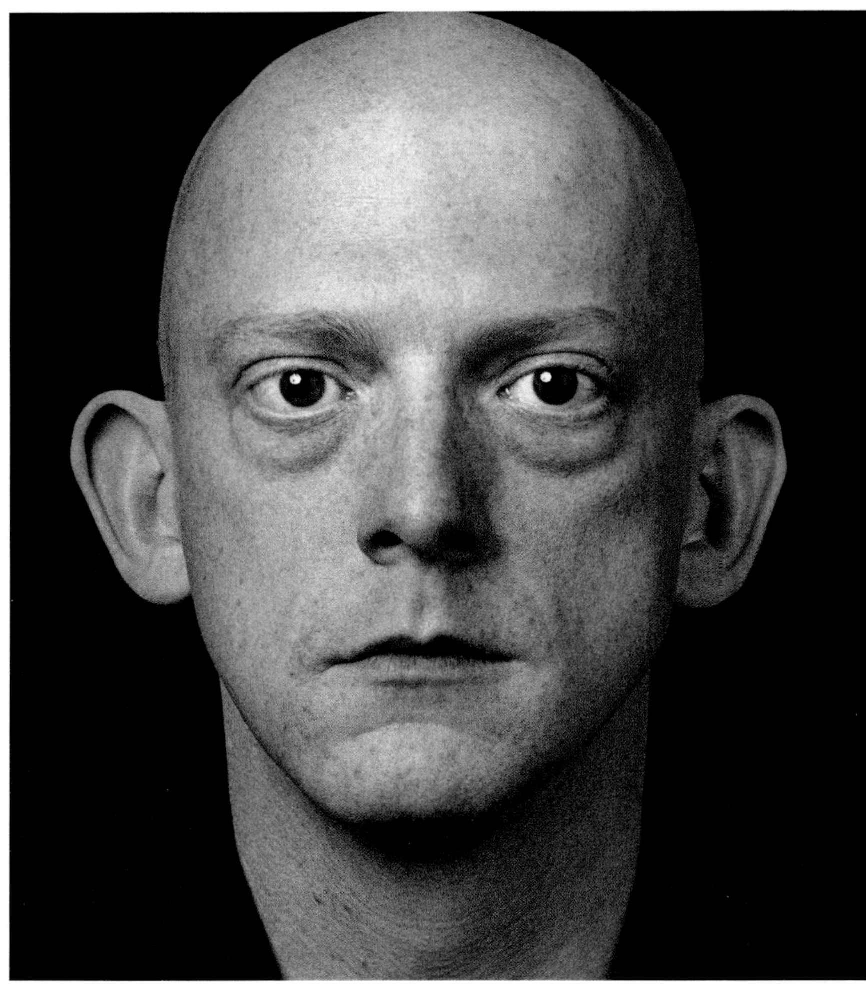

David Gibson, London: actor

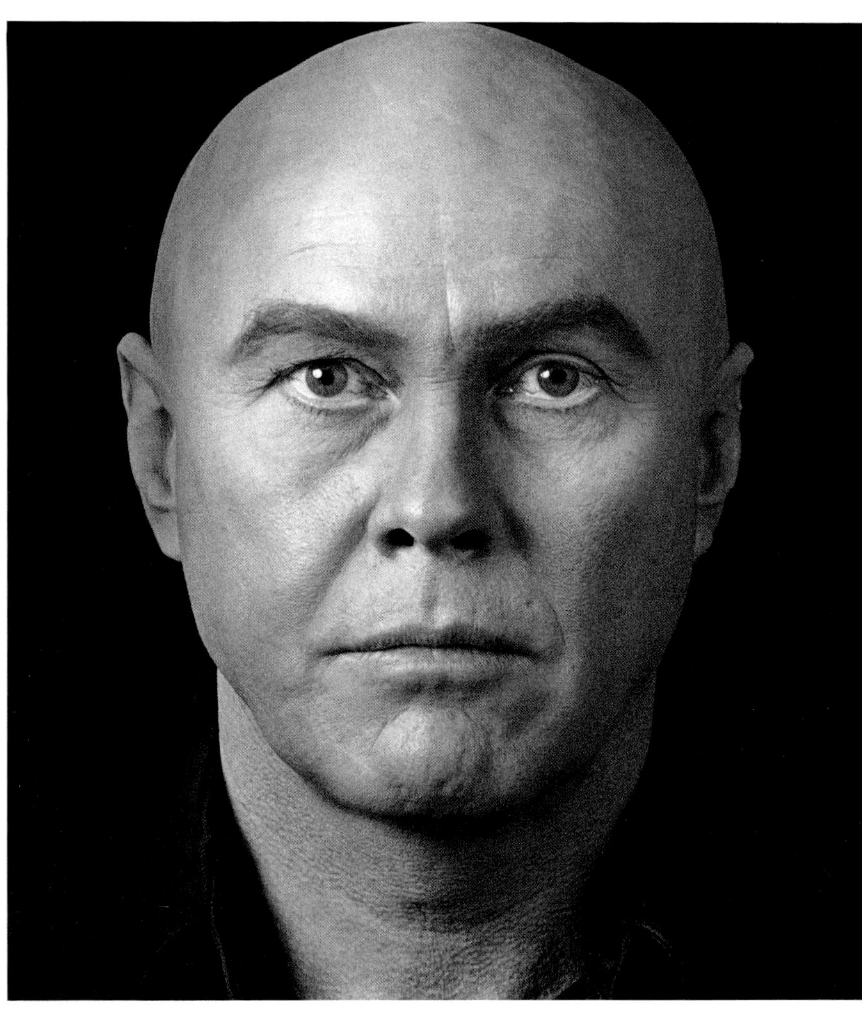

Harve Presnell, New York City: actor; featured as Daddy Warbucks in the Broadway musical *Annie*

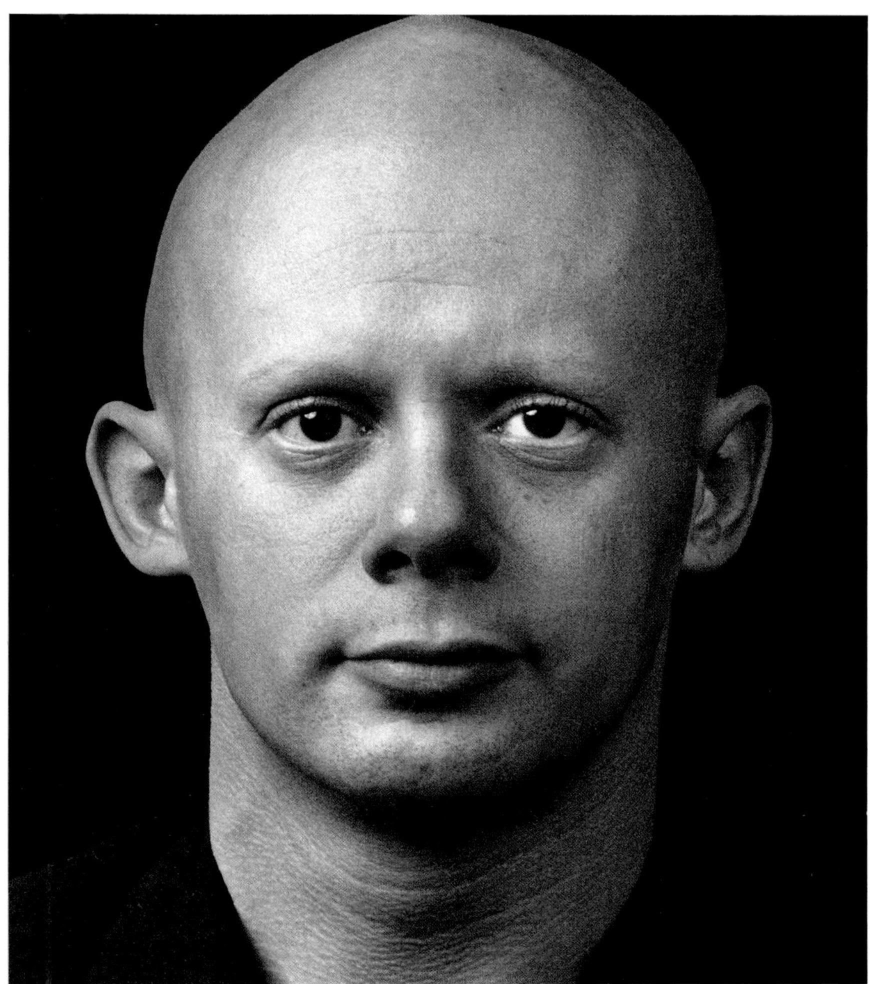

Dean Kartalas, New York City: theatrical make-up artist and actor

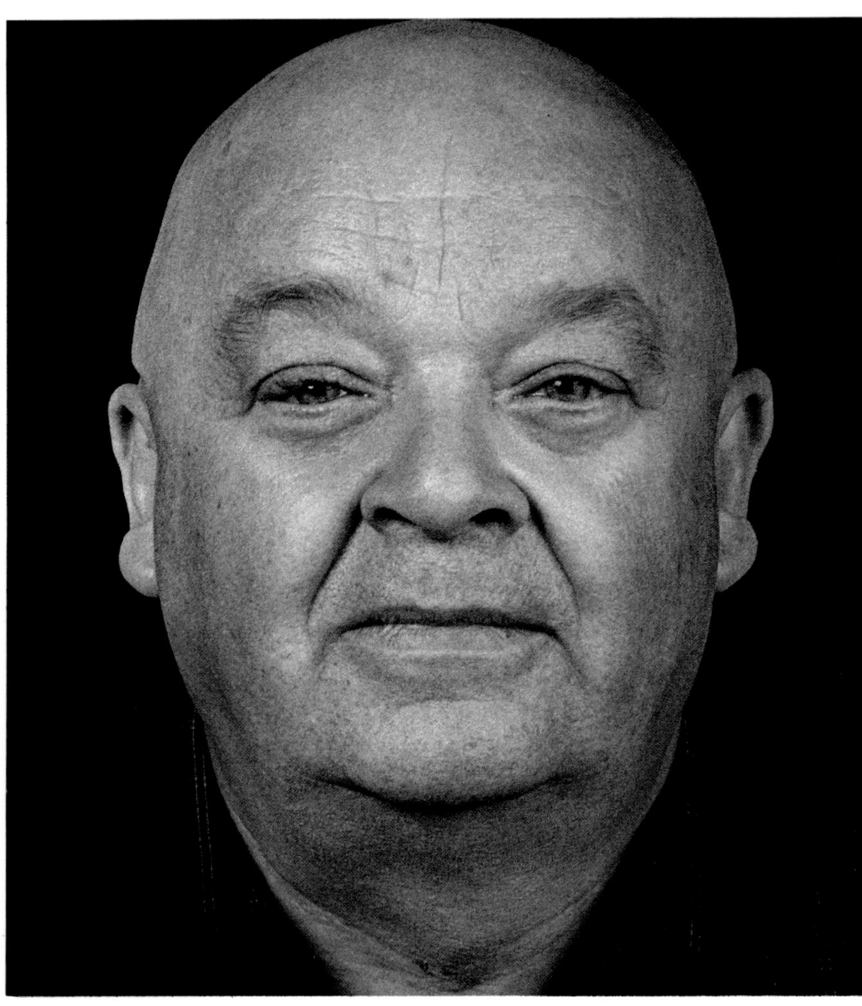

John G. Ayer, Los Angeles: investment manager

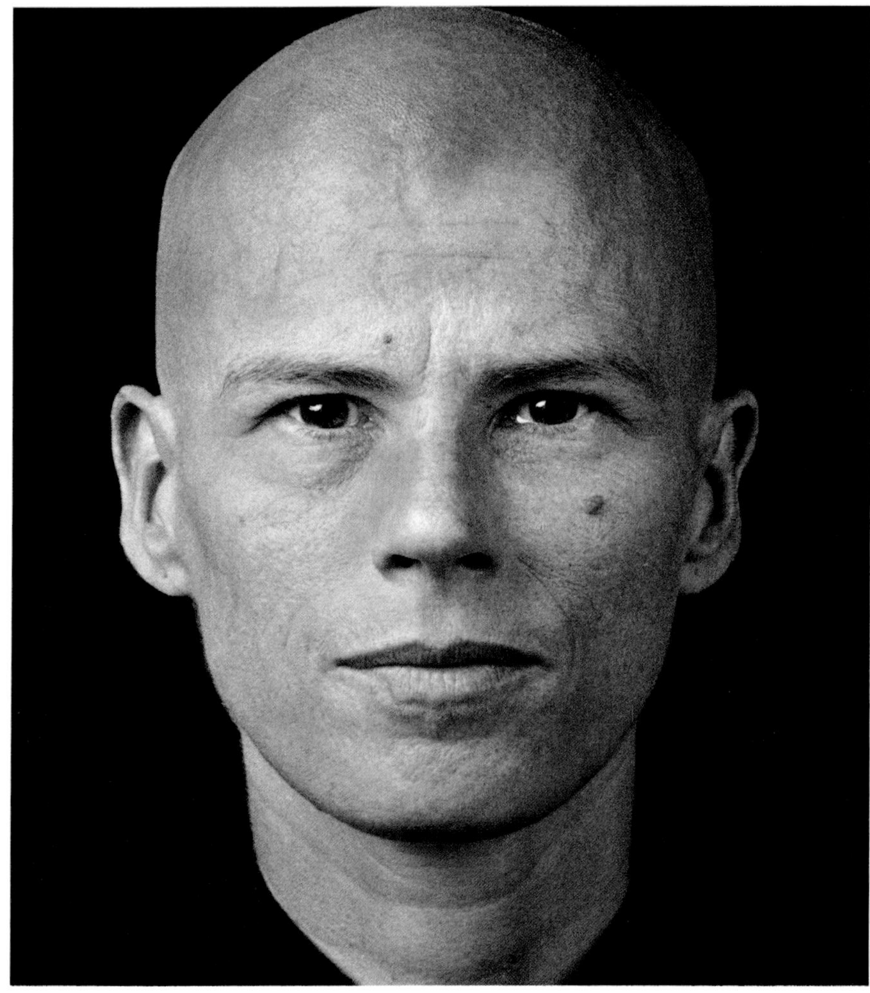

Julie Costain, New York City: works at Trana Health Food Store

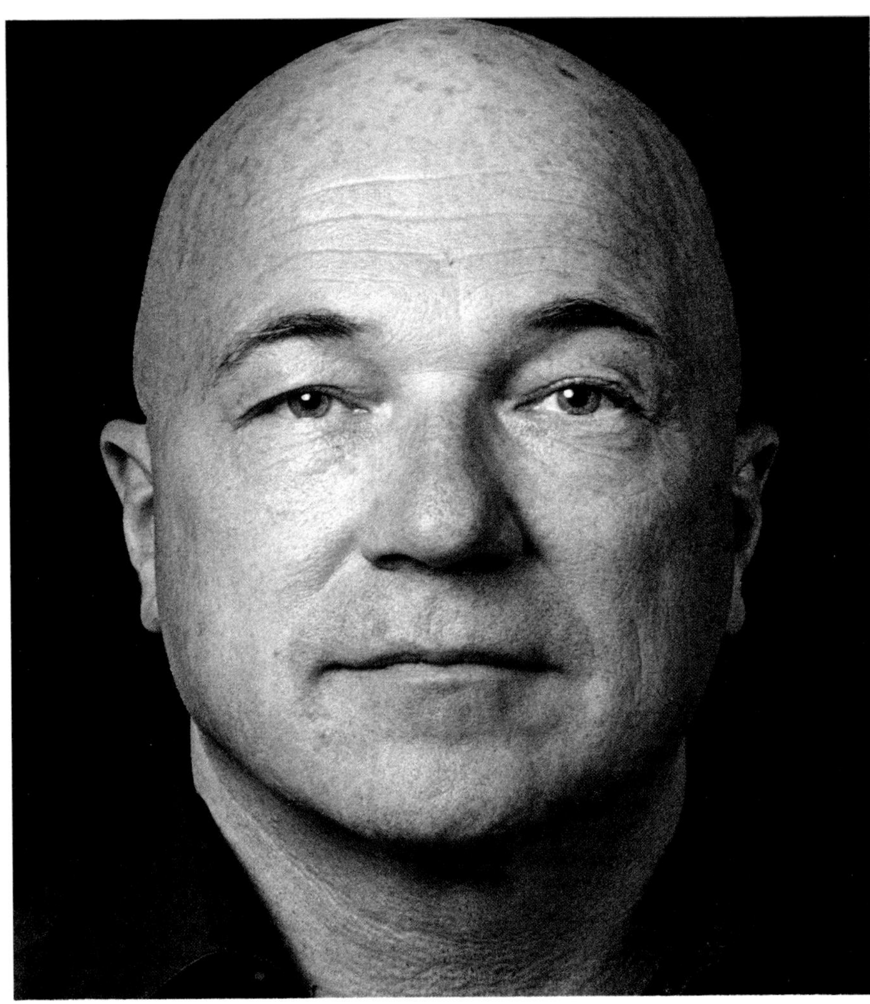

Robert Kirchmyer, New York City: tapestry and textile designer

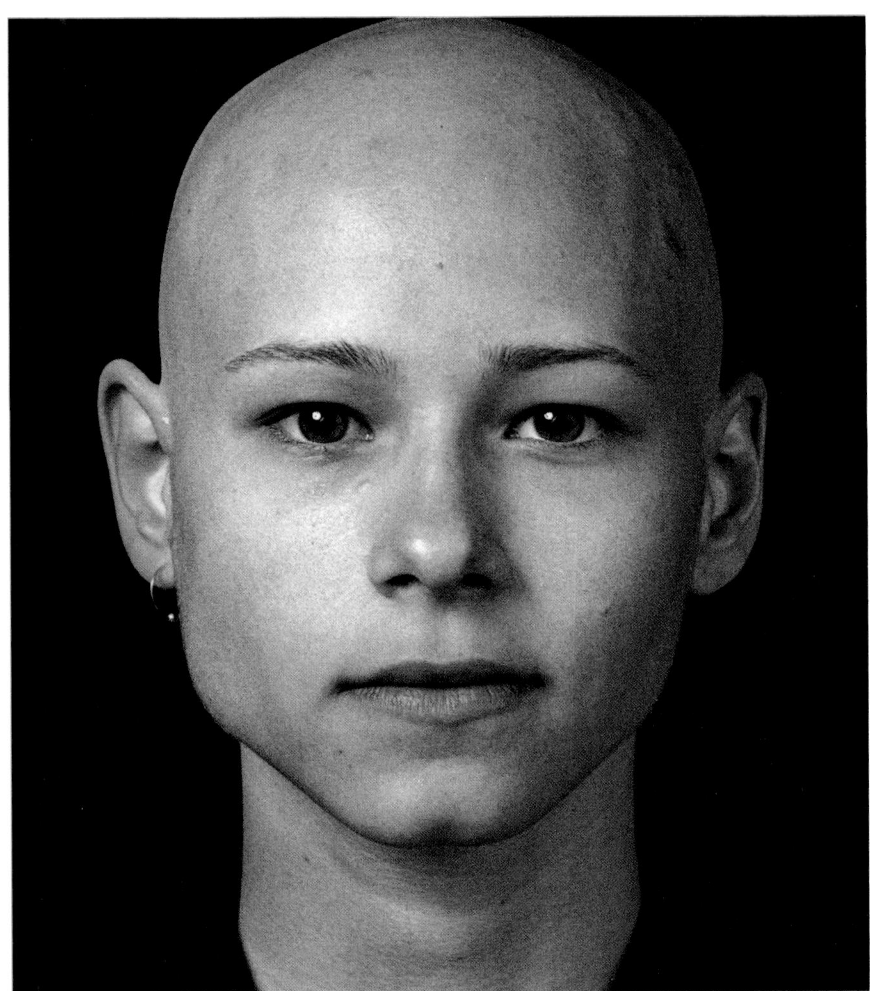

Perri Masco, New York City: musician

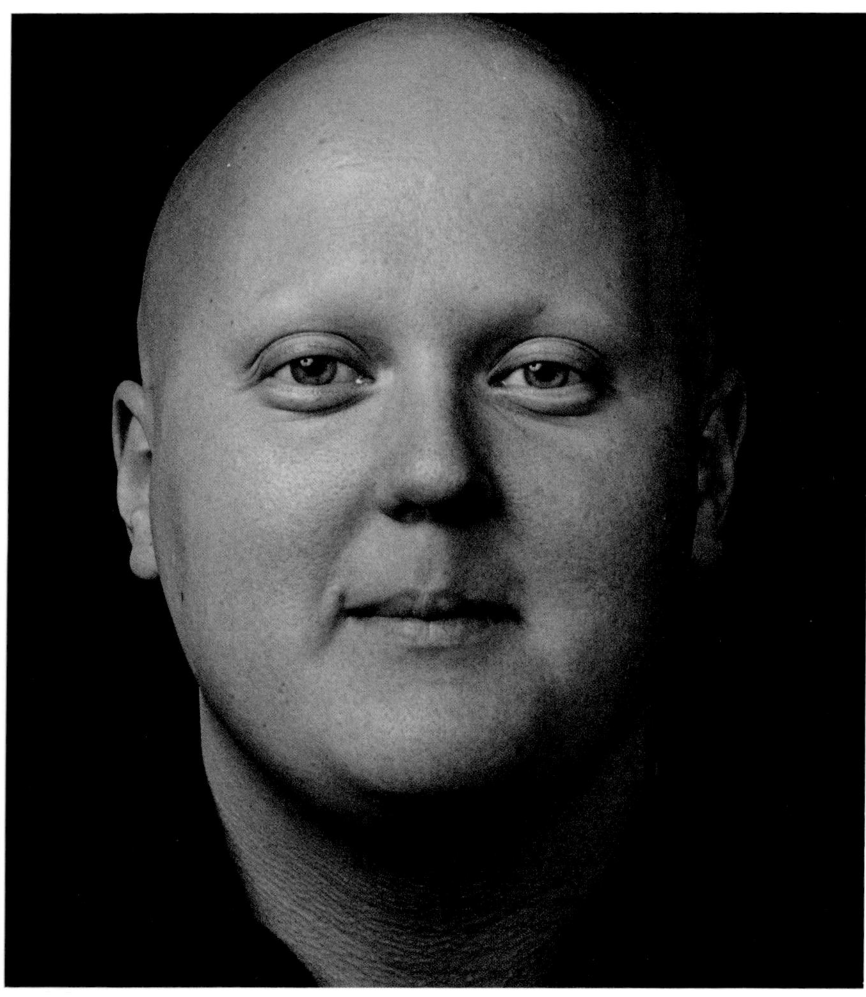

Kjell Persson, Stockholm

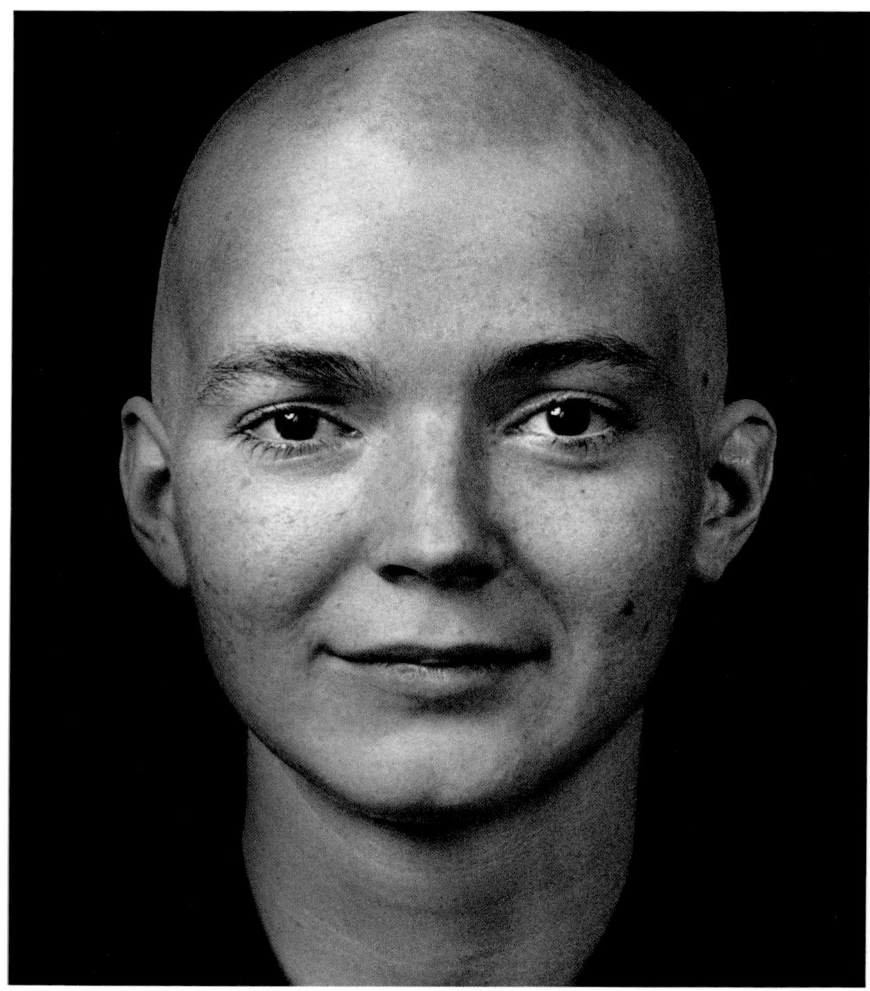

Alexandra Halász, Budapest: philosopher

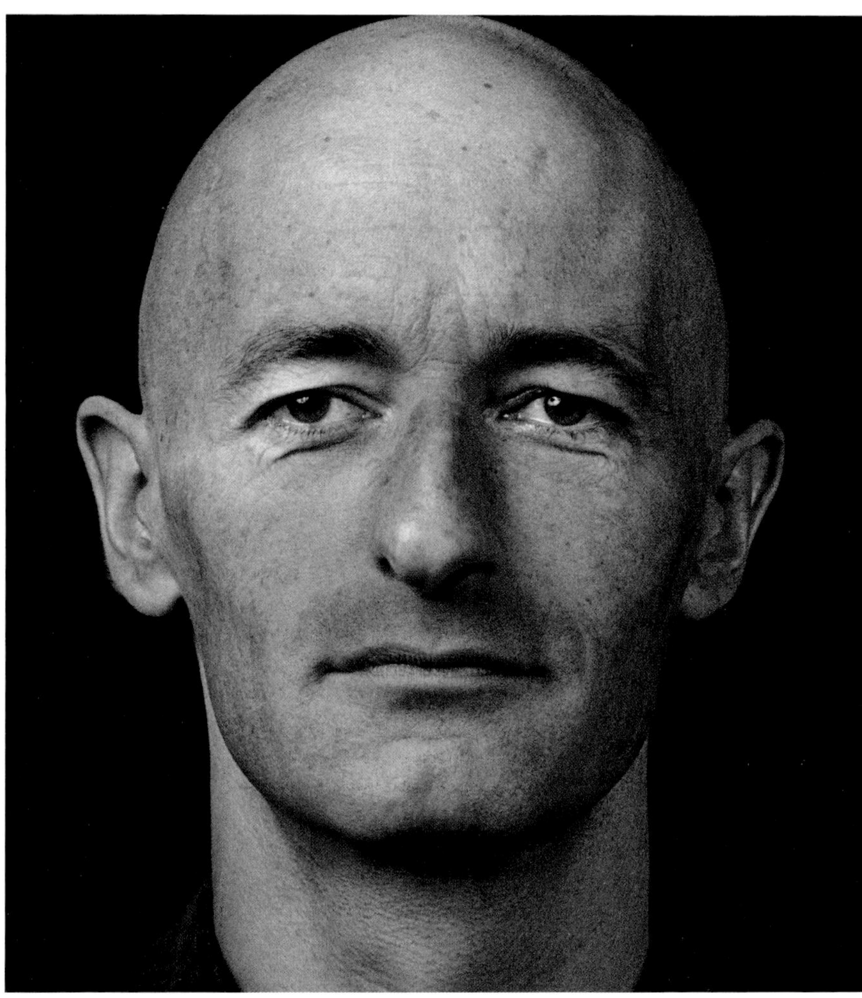

Jurg Altherr, Zurich: artist

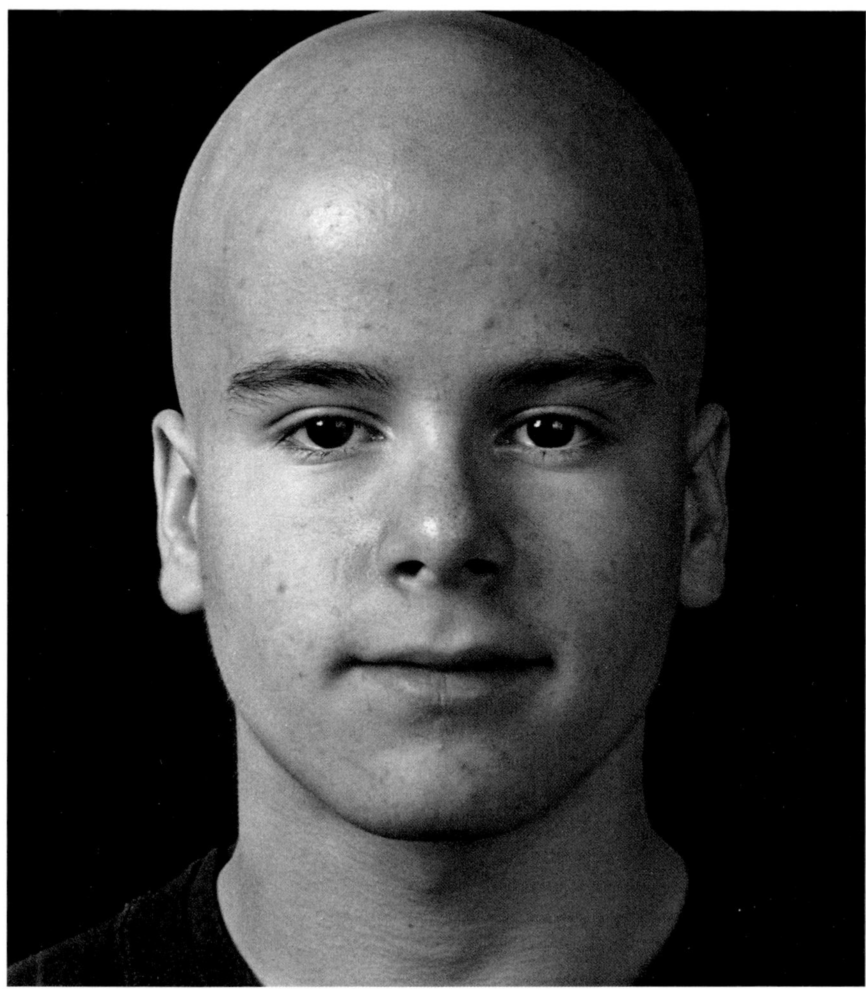

David Scilken, New York City: singer in New Wave group, The Young and the Useless; graffiti artist, exhibits at Fun Gallery

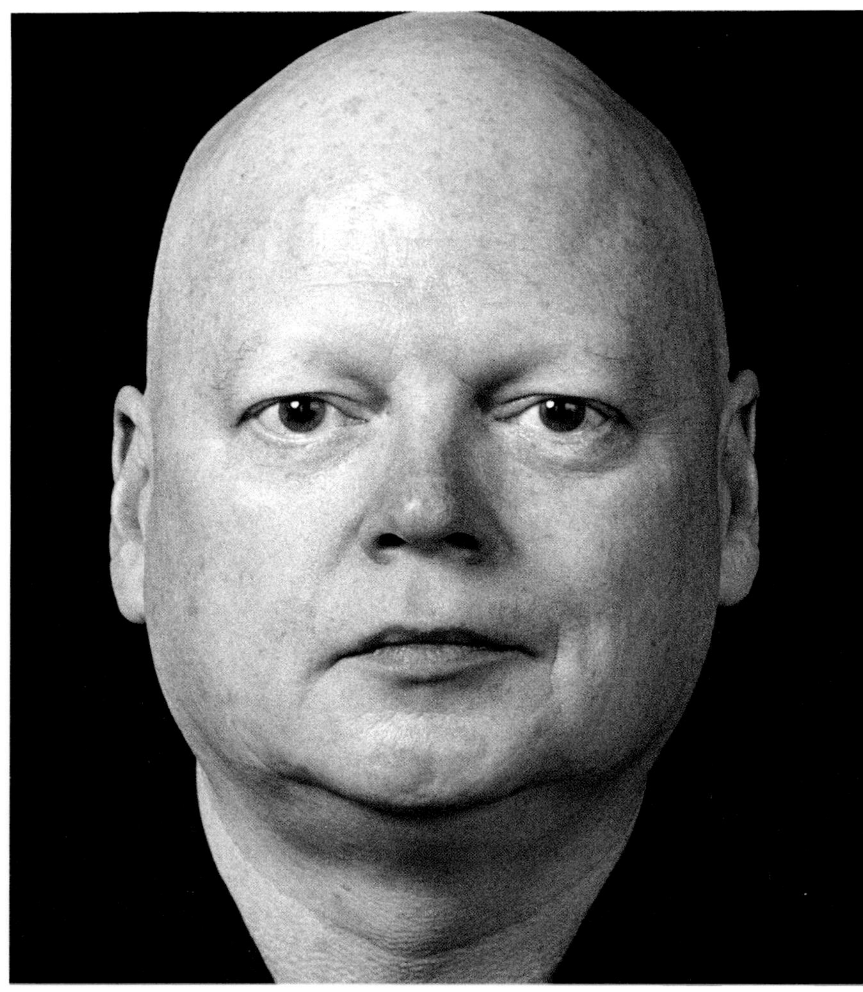

Price Garland, New York City: painter of surrealistic landscapes

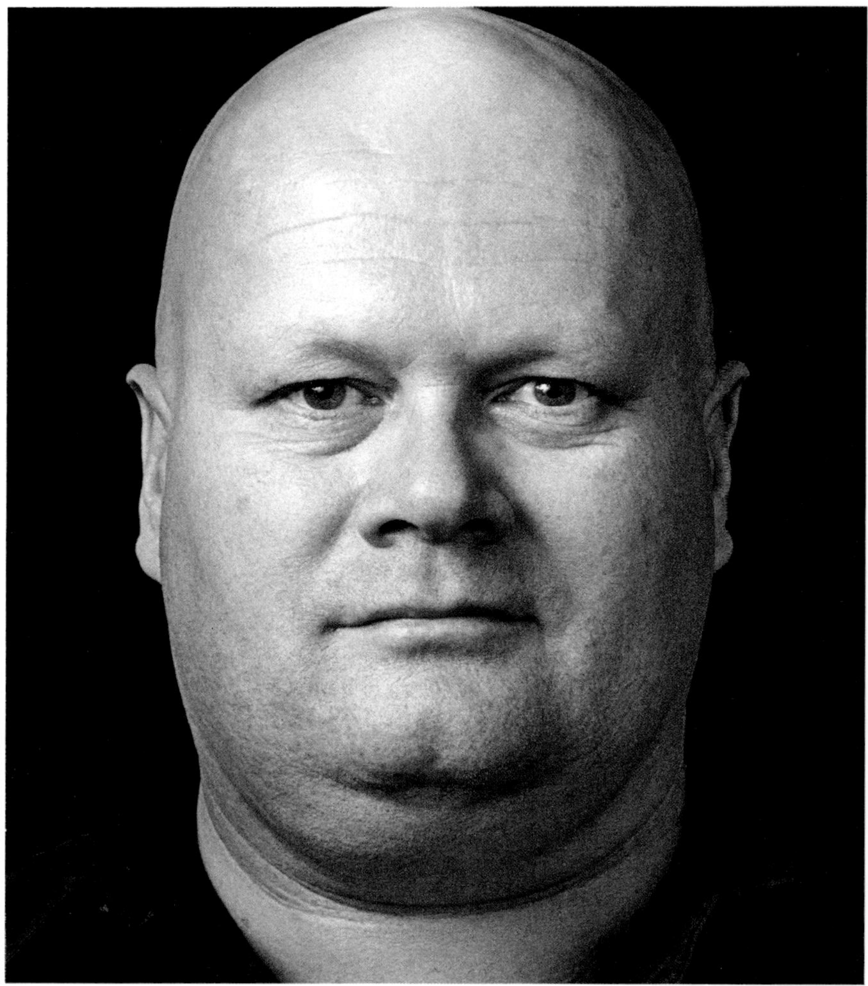

Captain Haggerty, New York City: founder of Captain Haggerty's School for Dogs; trains dogs for special clients and for television commercials and movies

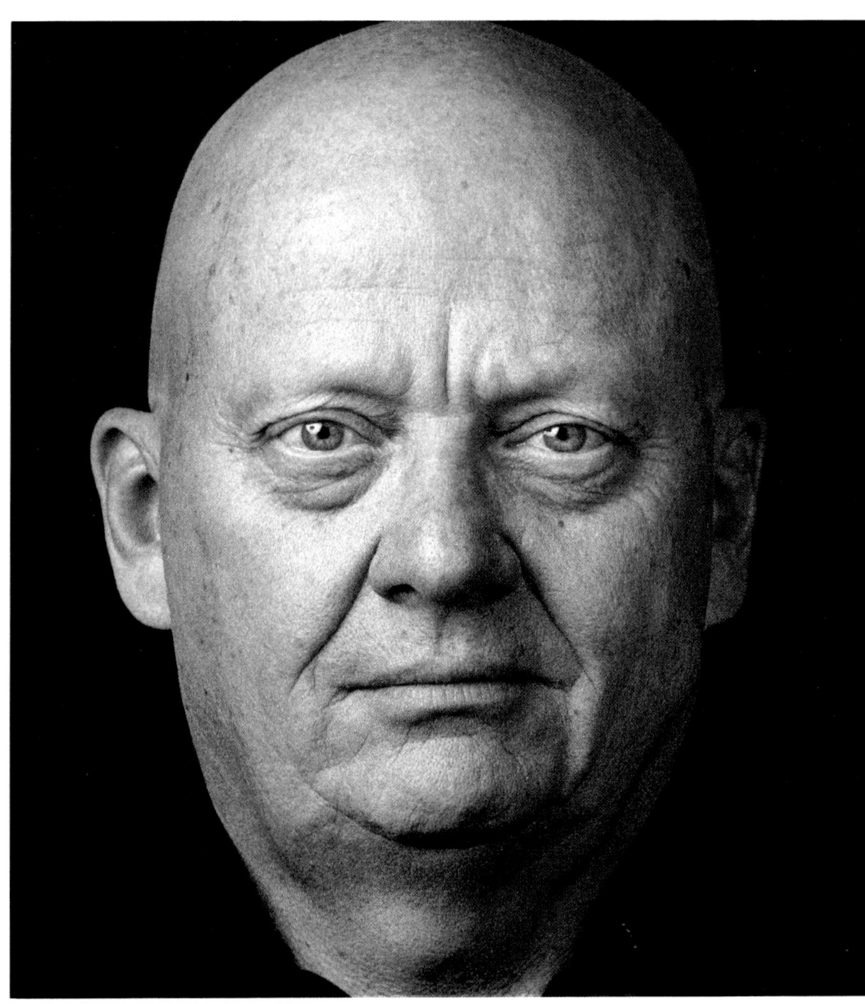

Clifford Oviatt, Washington, D.C.: management labor lawyer

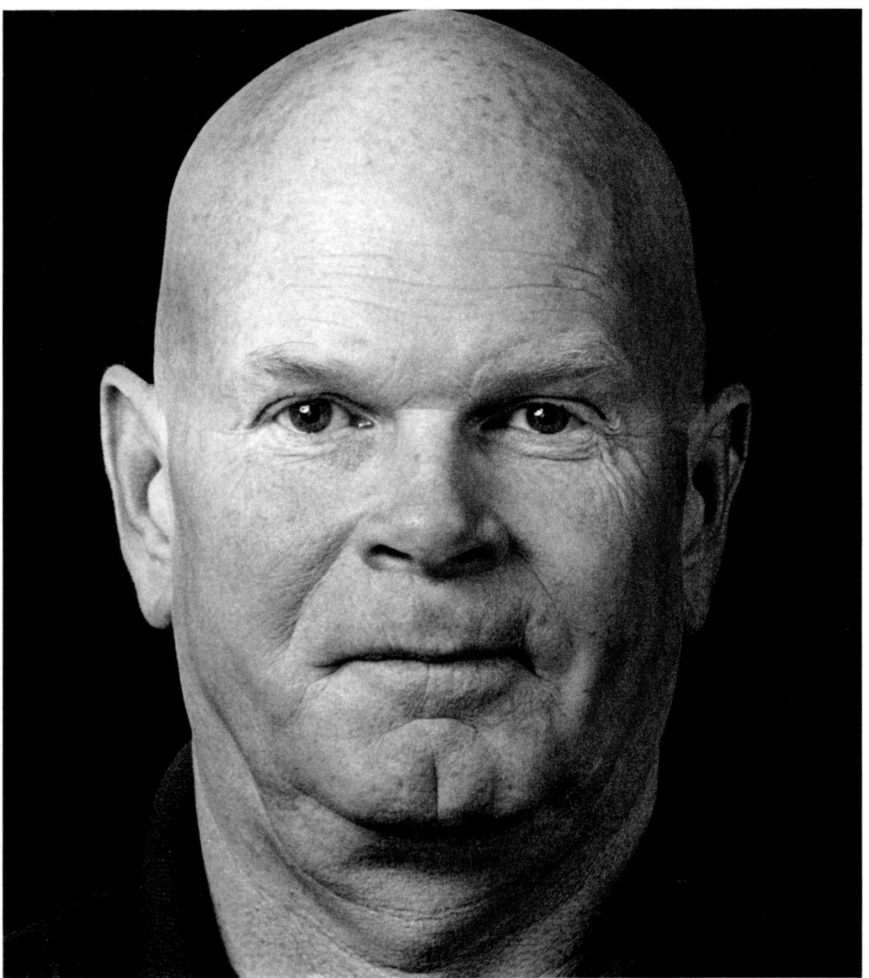

Robert C. Myles, New York City: banker

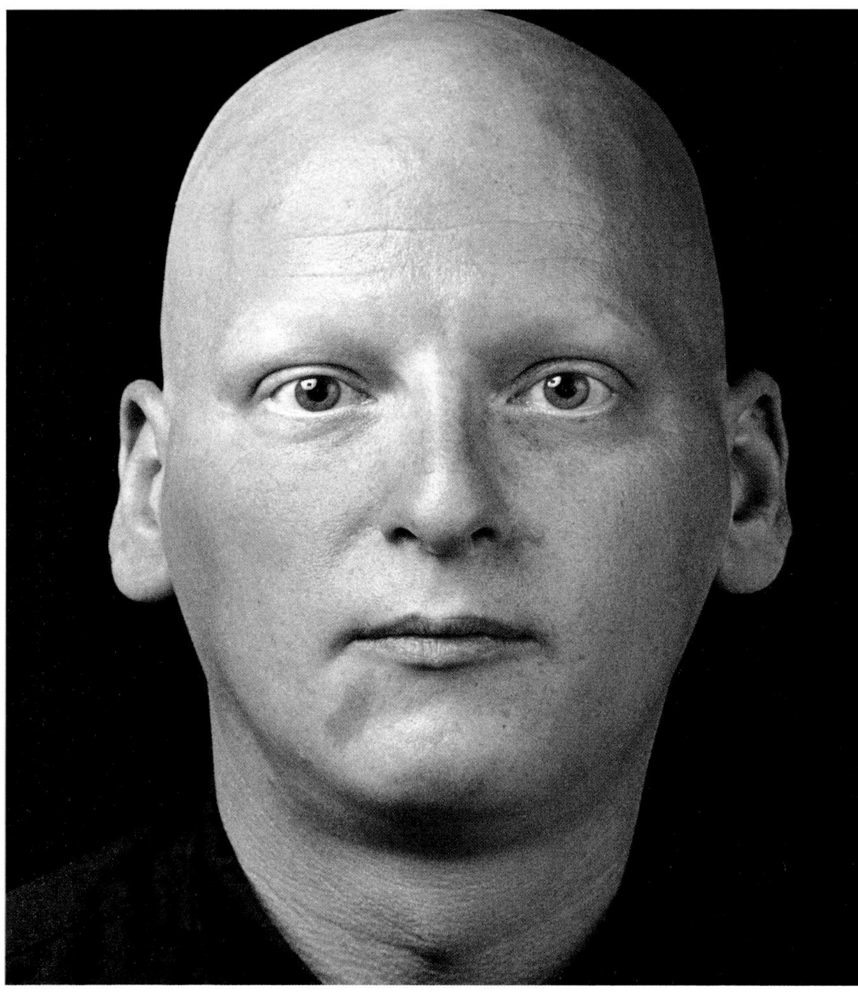

Win Zibeon, Blauvelt, New York: painter; three-dimensional surreal illusionist

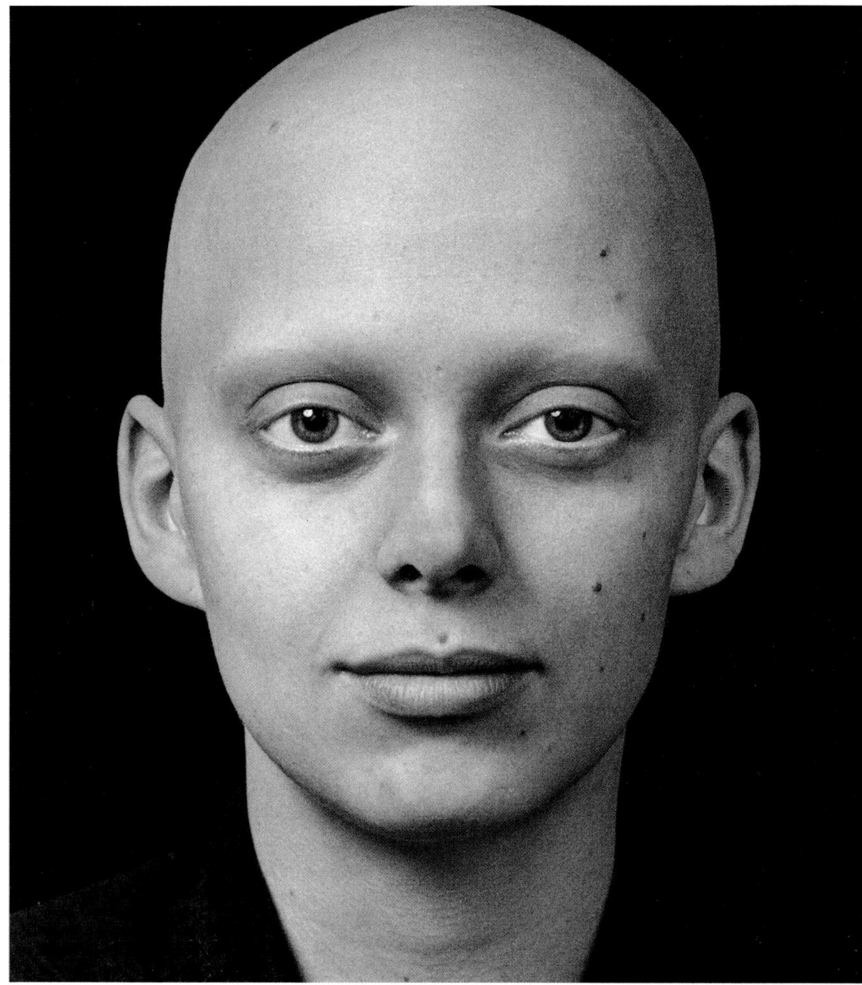

Jenny O., New York City: antique dealer and fashion model

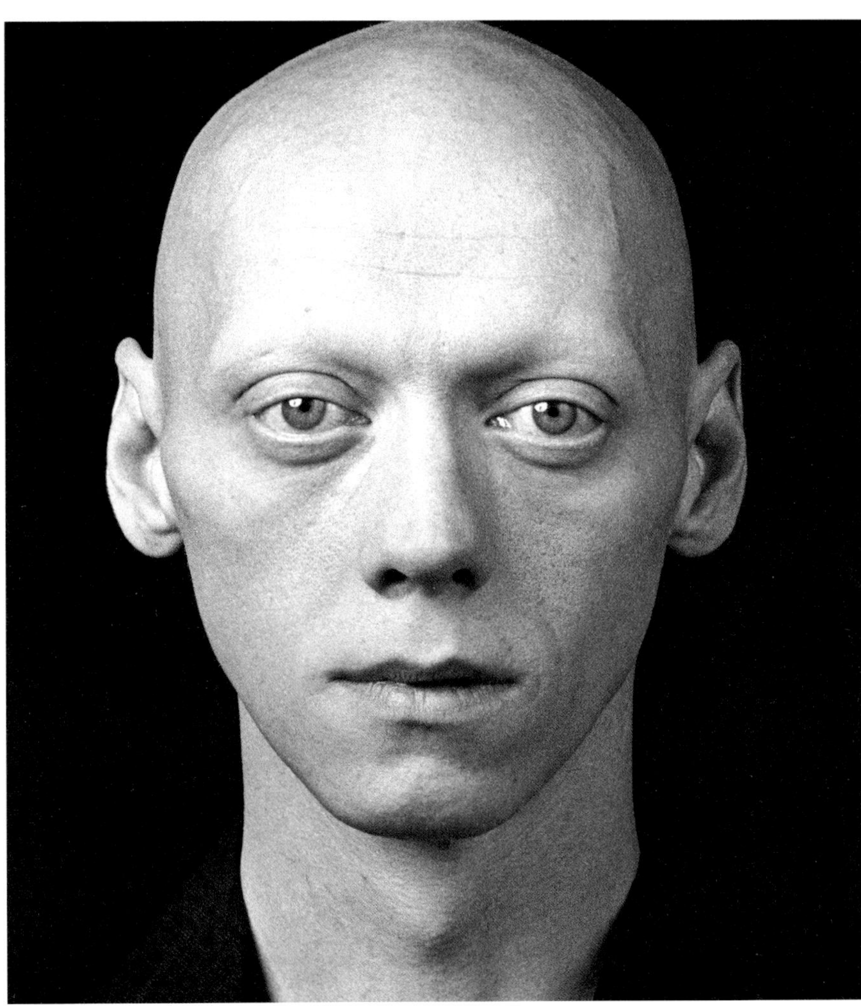

Michael McNulty, New York City: bank teller, Chase Manhattan Bank

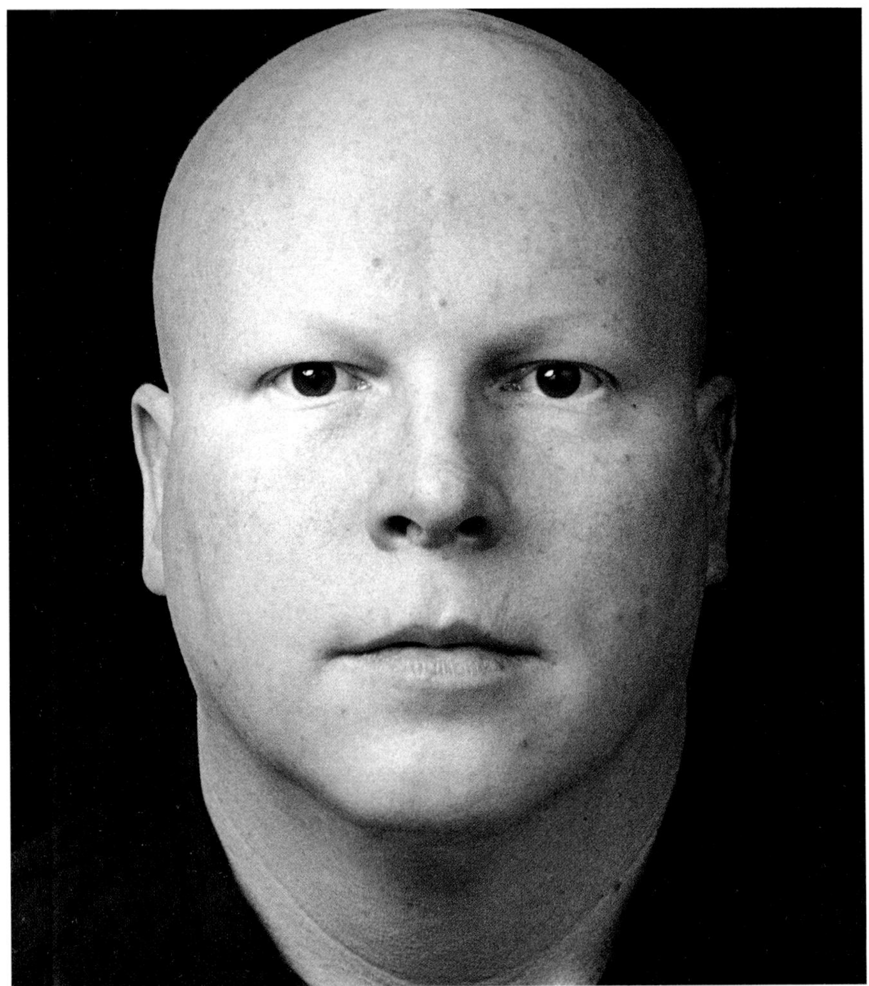

Bruce Deichl, New York City: stockbroker and art dealer

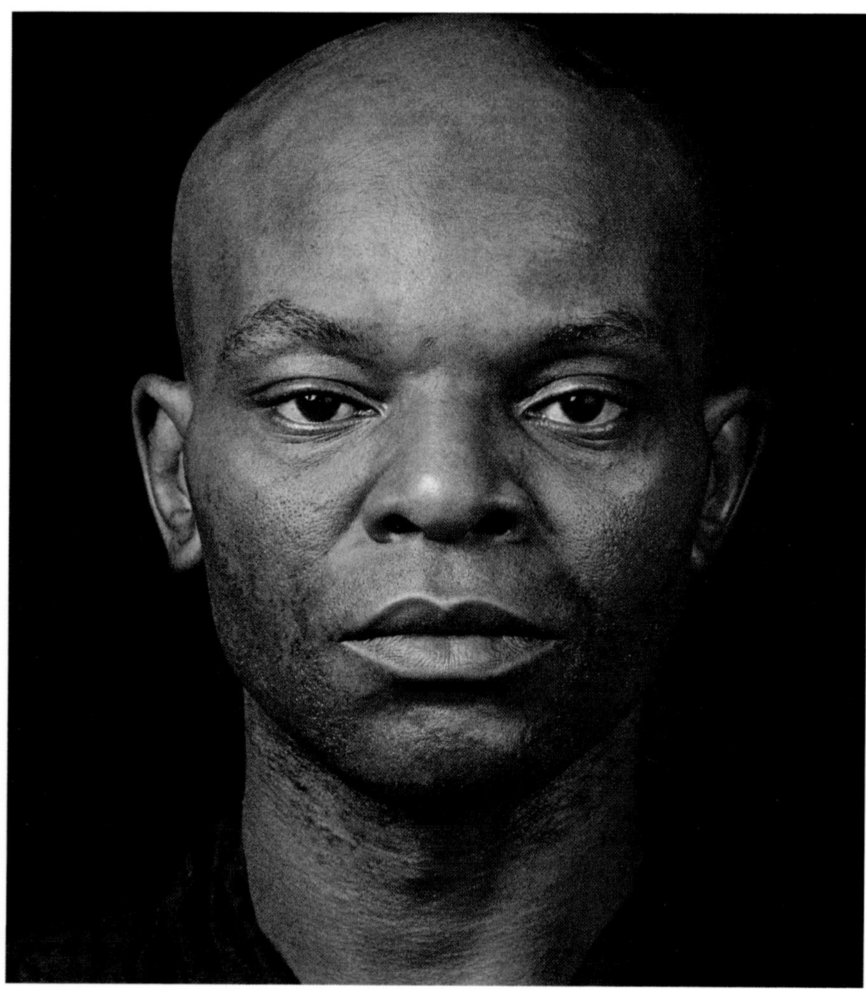

Richard Fillyaw, New York City: artist's model, School of Visual Arts

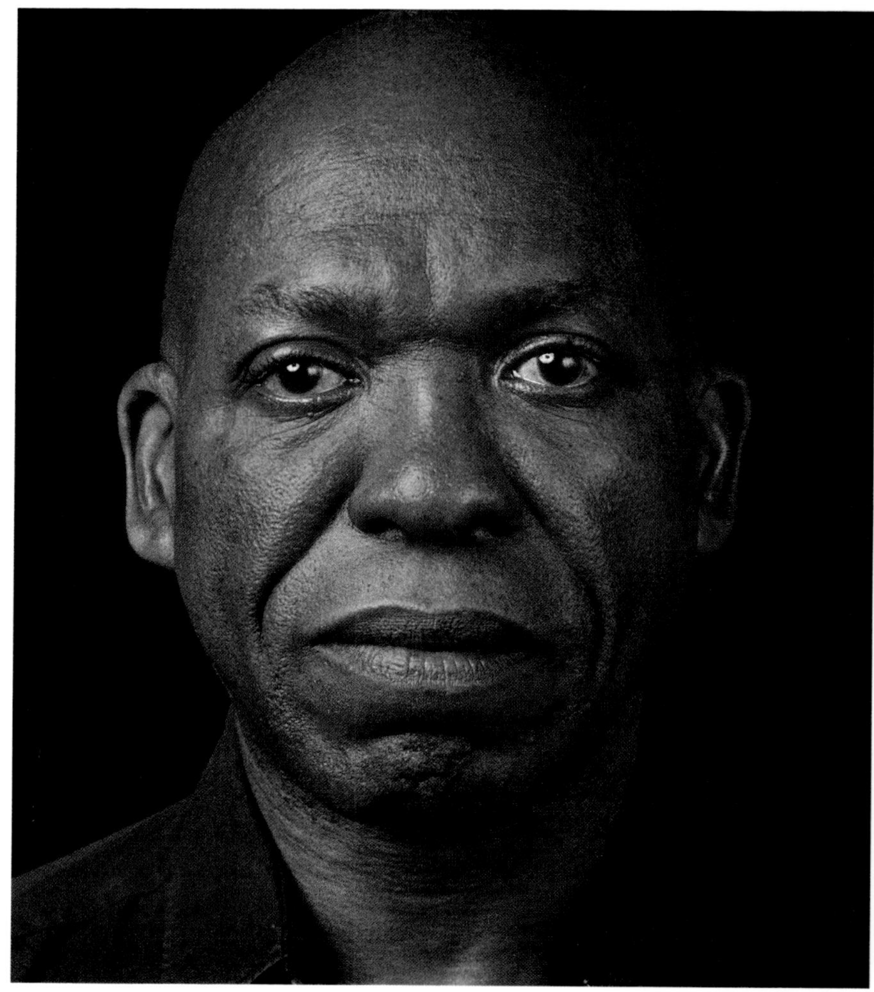

Jim Willis, New York City: social worker

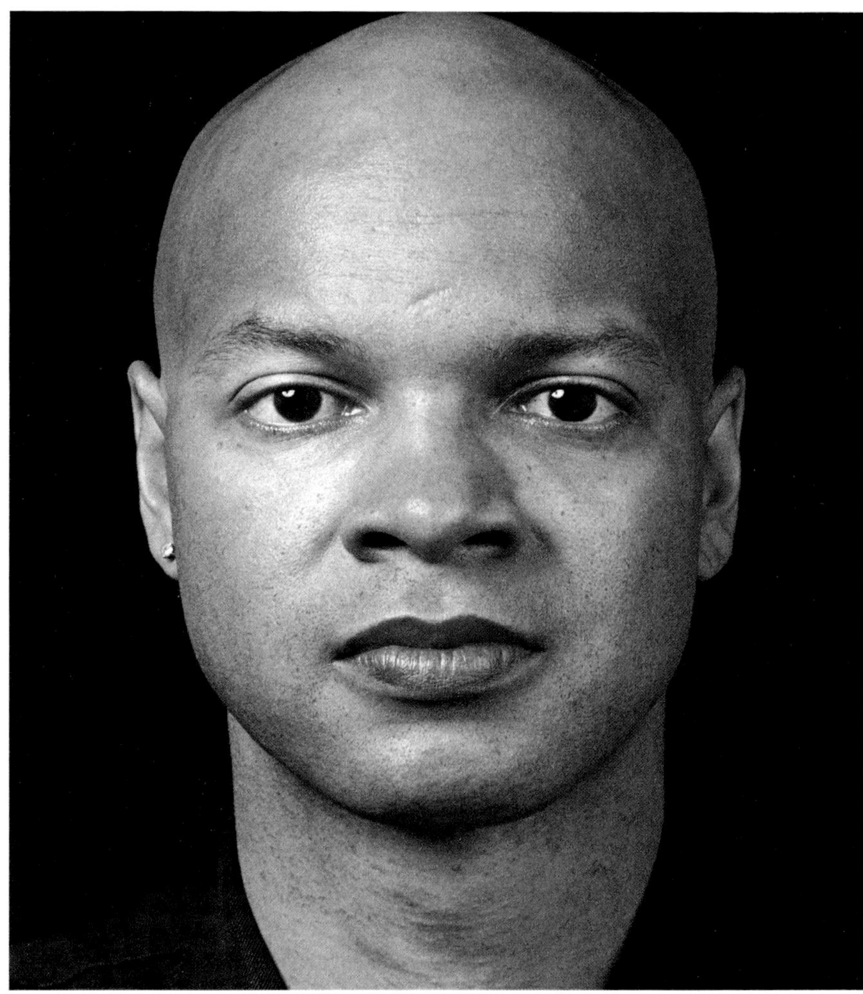

Ronald Jackson, New York City: fashion designer; clients include Diana Ross, Liza Minelli, Henri Bendel, and Bloomingdale's

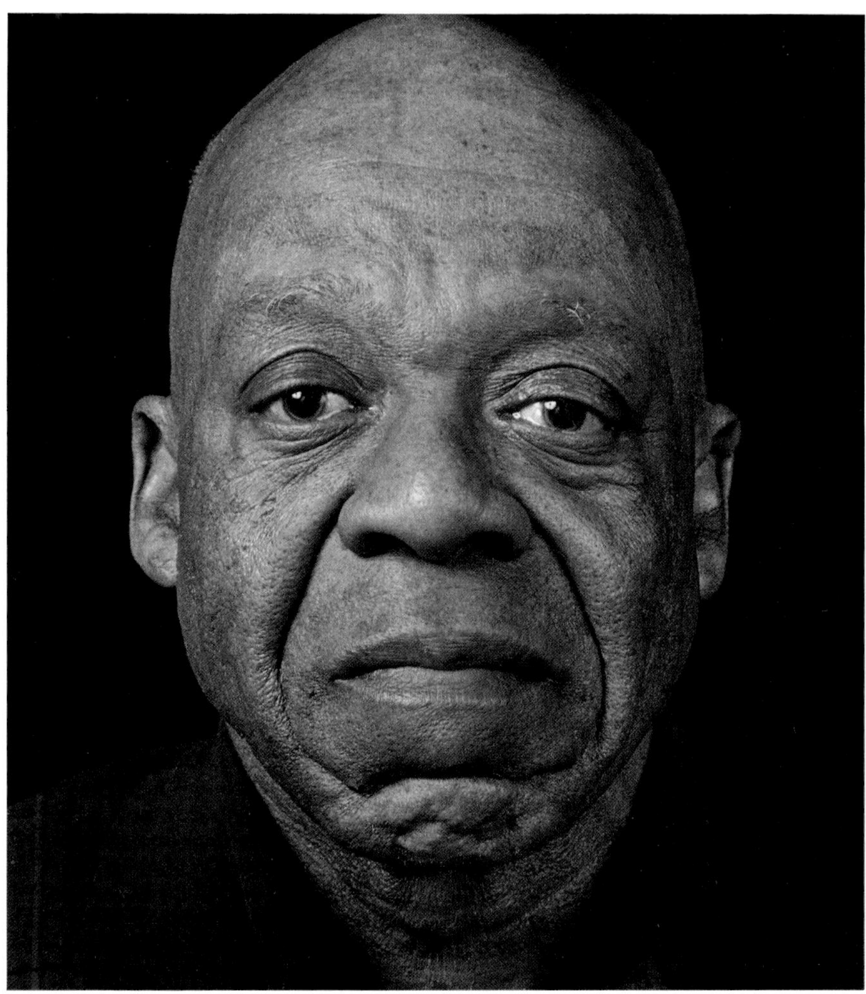

G. C. Smith, New York City: World War II Air Corps veteran

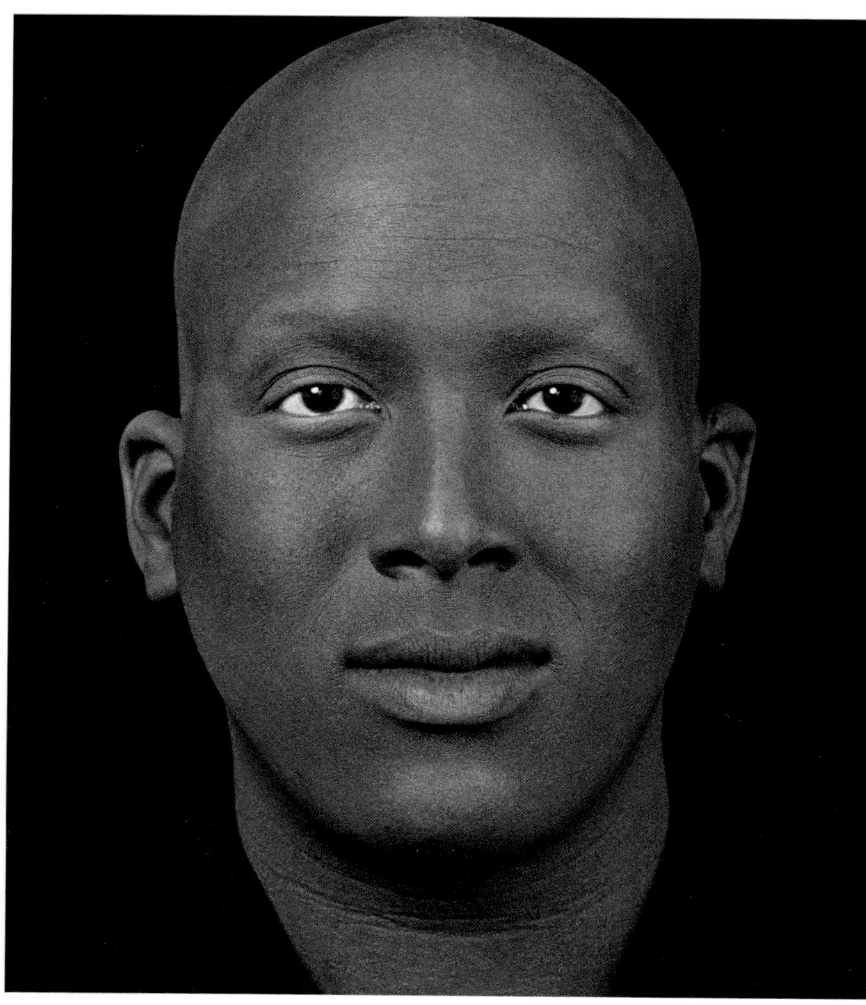

Michael Stein, New York City: fashion designer

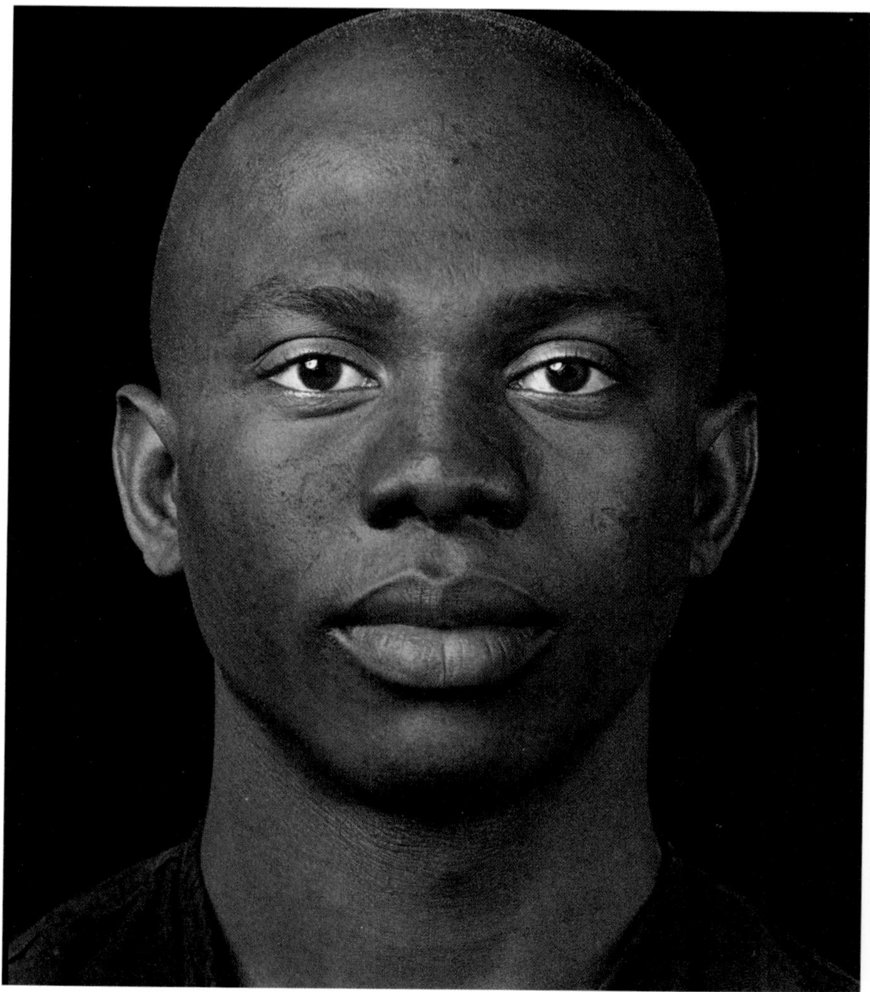

Tridam Das, New York City: dynamic yoga instructor; gives classes at Riker's Island prison and elsewhere

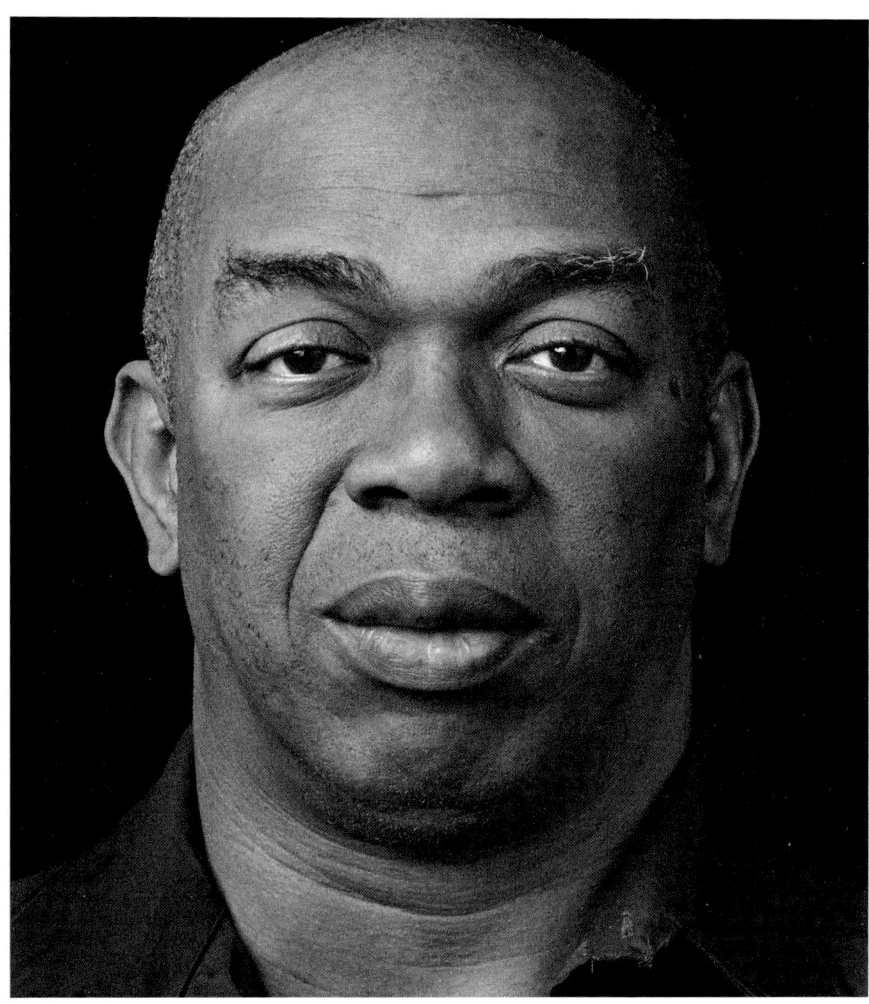

Geoffrey Holder, New York City: actor, famous for appearances on 7-Up commercials; artist, exhibits in many Upper Manhattan galleries

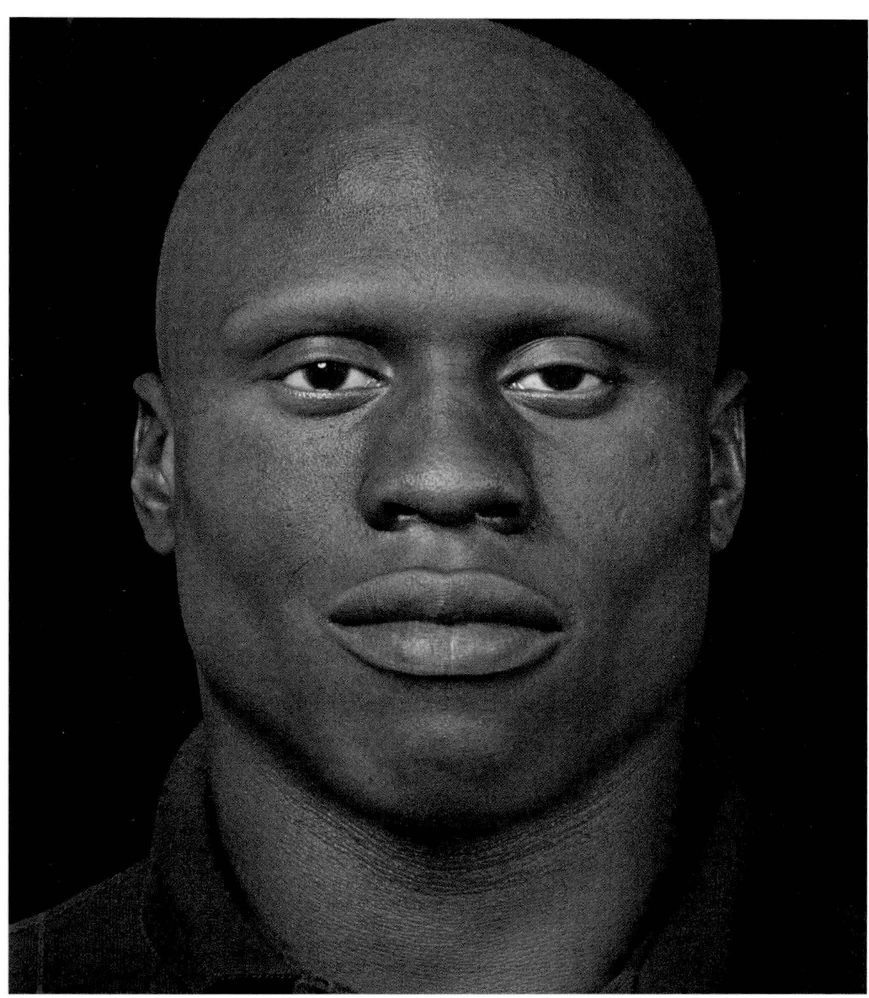

Kenneth Moody, New York City: movement and body-alignment instructor; part-time model

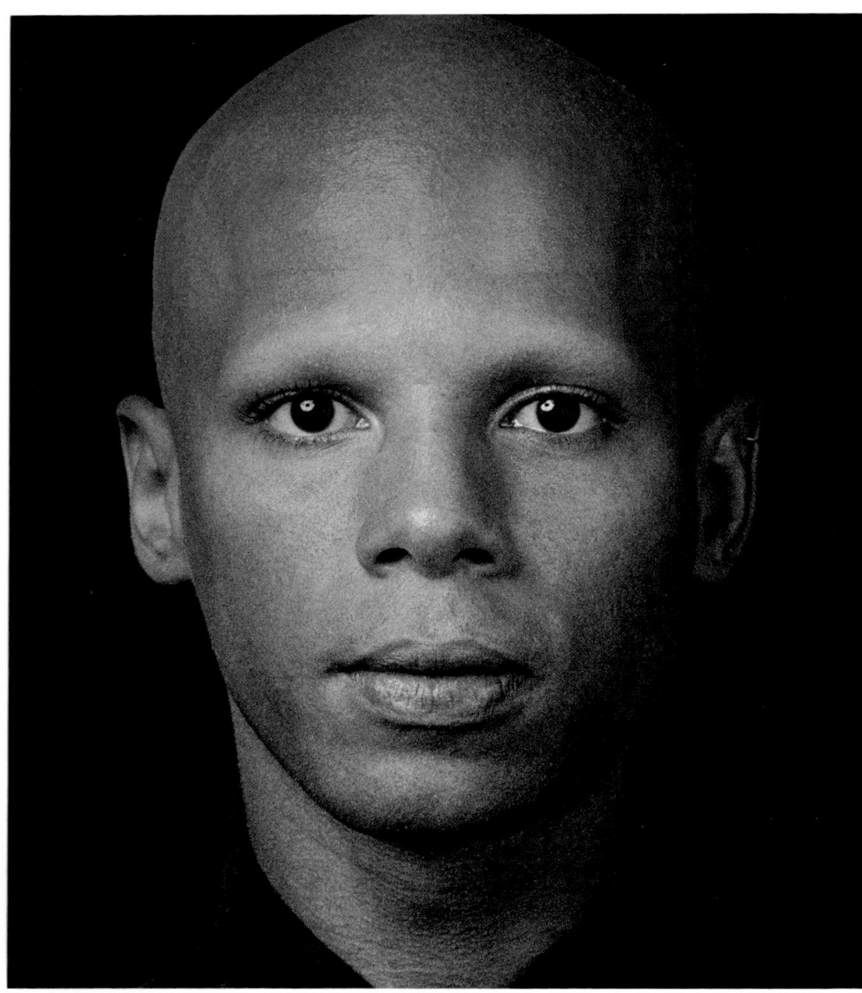

André Alexander, Berlin: works in audio communications; disk jockey

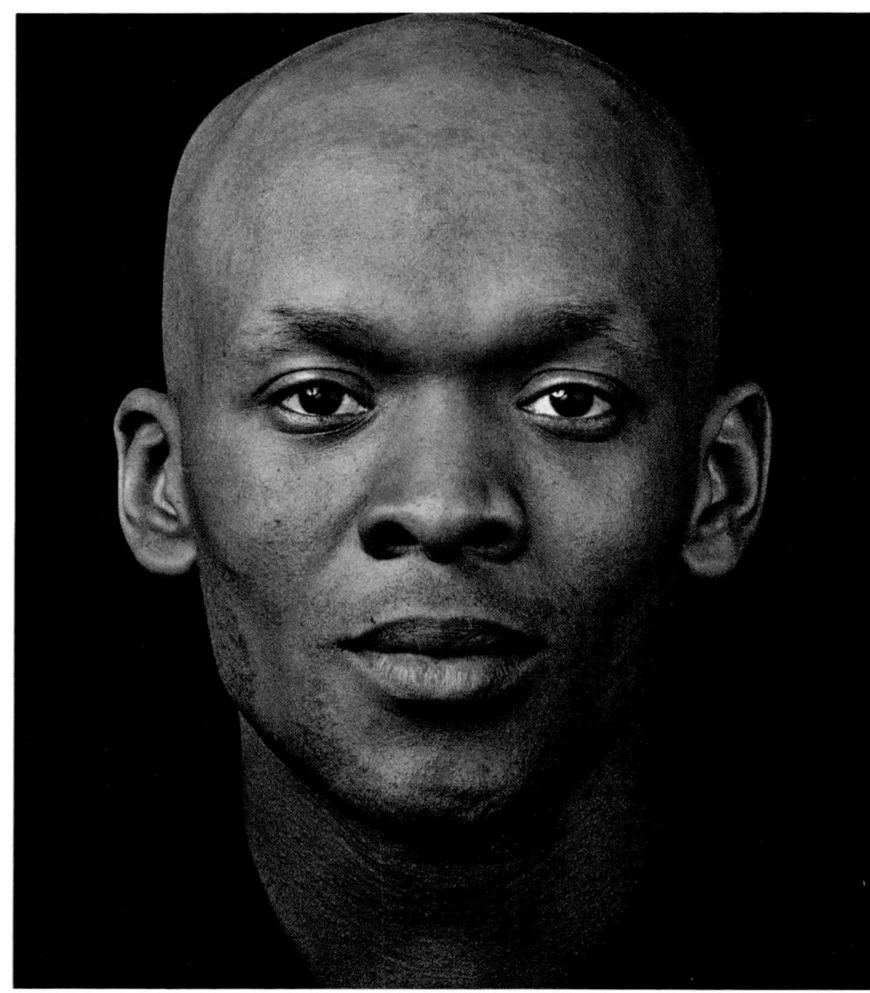

Donald Cann, New York City: illustrator and model

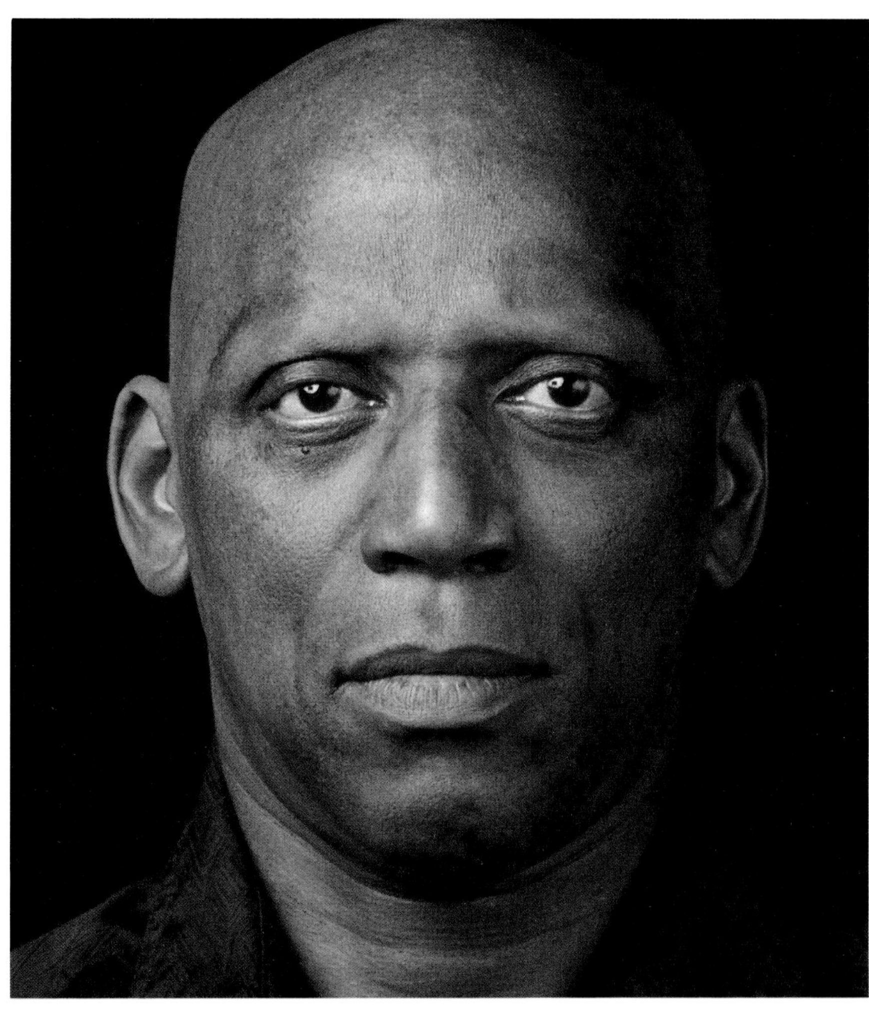

Abdul Rahman, New York City: visual artist; designed covers for James Brown and Melvin Van Peebles albums

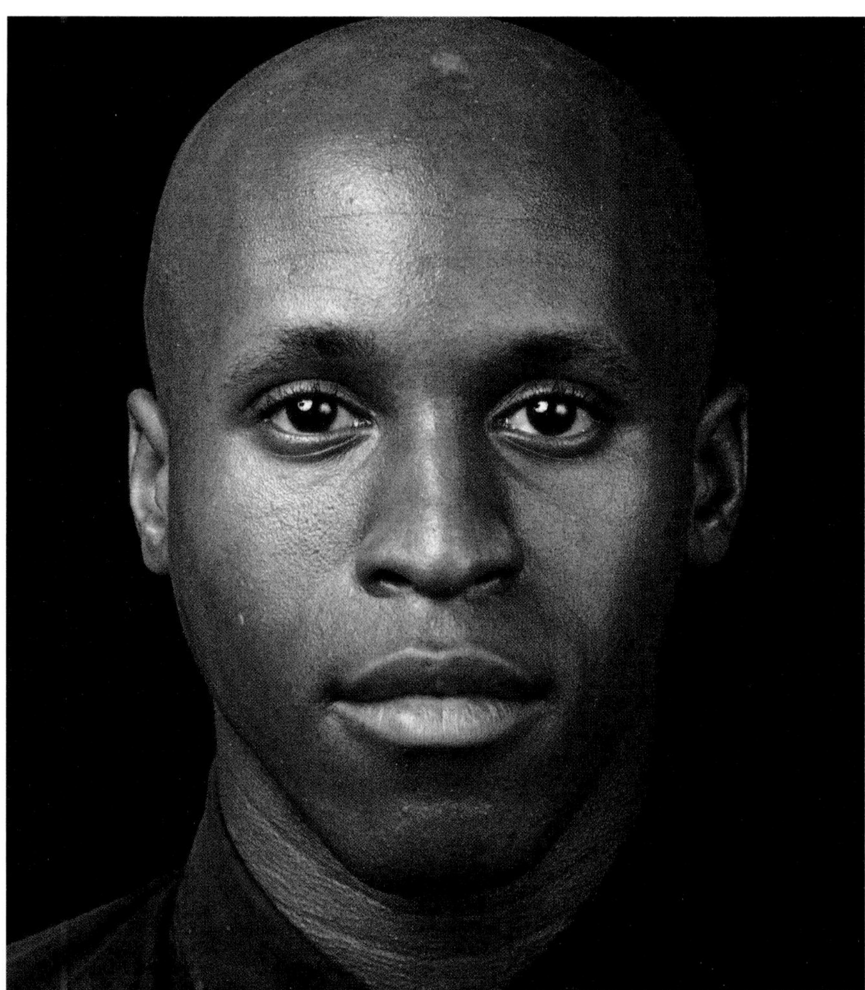

Peter Kea, New York City: fashion designer, Kea Menswear

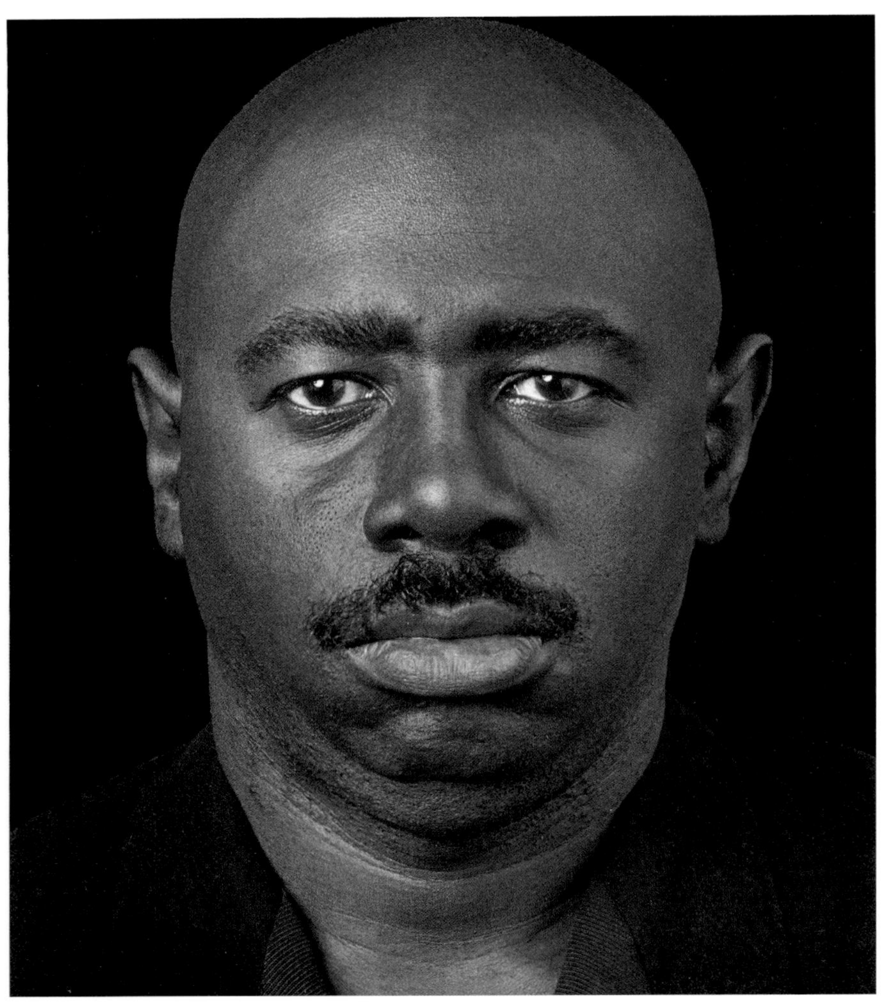

Robert Simmons, New York City: security guard responsible for the safety of many Upper-East-Side store owners

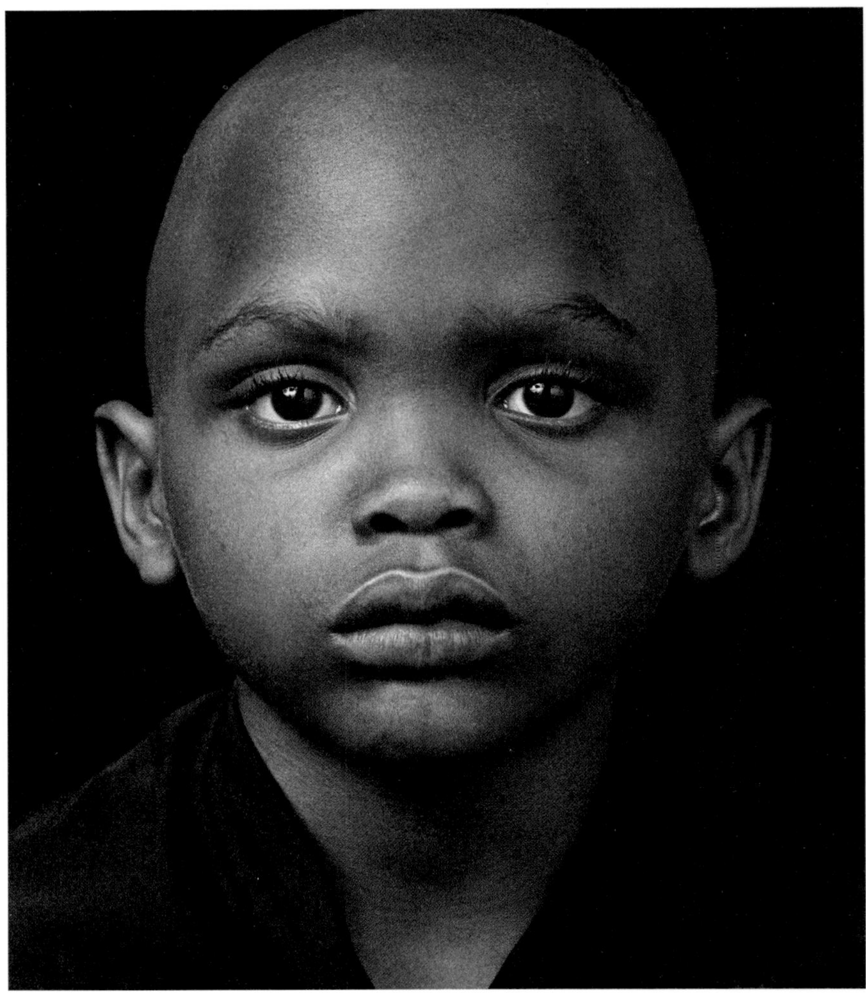

Devon Eskridge, New York City: student

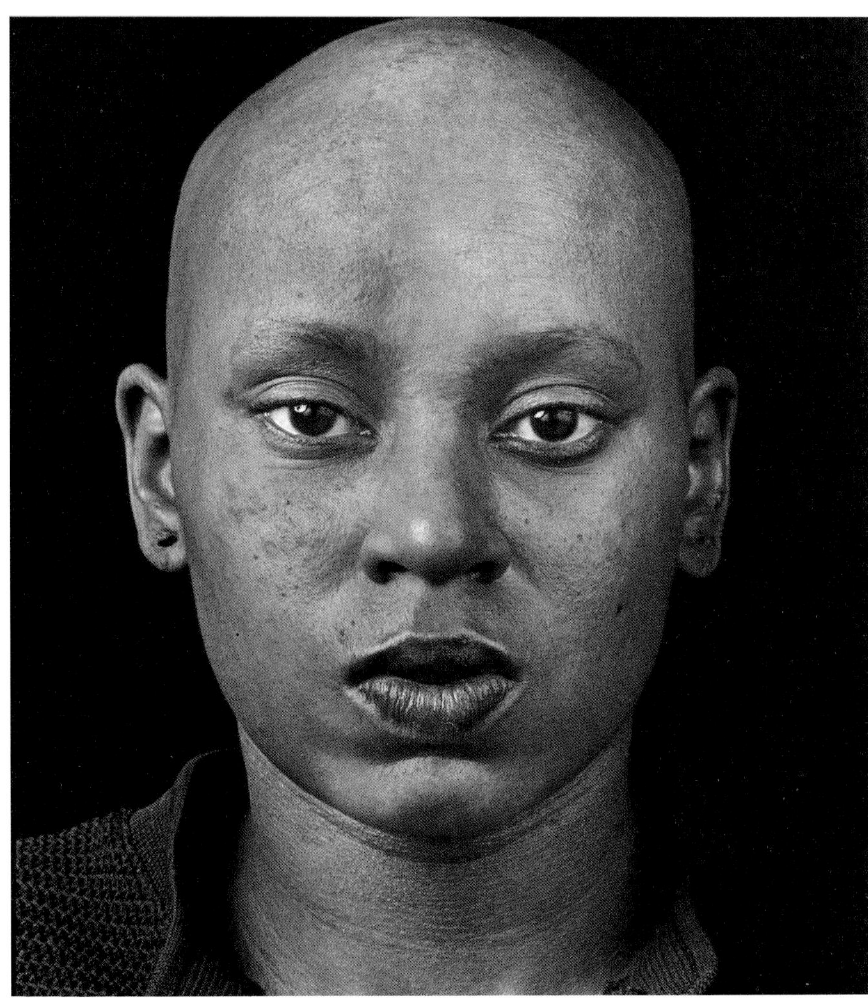

Brenda Adger, New York City: secretary, Western Union

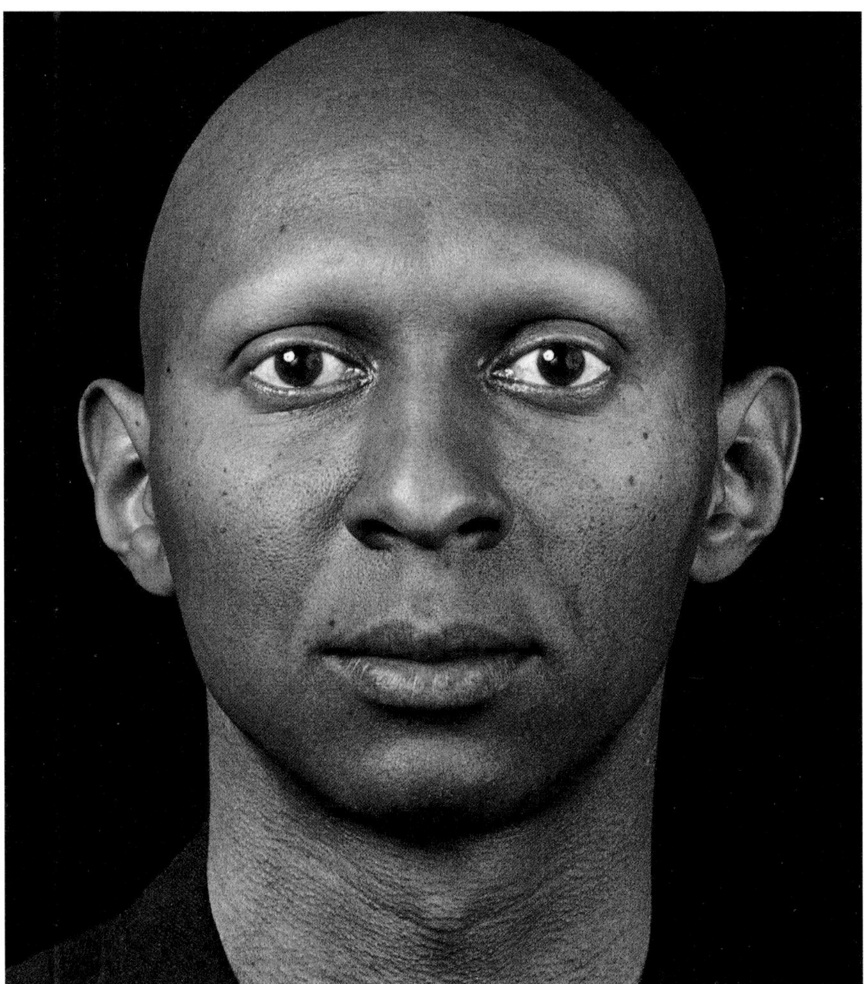

Eroll Hamilton, New York City: fashion photographer

I have studied various cultures and found in each something I could use to make my life better, including what I eat.

—Donald Cann

I grew up in the Midwest, where everyone conformed steadfastly to the status quo. I always took a radical stance politically, artistically, and in the way I dressed. New York has been my home for several years now, but the older I get the more my values become Midwestern. I am an extremist.

—Berns Fry

1981—I moved to New York with all I owned in the back of my pick-up. I have survived since that time, and I am not quite sure how. Being here tomorrow has a certain significance, but it is not my prime motivation anymore. I have made it over the difficult hurdles. My astrological aspects are sensational. Psychics have said that I have masters guiding me. The future is all positive.

—Bartholomew Gianformaggio

continued from page 57

in the morning. It felt as if all your erogenous zones were on your skull.

AA: Were all the pictures done here in your Manhattan studio?

AK: Yeah . . . almost all. There is one whole group from a baldheaded association. I was amazed when I heard on radio's "All Things Considered" about The Baldheaded Men of America, an association of about 10,000 members that was going to have its yearly convention. So I called John Capps, their president, and he invited me to attend the meeting down in Morehead, North Carolina. He organized a little studio space for me. People came from all over, one guy even from Sweden. It was great, a nice little ballroom with more than a hundred people who met specially to celebrate their baldness. A big American flag was erected on a little stage, and the club's leading figures were seated at a head—I mean the main—table. To start the convention, everyone together said the Pledge of Allegiance to the Flag of the United States of America. Then a bald priest said a prayer and, after a few speeches, it was time for the big contest. A jury of a dozen dazzling North Carolina girls had to elect "the smoothest," "the sexiest," and "the most kissable" bald head. It was wonderful.

AA: What did they think of your coming down there to take their pictures? How were you received?

AK: I was received royally—treated like an official.

AA: Did you do any other work outside of New York?

AK: Yes, a few pictures, maybe five, I took in Switzerland. For the boxer Marvin Hagler, I set up my little studio in his training camp in Cape Cod. A crew of five from Swiss national television accompanied me; they did a piece on *Heads* and some of my other work for a prime-time show.

I recently met a French lawyer who had just been appointed head of Interpol. He complained that in all his legal training he never had learned management, which he now needed so badly. The other day I ran into a colleague in Procurement and Contracts who had a background in public administration but complained that he had no legal training, which he now needed so badly. A combination of European and American schools might help to close these gaps.

—Prof. Dr. Jur. Ingo von Ruckteschell

AA: So they were shooting you shooting Hagler?

AK: Yes. But the best shot Hagler landed himself a few days later, when he made eight million dollars in his fight against Roberto Duran—the highest fee ever received for a single fight.

LM: How did that Swiss TV show turn out?

AK: Oh, it was fun. Its highlight was a party we gave for all the models of *Heads*, those I had photographed to date.

LM: Weren't you nervous, inviting all these people who didn't know each other and had only one thing in common: no hair?

AK: Well, at first the idea seemed a little weird, but soon people started calling in, saying they looked forward to the event. And then, that very night, it was fantastic. People arrived by subway or limousine. Some came alone, others brought their wives or boyfriends. A few people started dancing right away. A rock musician was in a hot conversation with a Wall Street broker and a mailman about some Whitney art show. I was surprised to find black leather mixing so well with black tie. Robert Sherman, in a long-curled-hair drag look, helped as a barmaid and suddenly took his wig off for the TV cameras, opening bottles of champagne at the same time. Kirk Lightsey played wild tunes on the piano, which my musician neighbor kindly lent me for the night. Lenny Tepper from Buddha-Gram, New York, let people rub his huge belly to bring them luck and financial success. Henry Boyer and Theresa Benzwie performed a dance improvisation that made it hard to believe they had just met that night. Someone read poetry, and Dr. Rosa introduced his well-trained baby-oiled muscles. The studio was packed, and since noise and loud music usually draw people from the street, we were lucky to have The Crusher as a doorman.

continued on page 97

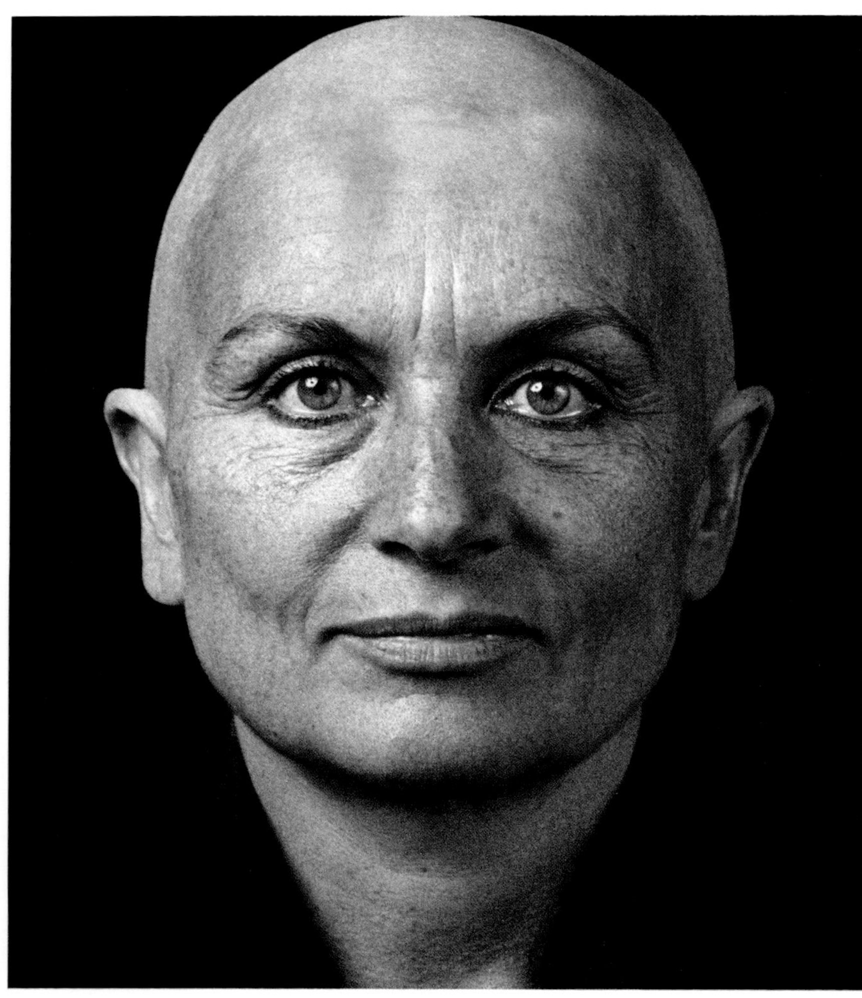

Claude Torey, Paris: video artist

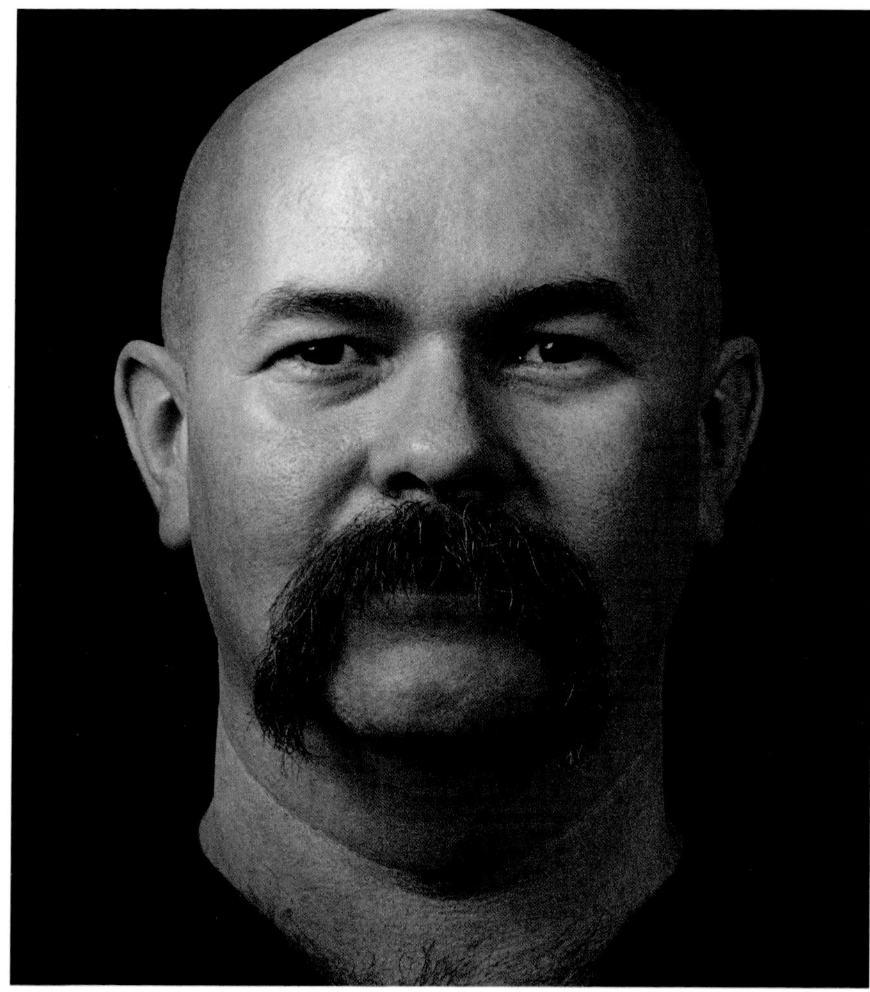

Dennis Pilkington, New York City: painter

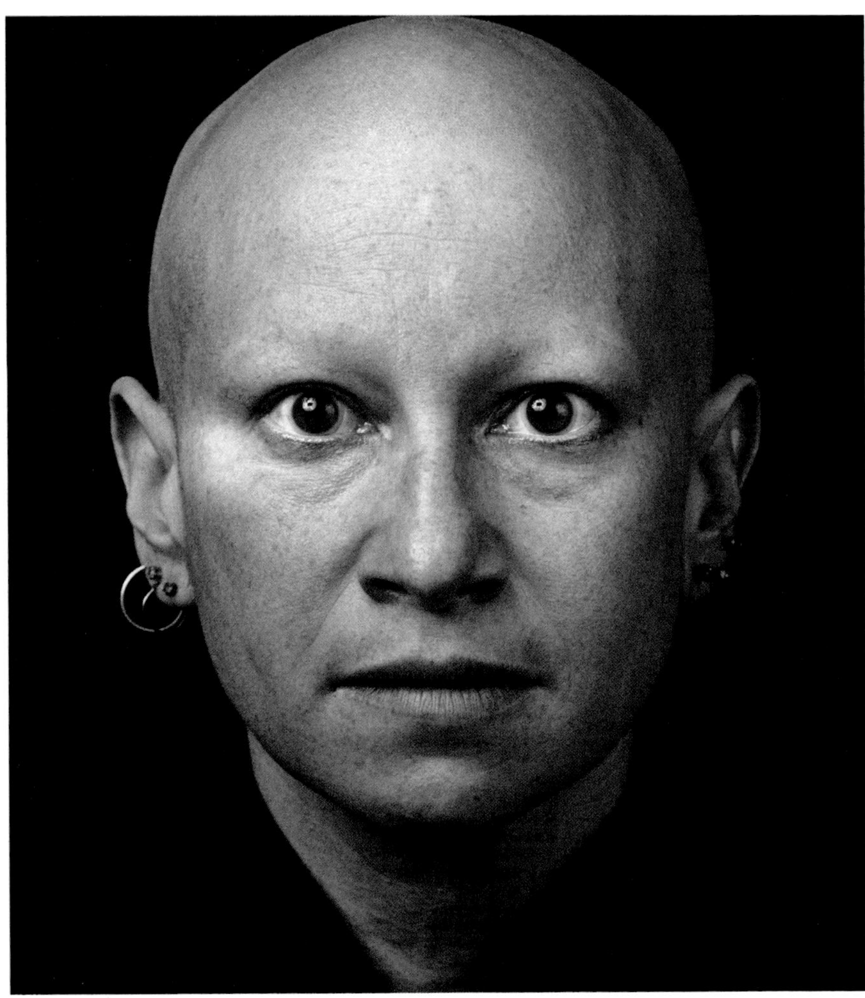

Hermine, Los Angeles: owner of Endangered Species, a mail-order exotic flower business

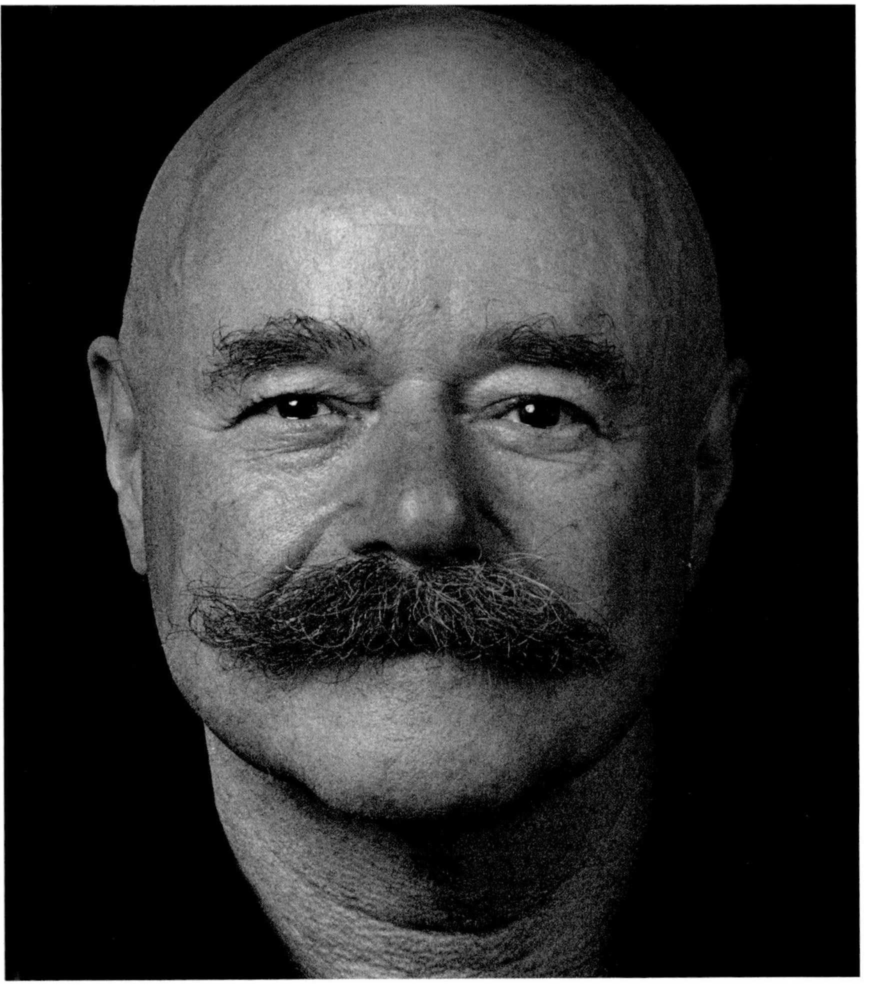

Robert G. Fleischer, New York City: accessories buyer and merchandiser, Bergdorf Goodman; product designer, Mary Quant Cosmetics and Hubert Givenchy

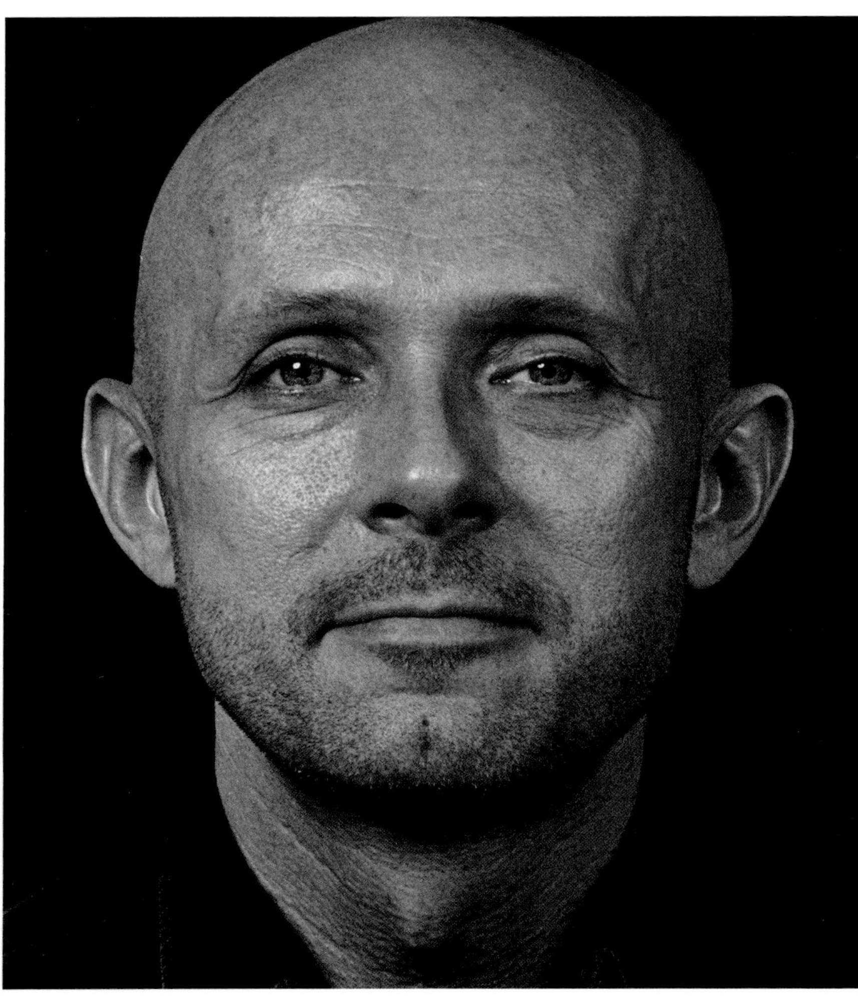

Adam Hayes, New York City: lighting designer

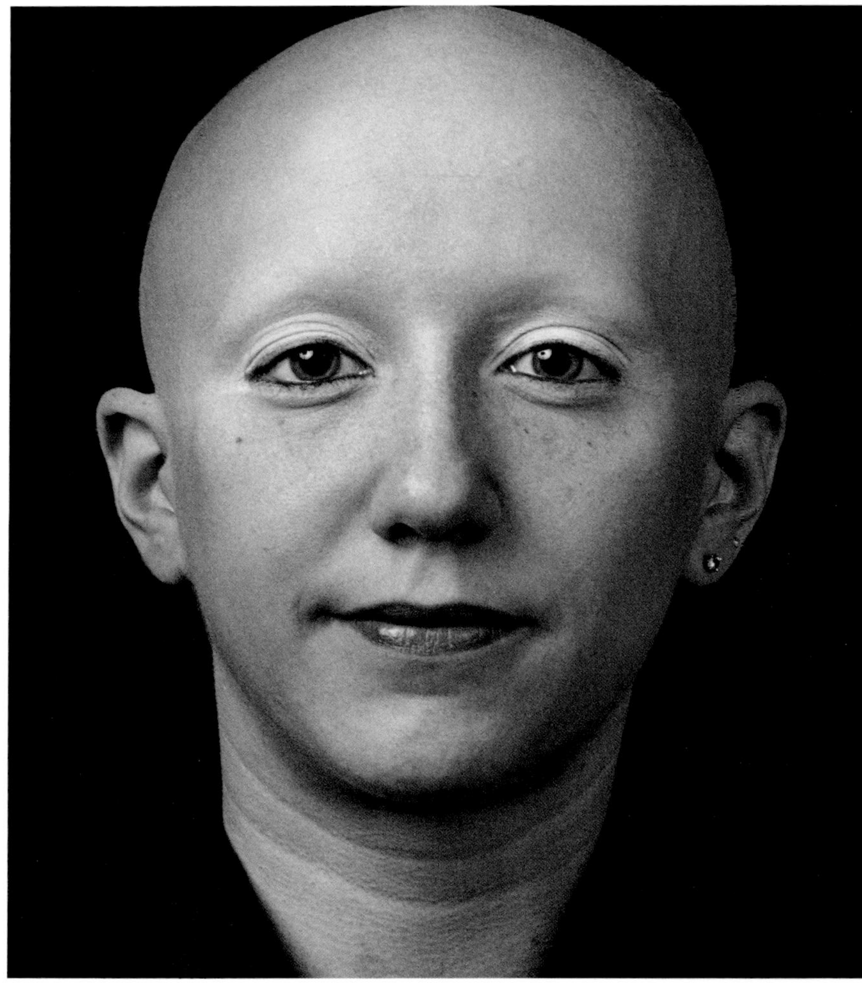

Cindy Allen, New York City: owner of Black Market, an East-Village clothing store—sells only things that are black

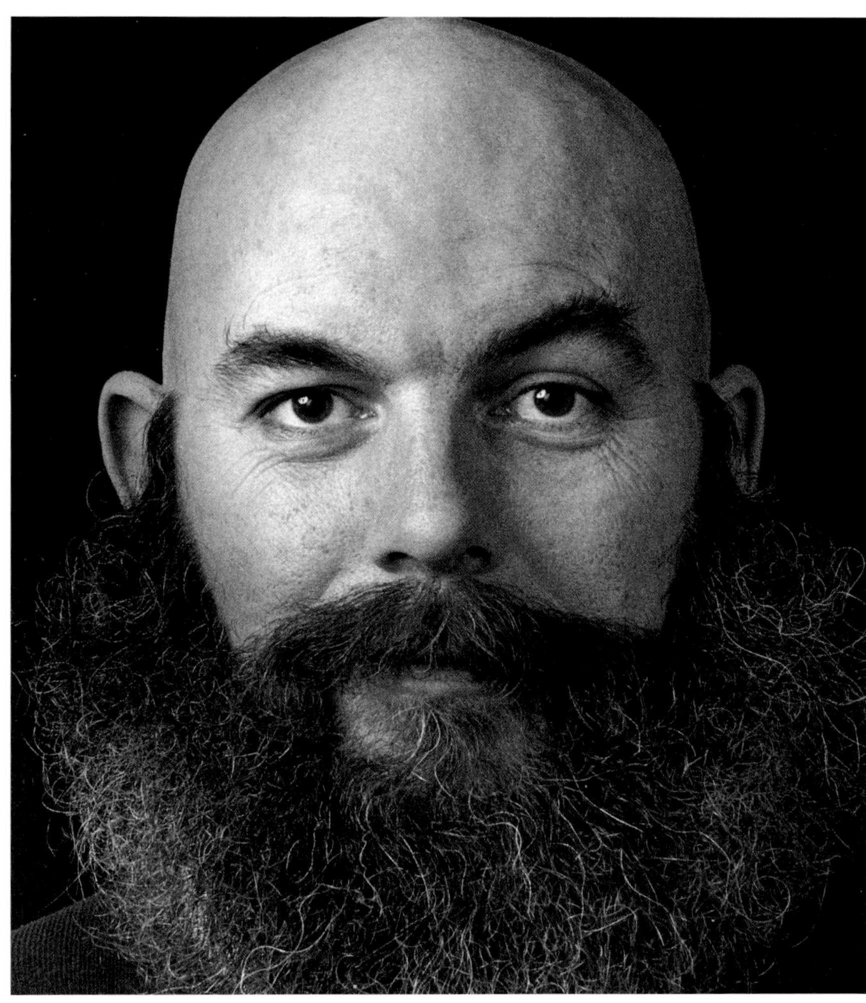

Ronald Dayton, New York City: puppeteer

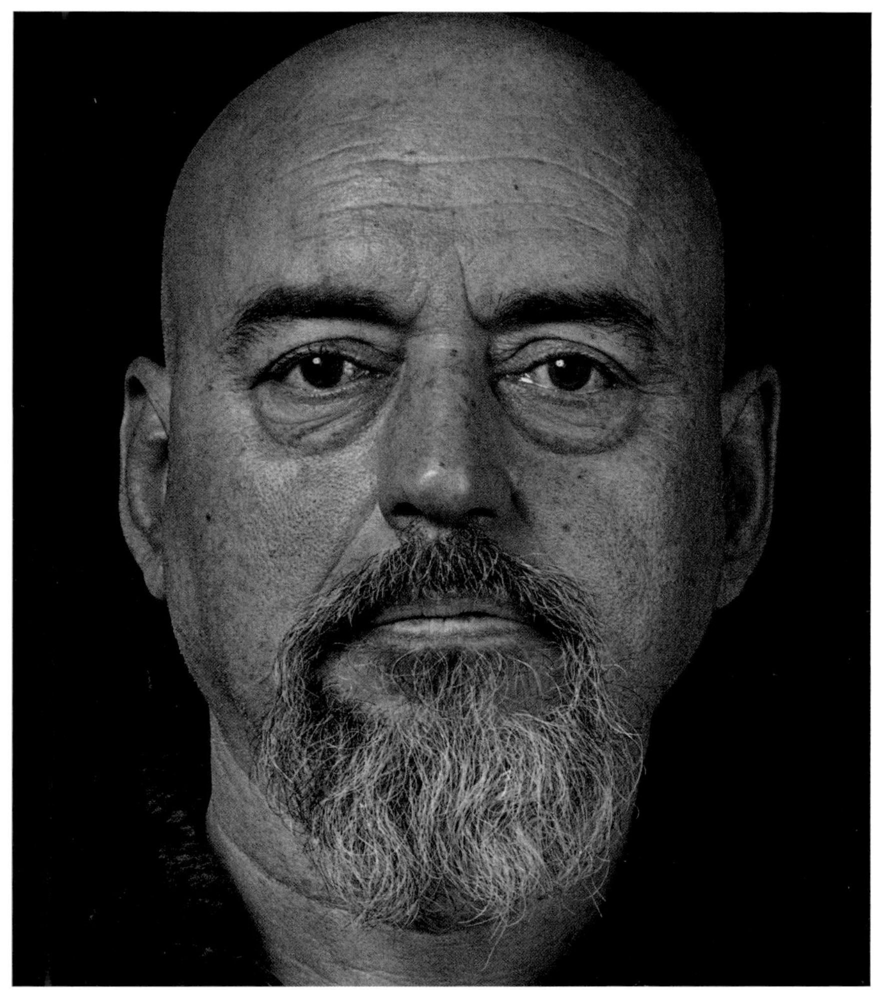

Leo Torres Agüerro, Buenos Aires and Paris: painter

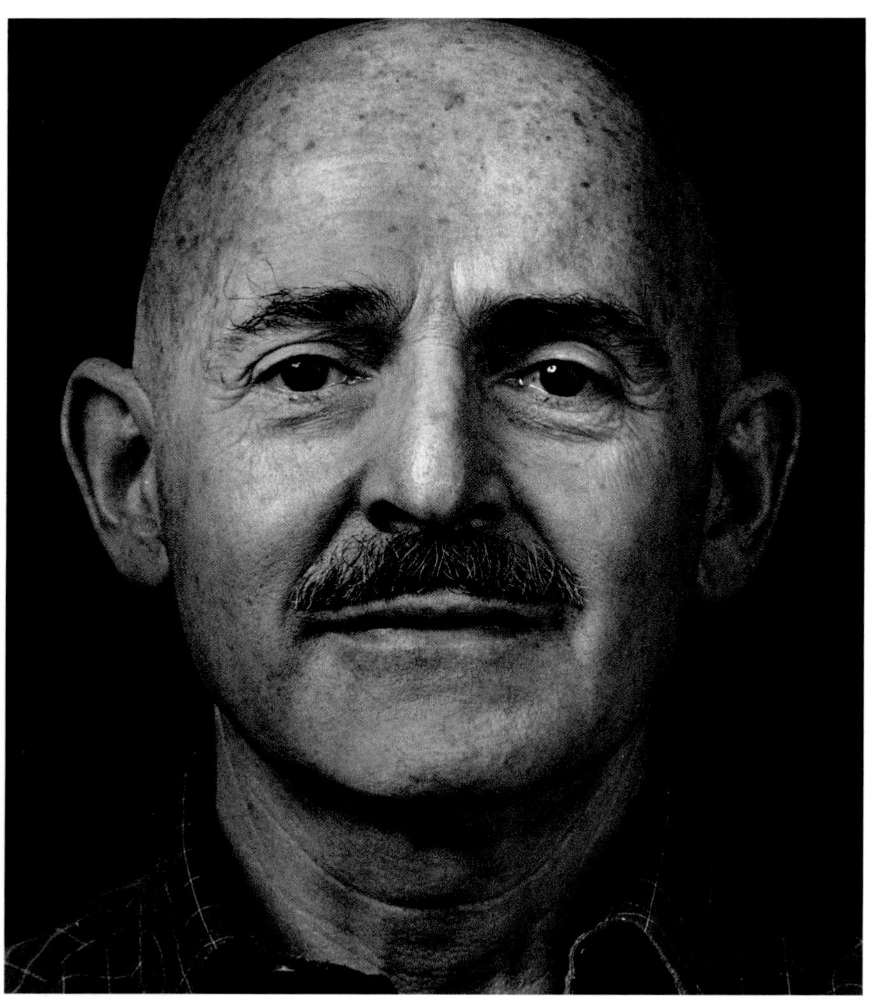

Joe Caroff, New York City: graphic designer; designed for ABC News; designed ABC Olympics logo, graphics for *West Side Story, Cabaret,* Woody Allen's *Zelig* and *Manhattan*; book-cover graphics for Norman Mailer's *The Naked and the Dead*

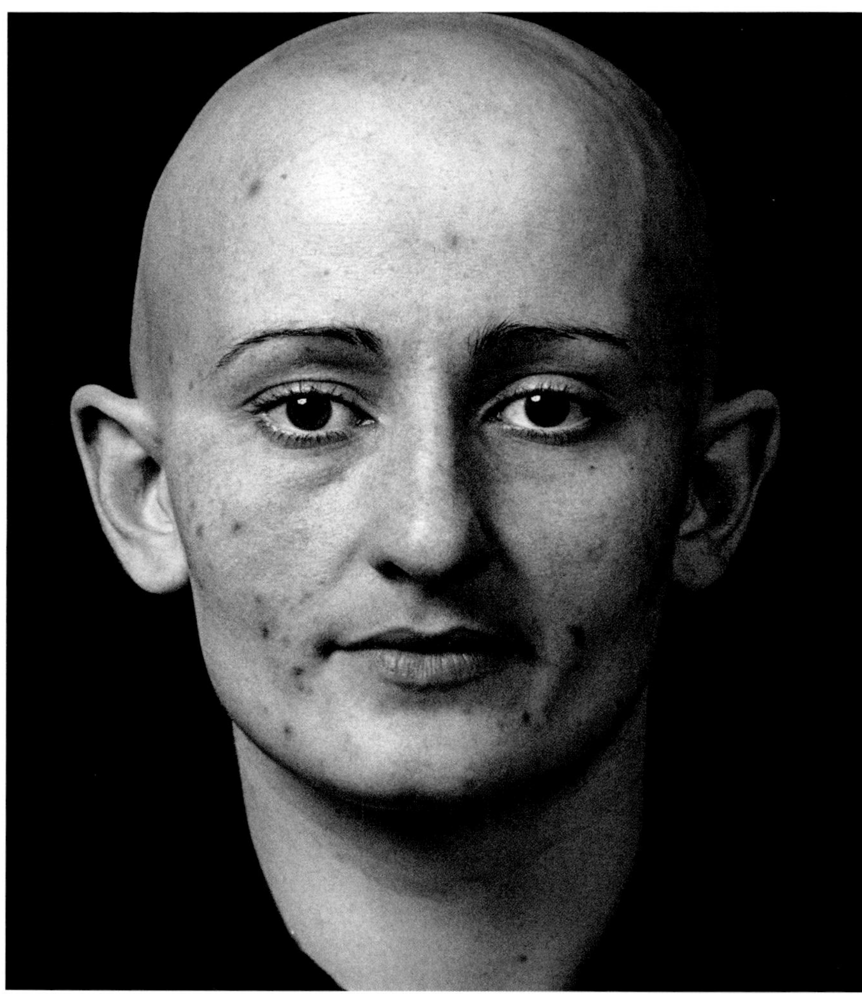

Anita Wahl, Berlin: painter and performance artist

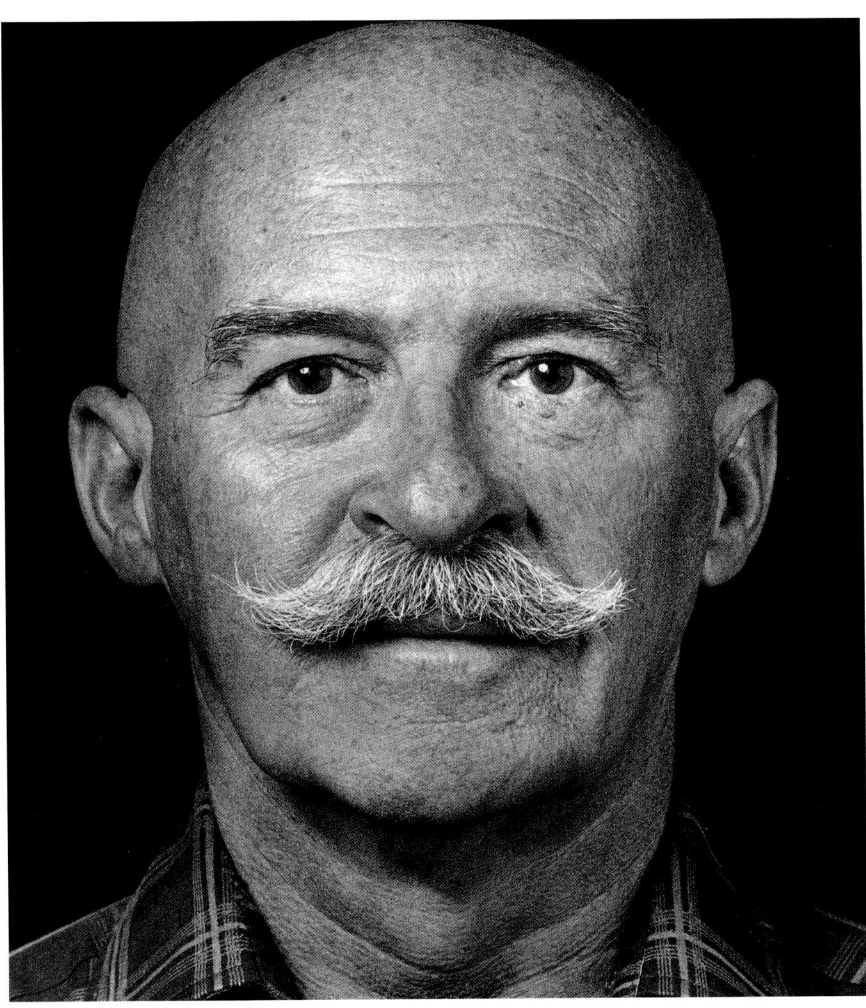

John Harbster, New York City: retired medical technician

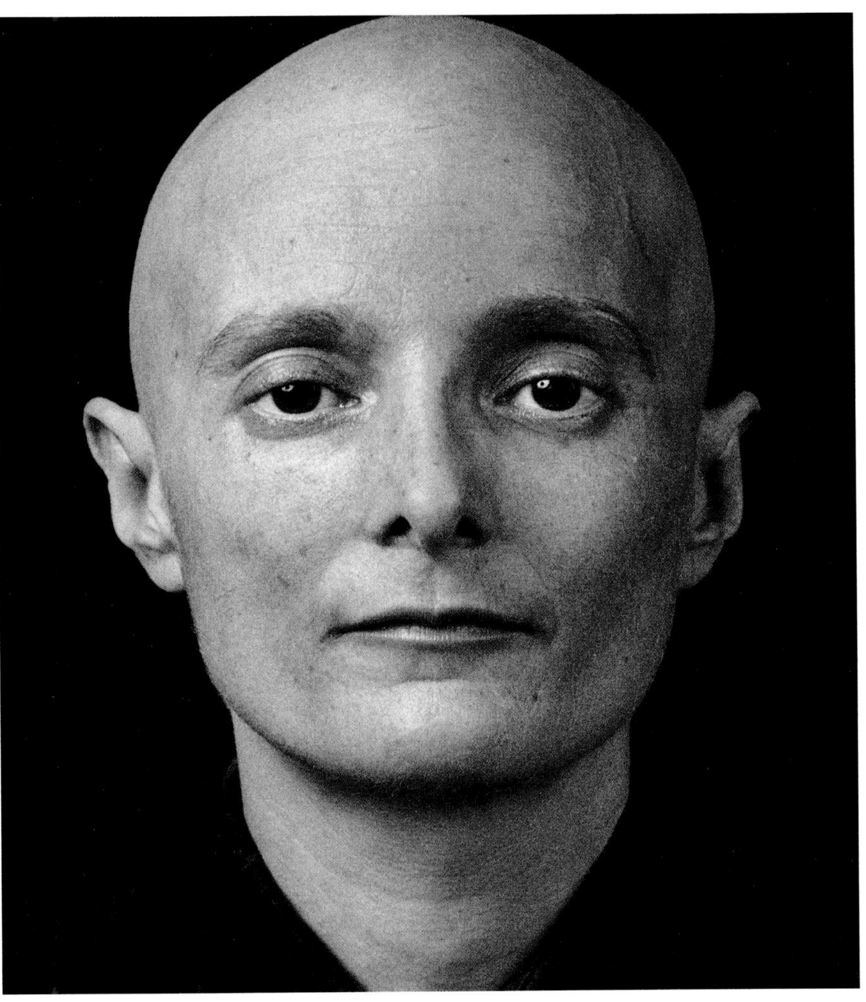

Ann Bar-Tur, New York City: painter, deceased; a memorial exhibition of her works has been held at the Levitt Gallery, New York

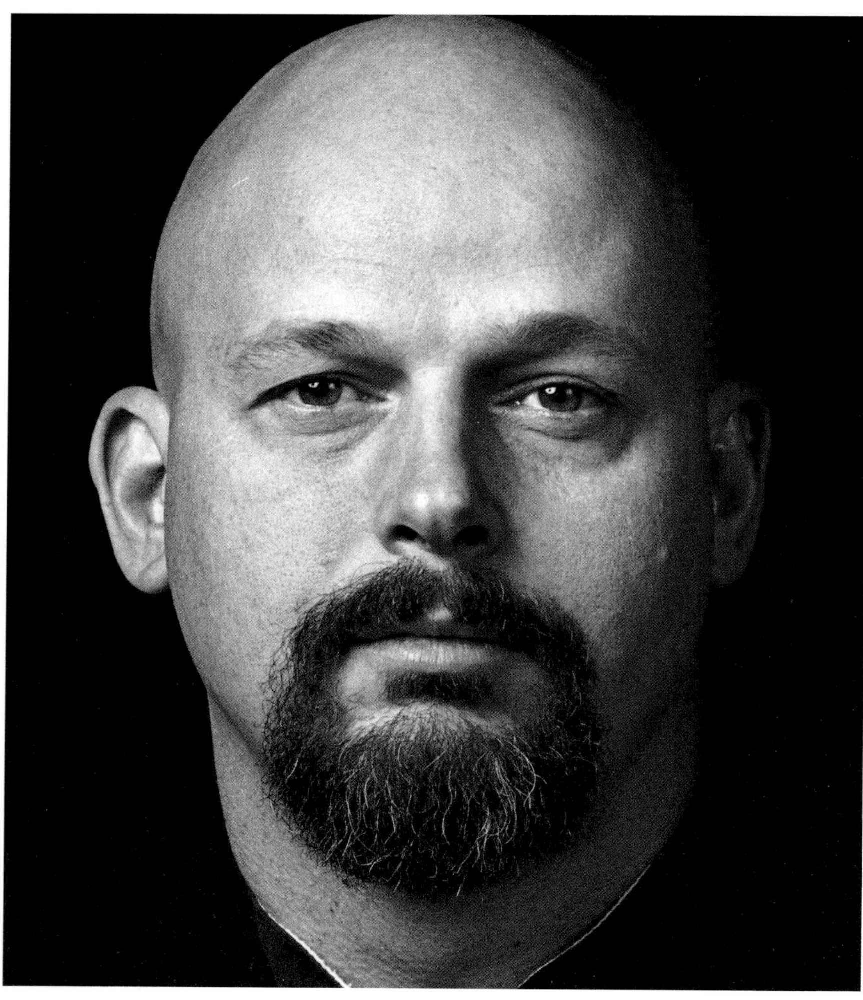

Richard Carlino, New York City: phototypesetter

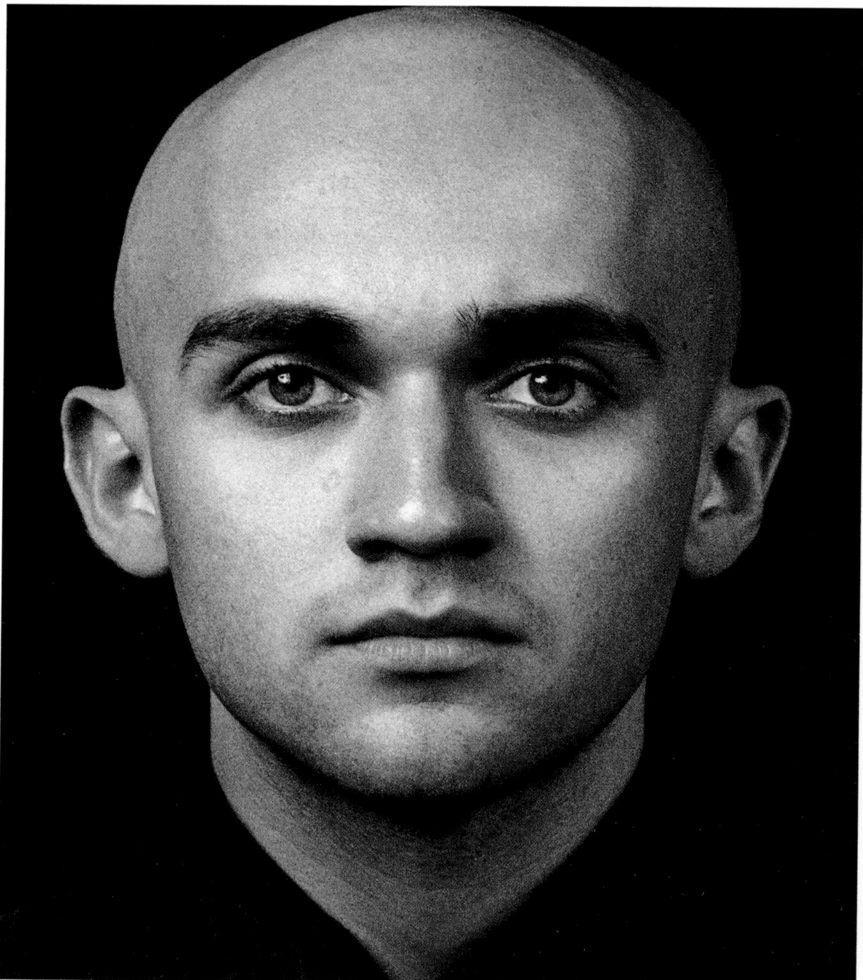

David Yarrito, New York City: actor and performer, various downtown clubs, including Area, Pyramid, and Danceteria

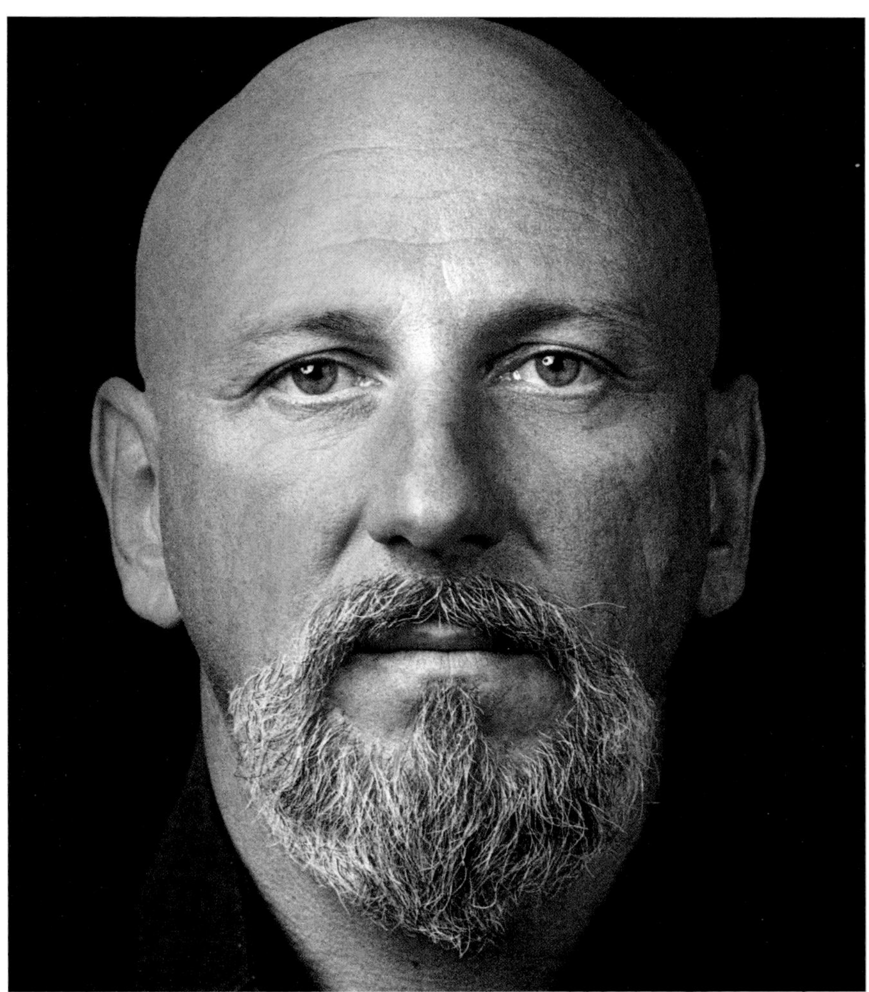

Lair Parent, Los Angeles: theatrical technician, technical director, stage manager for industrial shows; producer of multimedia and video for industrial clients, including IBM, Mobil Oil, Avon, Subaru, Cessna, and the New Zealand government

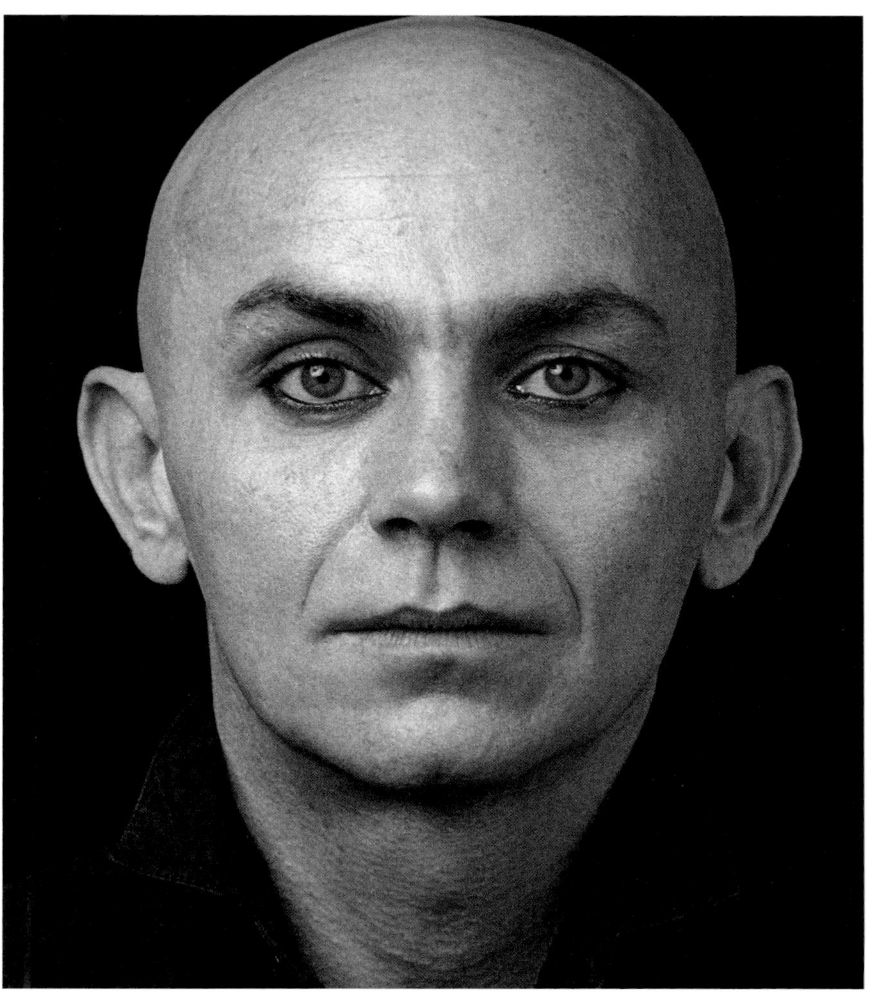

Peter Stack, New York City: hair and make-up artist

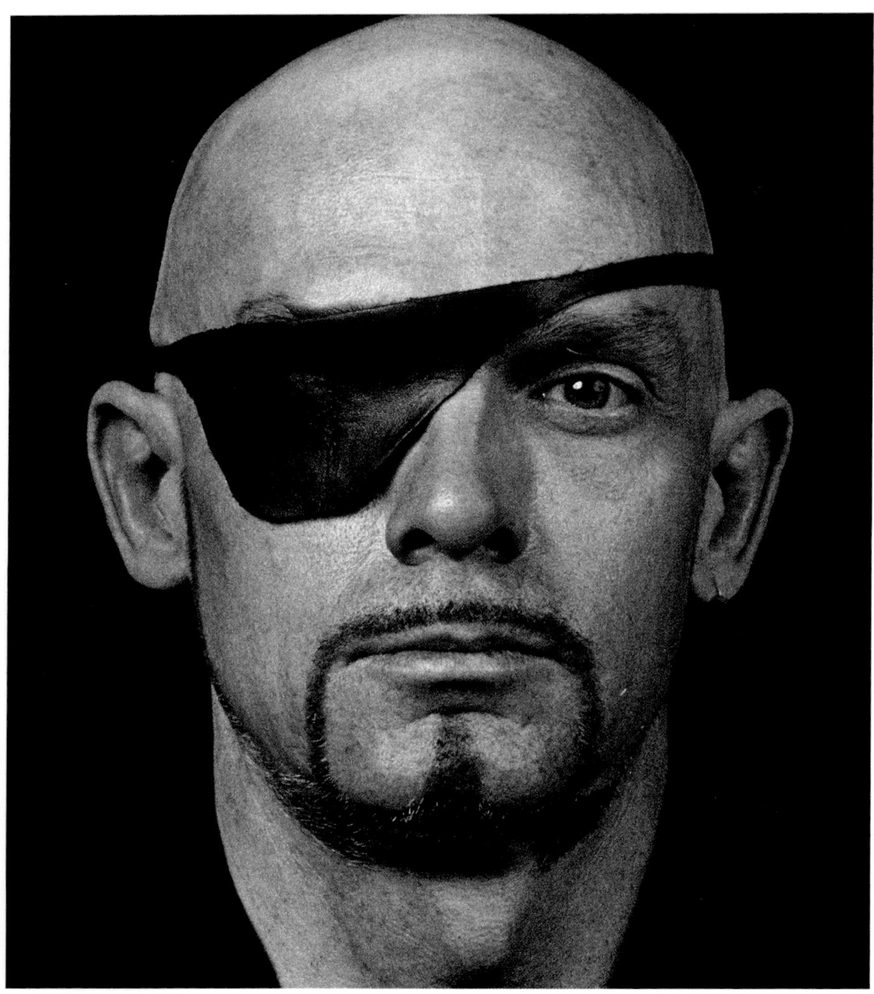

Frank Schwizt, New York City

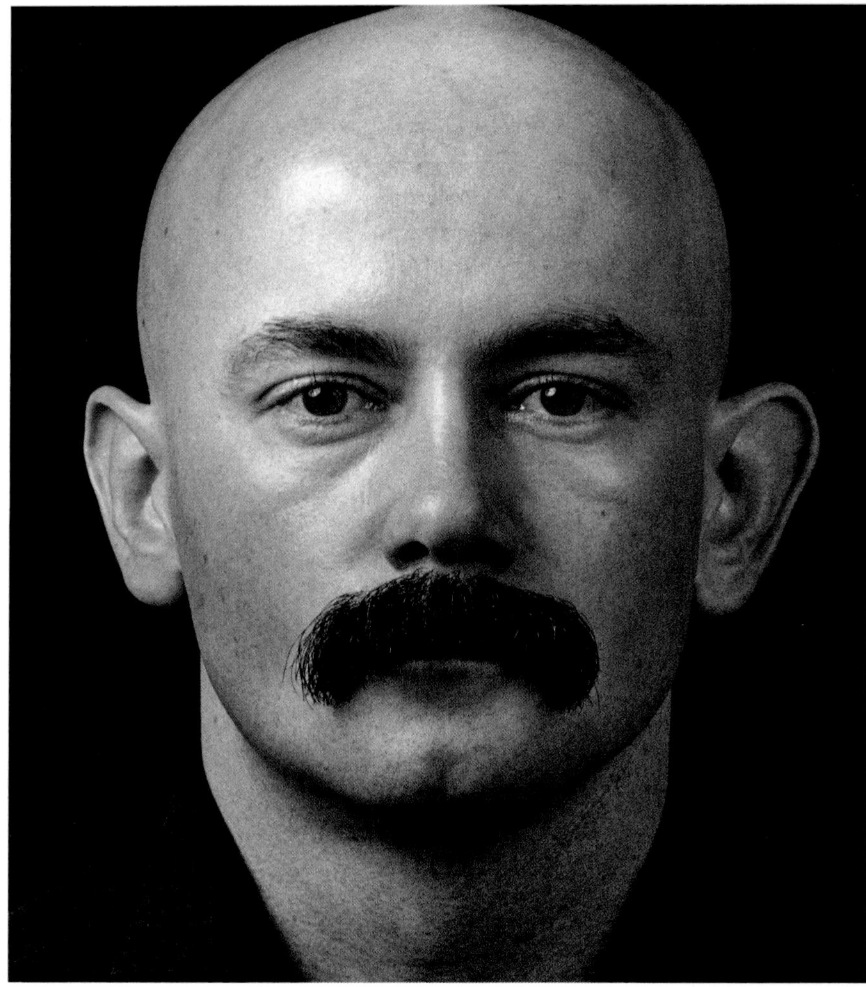

Wayne D. Purviance, New York City: owner, Red Star Cafe

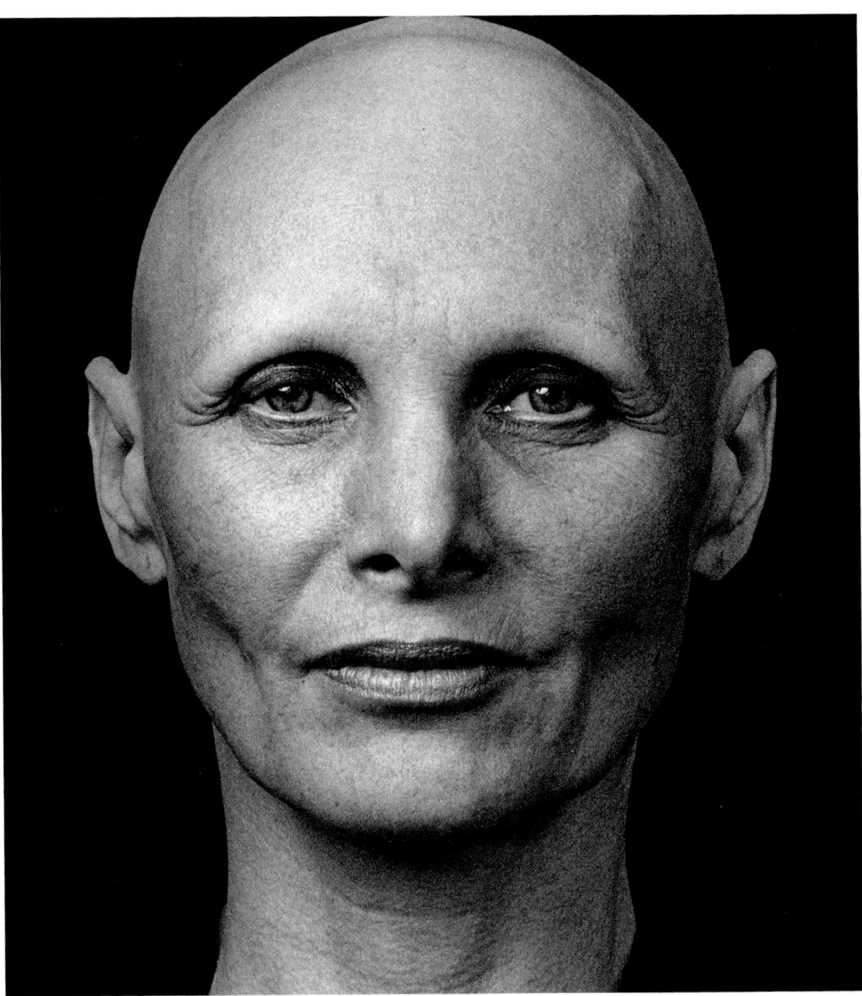

Teresa Benzwie, Cherry Hill, New Jersey: creative movement instructor; appears on television talk shows to discuss the role of movement education in schools

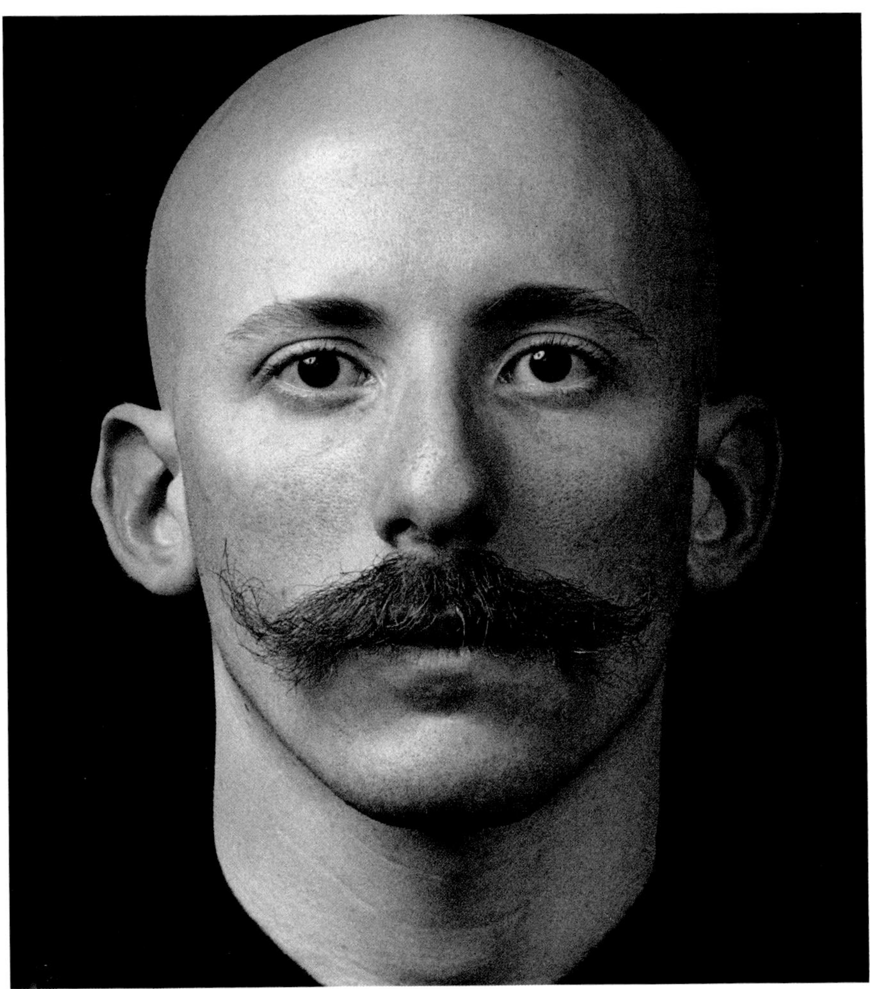

Michael Cooper, New York City: poet

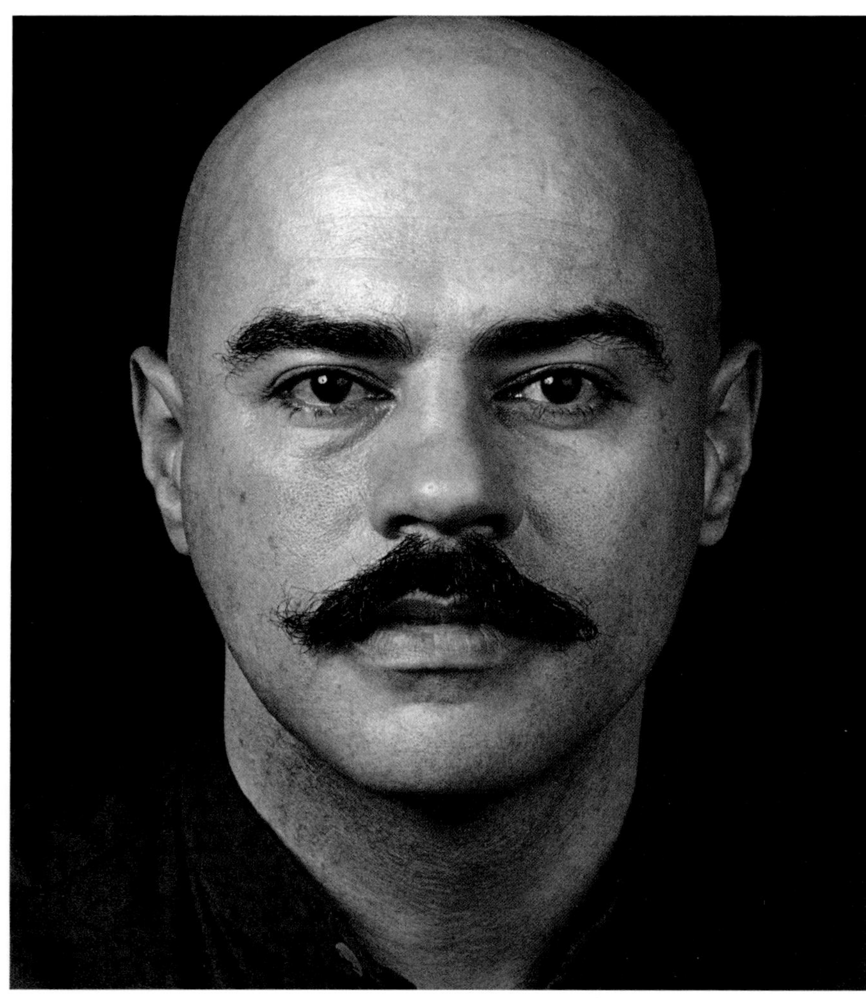

Papo, New York City: painter

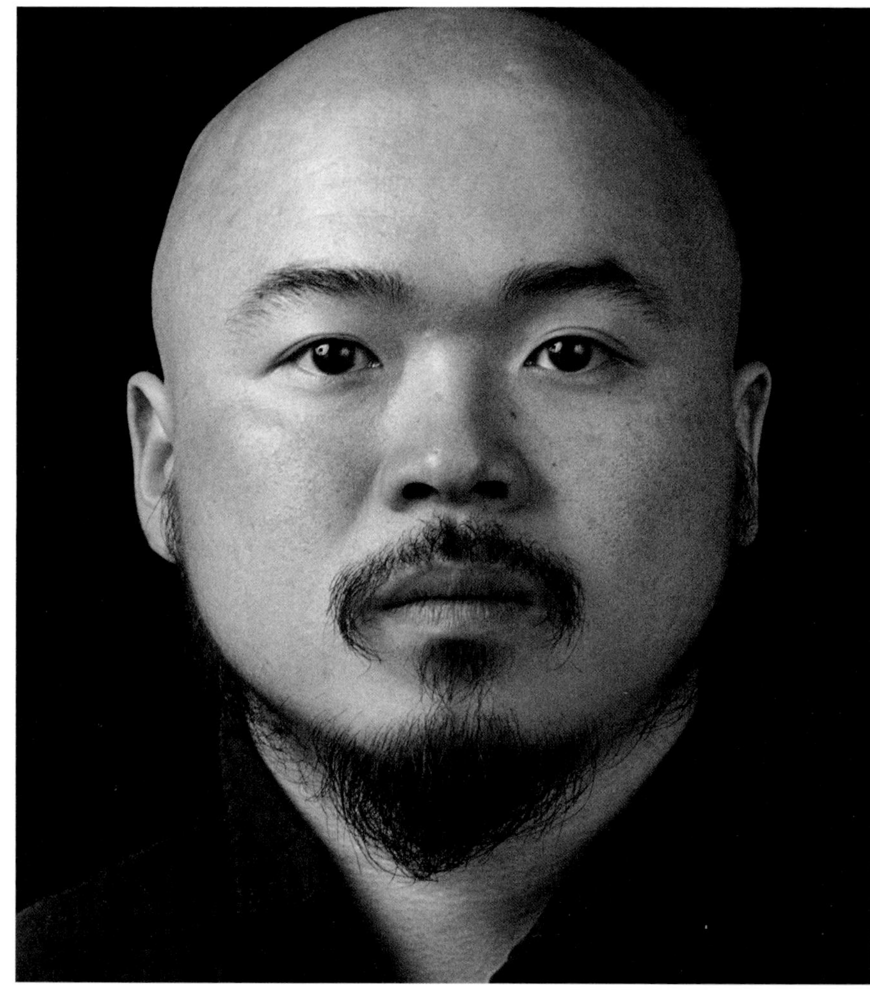

Ken Hiratsuka, New York City: artist and photographer

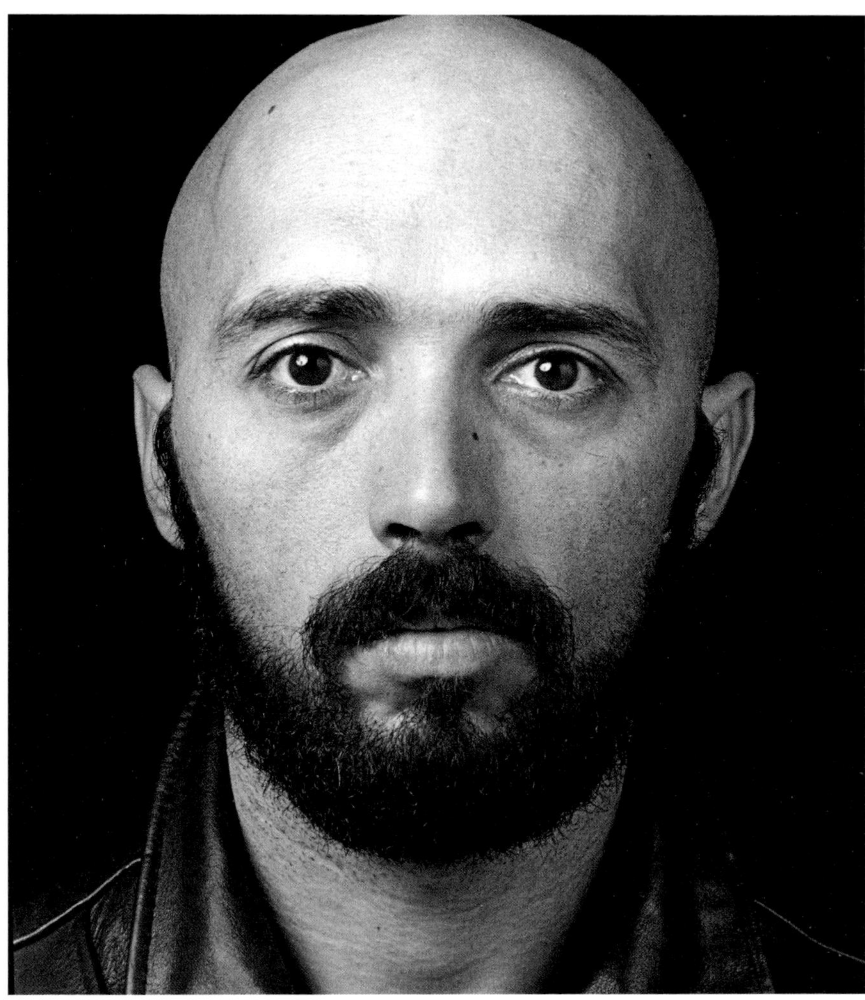

Fred Montelbano, New York City: longshoreman

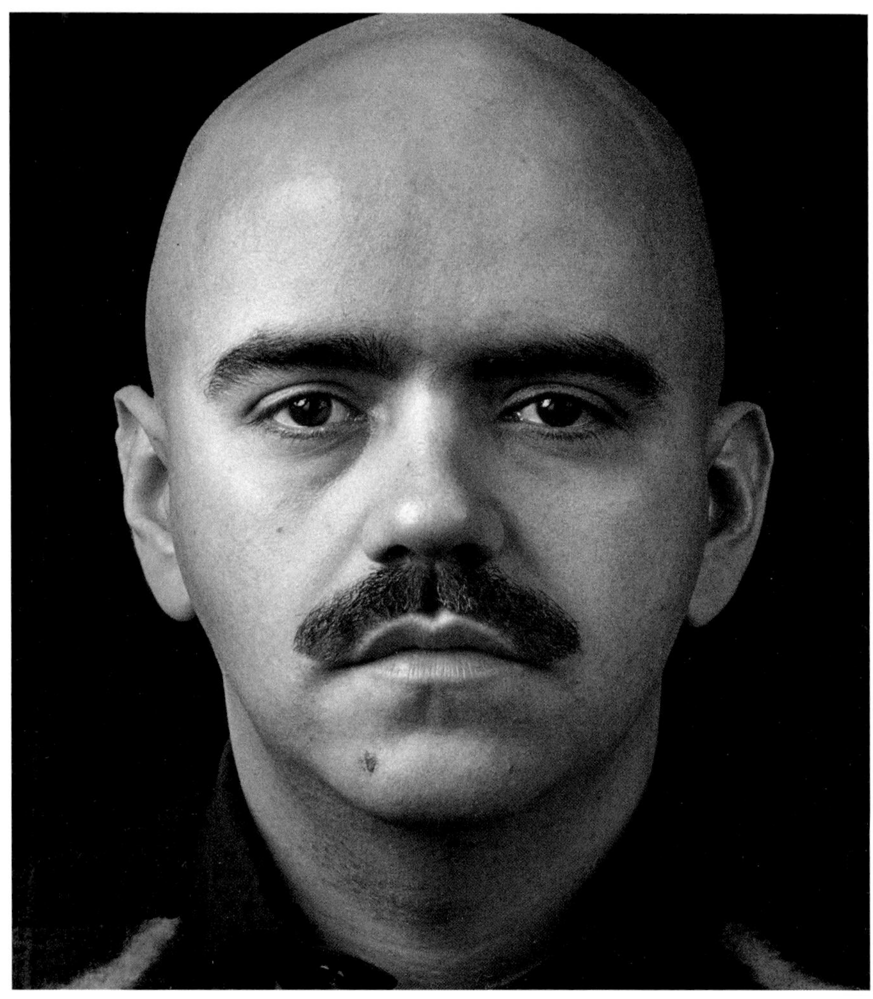

Araken Ribeiro de Oliveira, New York City: fashion designer for K.O.D. Productions

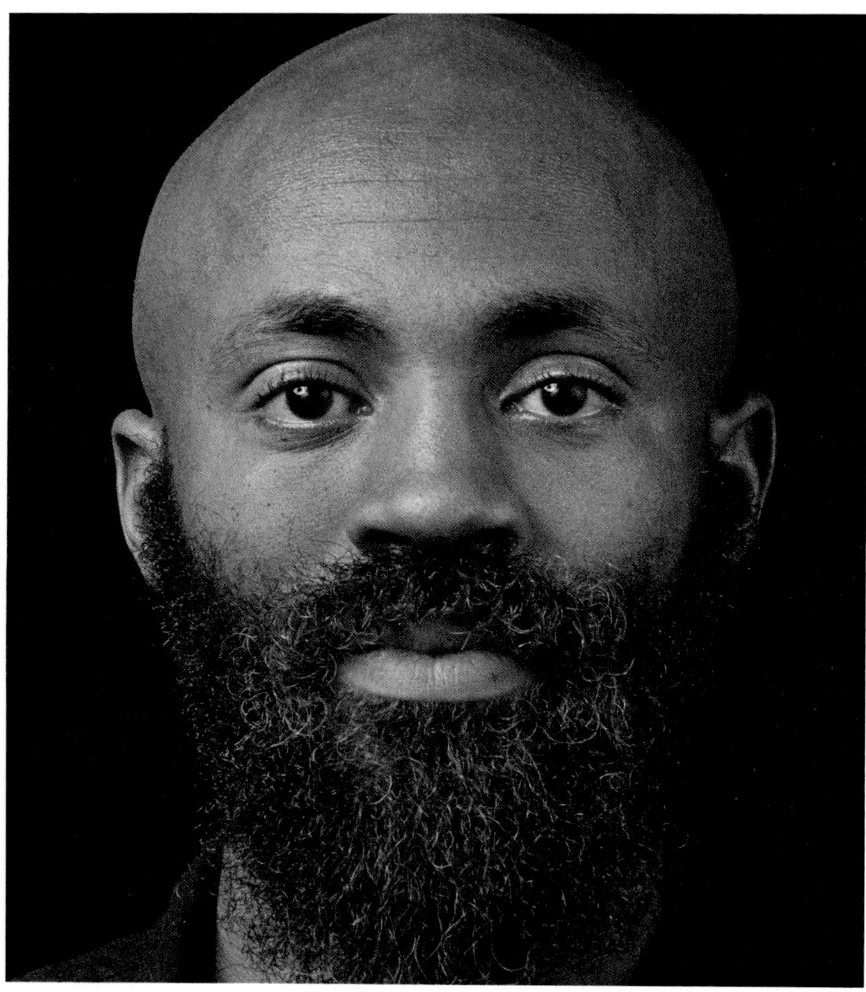

Phil Settle, New York City: gymnast and athlete

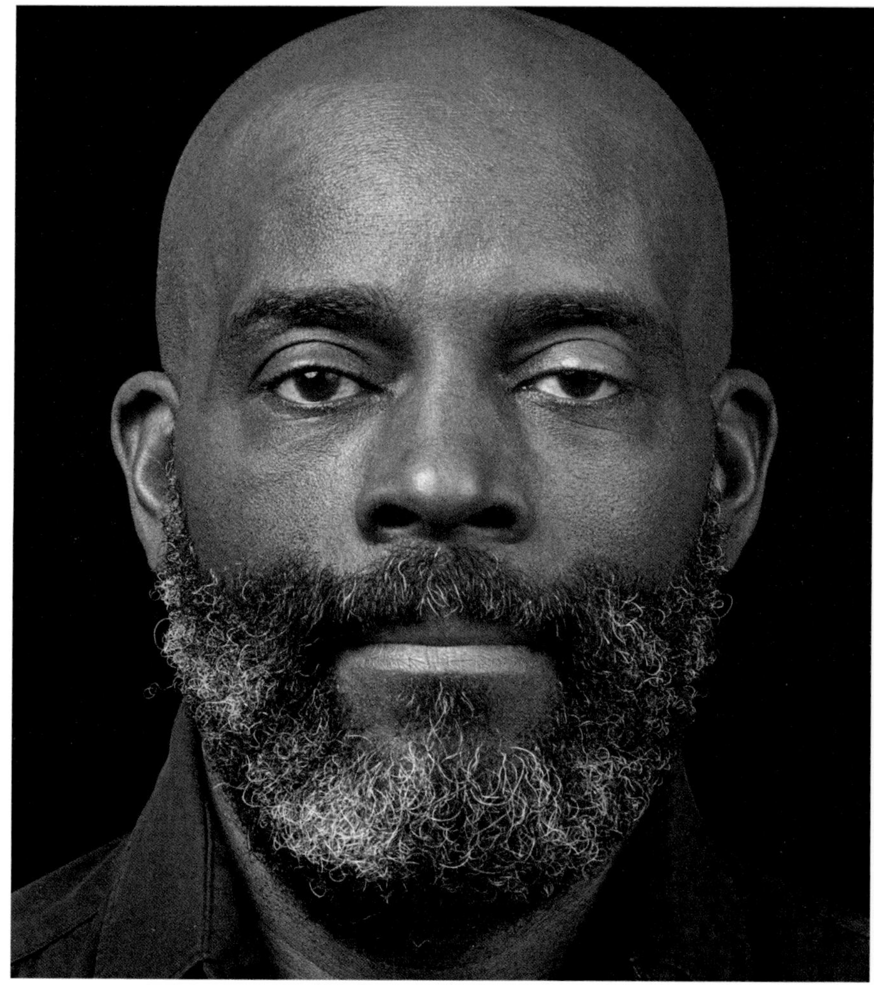

Mel King, Boston: politician; first black man to win Boston mayoral primary

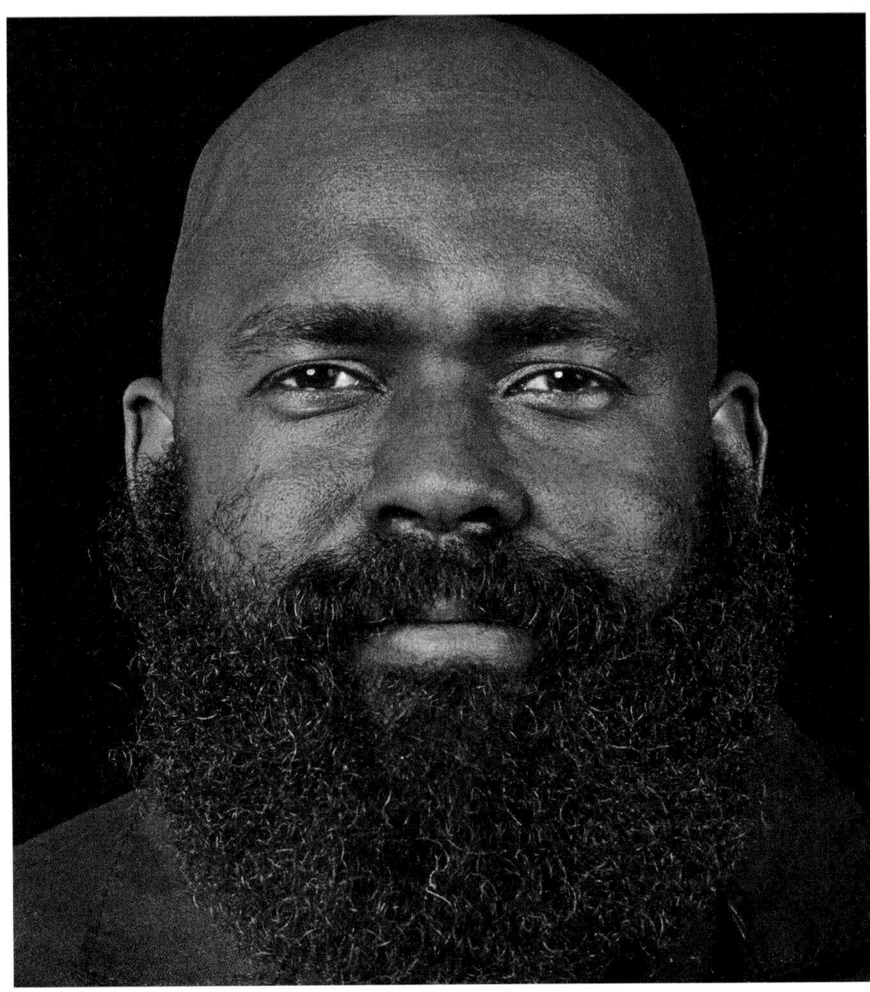

Victor B. Diaz, New York City: telephone technician, Nynex

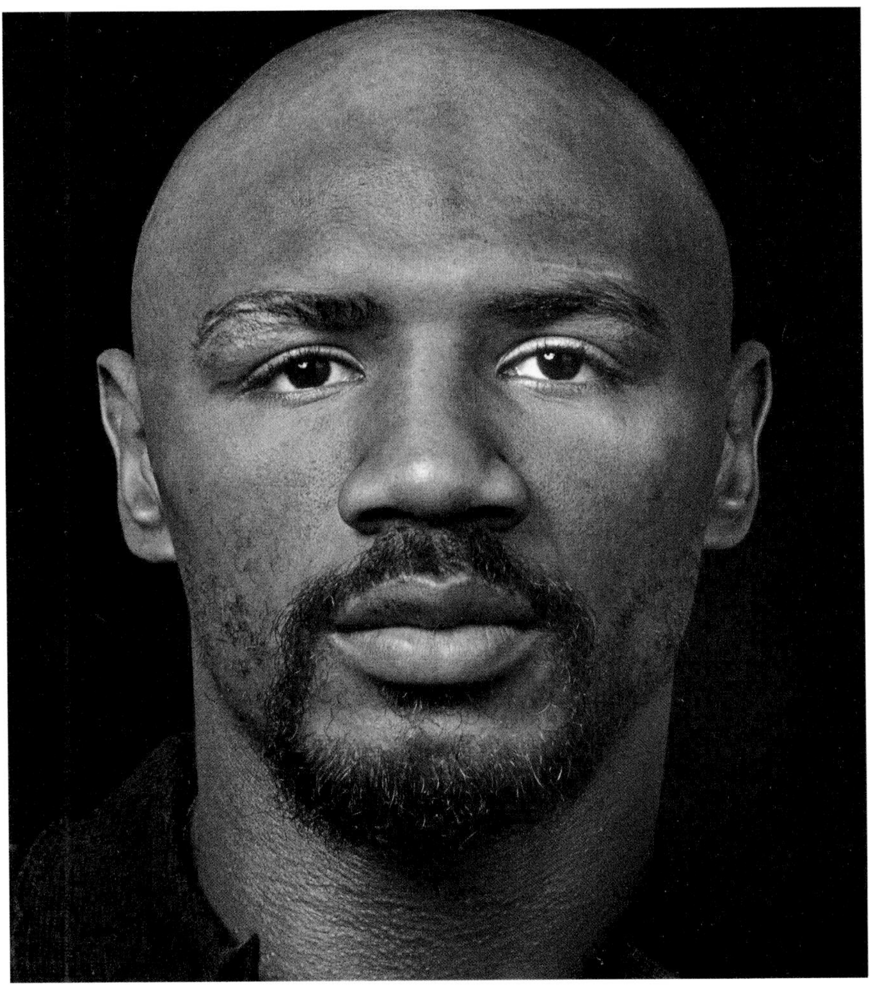

Marvelous Marvin Hagler: middleweight boxer; received $8 million for his November 1983 fight against Roberto Duran—highest fee ever paid in boxing

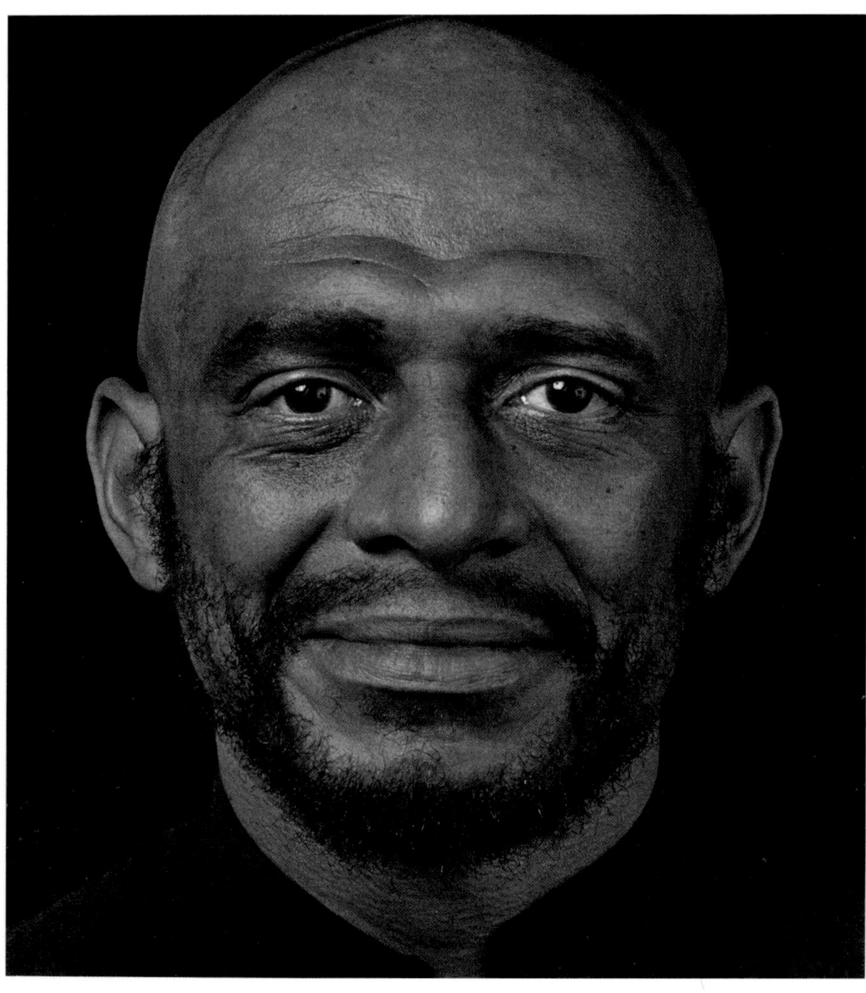

Kirk Lightsey, New York City: jazz pianist

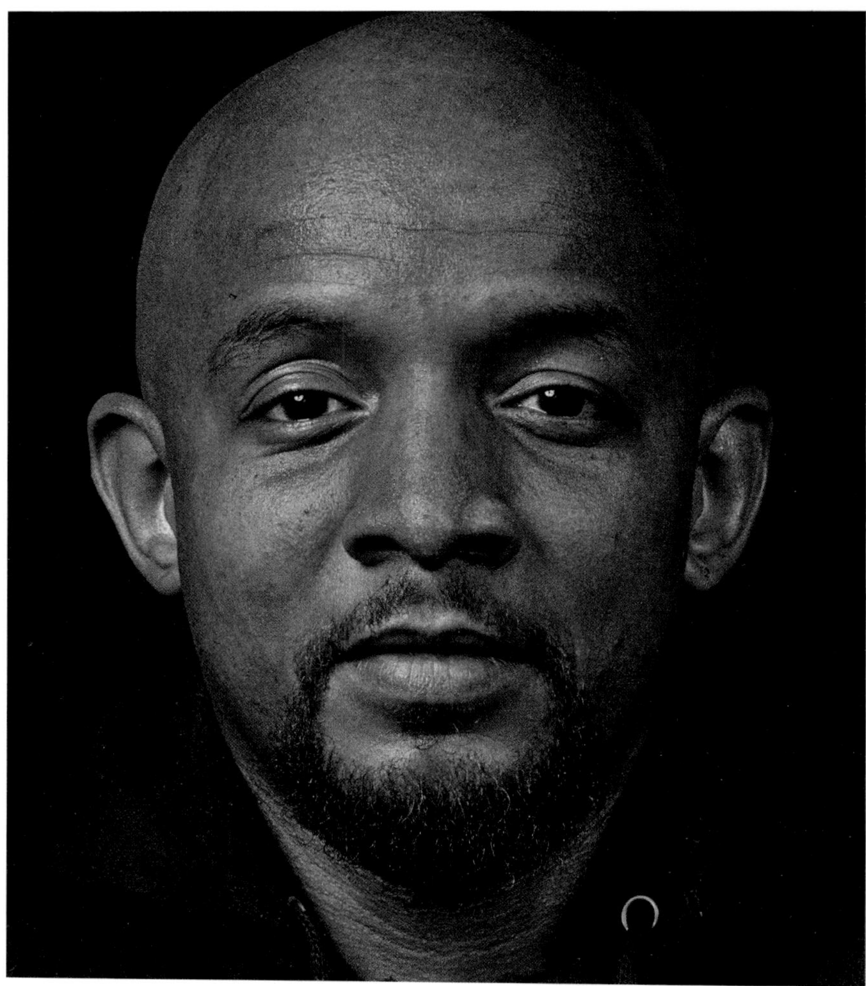

Rubin Carven, New York City: chauffeur and security guard at the fashion boutique, Comme des Garçons

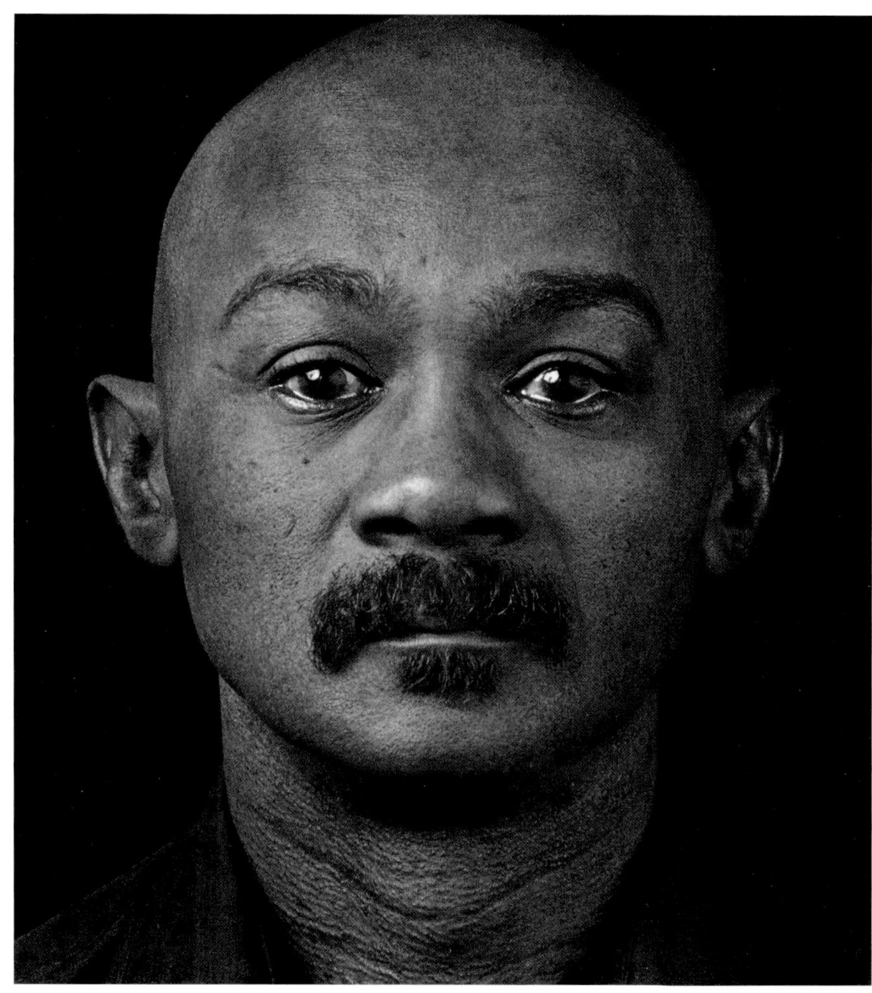

Sam King, New York City

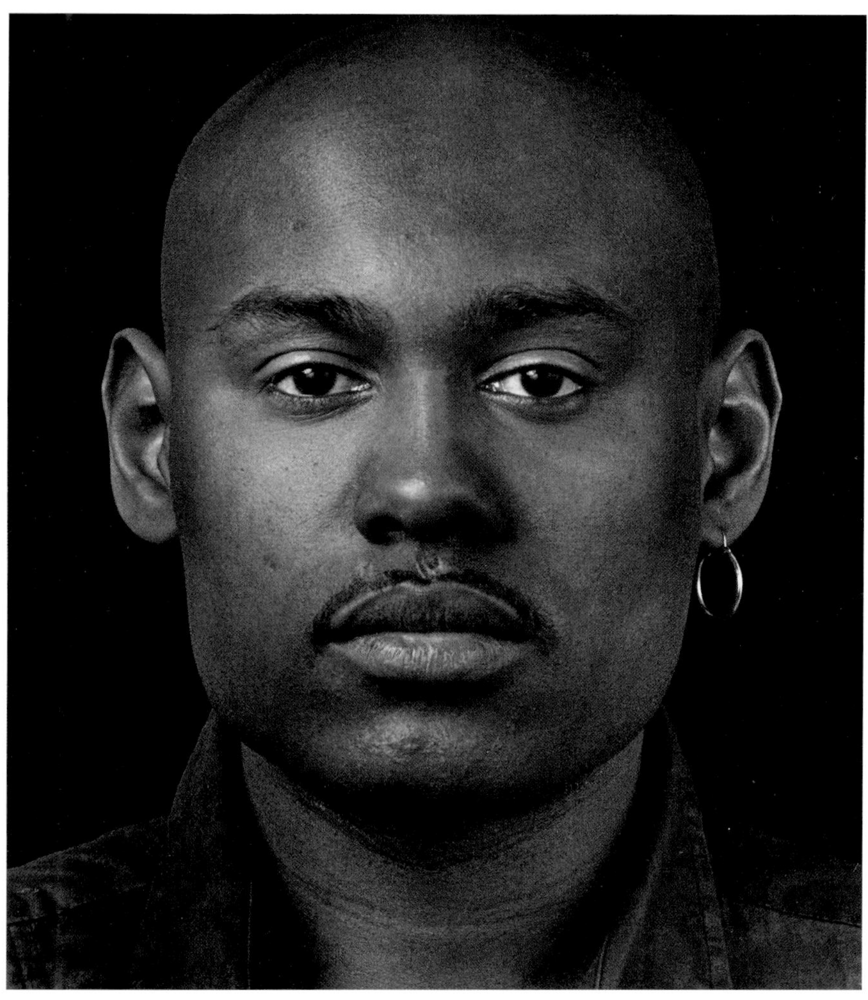

Pierre Marie Beauvoir, Paris: guitarist

Being a coxswain called for standing four-hour watches at the helm. There was still plenty of time left for painting bulkheads and swabbing decks. I enjoyed my tour of duty aboard the aircraft carrier *Constellation*. Learned a lot about people and life.

—John Jones

As with shaving one's head, through which the self becomes revealed to the world through the underlying scalp, the creative act not only builds up artifice, but peels it away: the fruit inside the orange skin.

—Michael Cooper

IN THE MATTER OF THE APPLICATION OF FRANK HERMAN SCHWUTTGE, JR., FOR LEAVE TO CHANGE HIS NAME TO FRANK W. SCHWIZT. On reading and filing the petition of Frank Herman Schwuttge, Jr., verified the 23rd day of November 1977, praying for a change of name of the petitioner, it being requested that he be permitted to assume the name of FRANK W. SCHWIZT in the place of and stead of his present name.

—Frank Schwizt

continued from page 79

AA: Who is The Crusher?

AK: The first experience I had with him was trouble, when he gave me such a hard time about getting backstage to see a friend after a fashion show. Years ago. Robert—The Crusher—Simmons is great. He's huge, and he can lift you up with one hand and throw you to the ceiling, if he wanted. He usually works as a security guard in several Upper East Side boutiques or as a bouncer at fashion shows in New York night clubs. But, one day, he got this special assignment from an East Sixties block association. The job was to sweep crime from East 60th Street. They told him to do it any way he wanted to, but to do it well. "I stood there in the street reading a paper, like waiting for the bus. I already knew the bad guys. So when they walked or ran by, I stretched out my left and grabbed them. The tough ones I had to knock out—BANG—since I knew they had a gun or knife."

AA: Didn't you also photograph a police photographer?

AK: Yes, Adrian Kellard. He's taken millions of mug shots in his life, and here he saw an idea of mug shots as art. He was amazed.

LM: Why did you dedicate your book to Otto Steinert?

AK: Steinert was my teacher. He was a man of no compromise, and, as far as I'm concerned, he was one of the few supremely competent people in photography in this century: as a teacher, a curator, and as a photographer. *Heads* and its straight form have something in common with the portraits Steinert did of Nobel prize winners and so on in the fifties and sixties.

AA: How was he as a teacher?

AK: Terribly authoritarian, merciless, but the best. Even when he was drunk, his sense of the real photograph was incredibly sharp, and he could tell you in a few words what nobody else could give you in a whole

Inga, my wife, is an airline employee, which gives us opportunities for travel. We try to dispel the image of the Ugly American. We stay in native pensions or boarding houses. We always carry a supply of small grooming kits, ball-point pens, chewing gum, Lifesavers, and, of course, American cigarettes.

—John Lukaszuk

I think that I shall never see
A poem perfect as an egg
So round so firm, so neatly packed
No leafy arms
No leg

—Wade Barnes

afternoon. He would accept anyone he wanted into the academy, if you survived the interview, which you would get only if he liked your portfolio. And then he threw out anyone who didn't work like hell or didn't progress fast enough. He would not look at any work below a certain standard. First you had to study with the other teachers anyway, and when you felt ready to deal with Steinert you could get the big surprise. It would happen that a student would lay out on the table the result of two weeks of hard work, and Steinert would throw everything on the floor without further comment, except to say, "Next one, please." So sometimes his lectures were spiced with tears. He also had this huge rubber stamp with bold capital letters: SCHEISSE—shit—and he could be quite generous with it, stamping all the pictures he didn't like.

LM: Do you keep in touch with your models?

AK: Some of them, yes. We would bump into each other on the street or at a party. A few of them I see quite frequently. Liborio comes over once in a while and cooks pasta for me and some friends. And Dr. Ken Rosa has become my chiropractor and nutritionist.

LM: Have you been taking more pictures of them?

AK: Yes, but totally different work. Mostly full-figure studio portraits—very much tailored to their individual personalities and activities, mostly in bright colors.

Lyn Mandelbaum is an artist and jewelry designer. She is a longtime friend of Alex Kayser.

Alan Axelrod is an editor at Abbeville Press and a jazz critic for *down beat* magazine. He met Alex Kayser only recently.

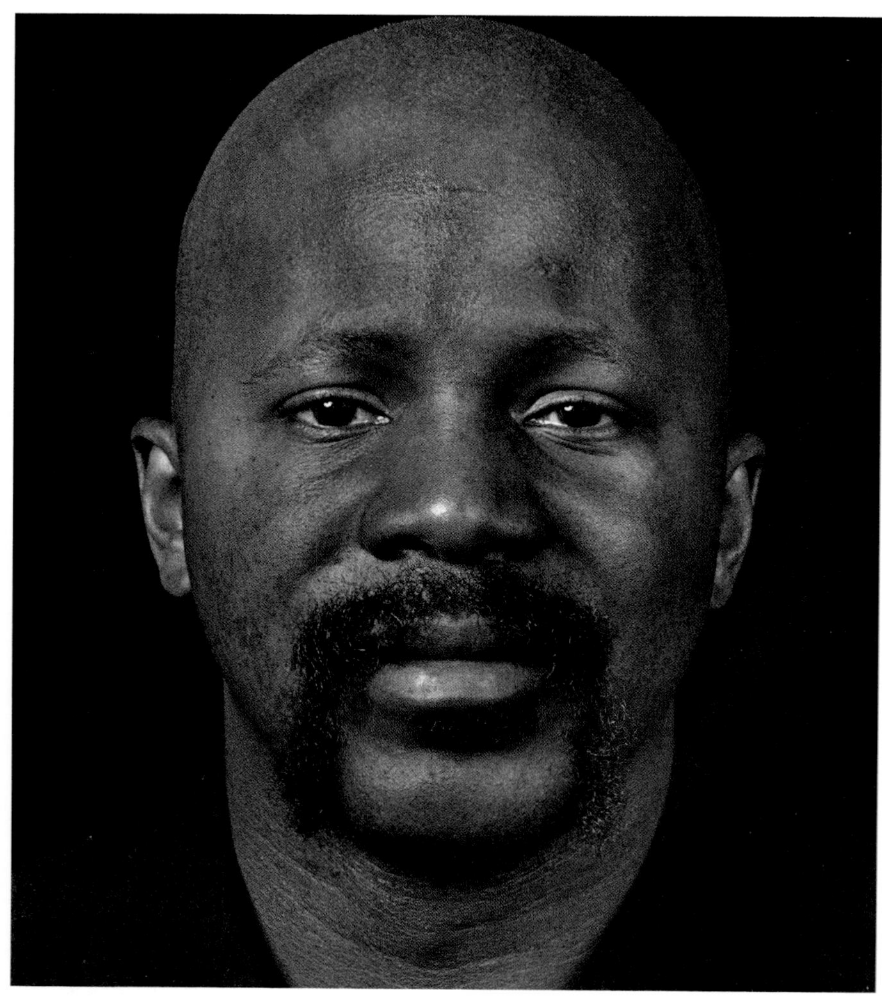

Thomas Johnson, New York City: contract officer

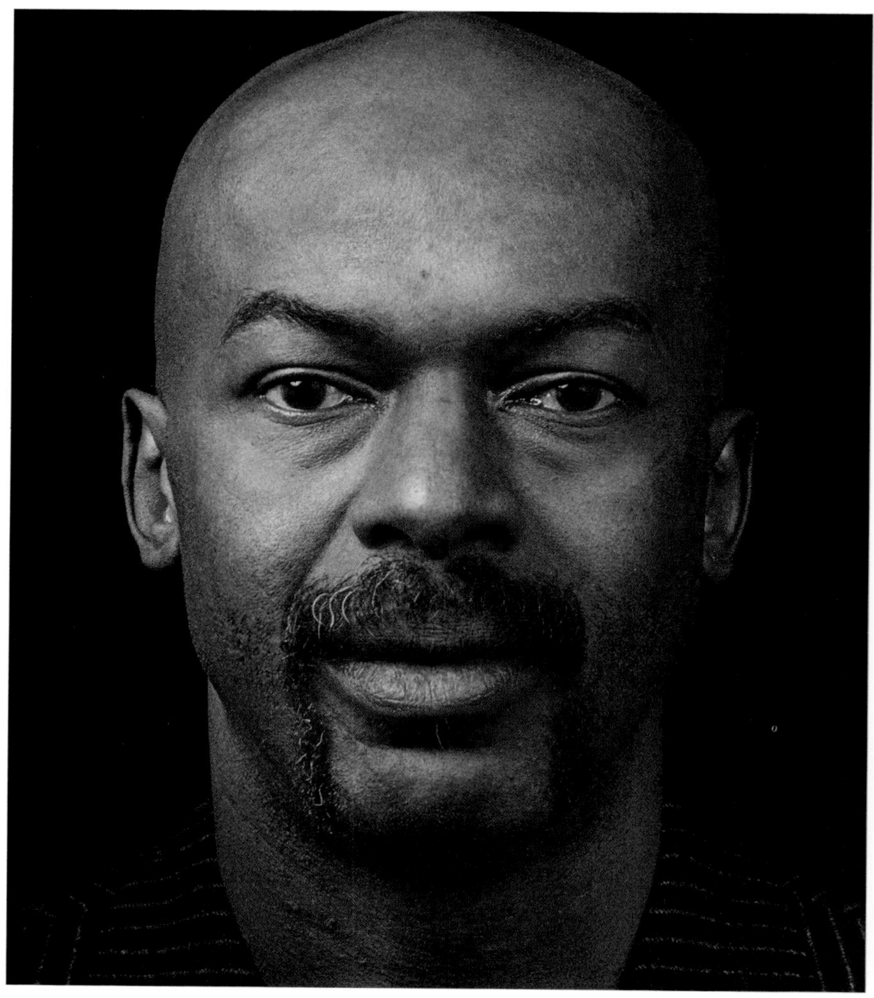

Spencer, New York City

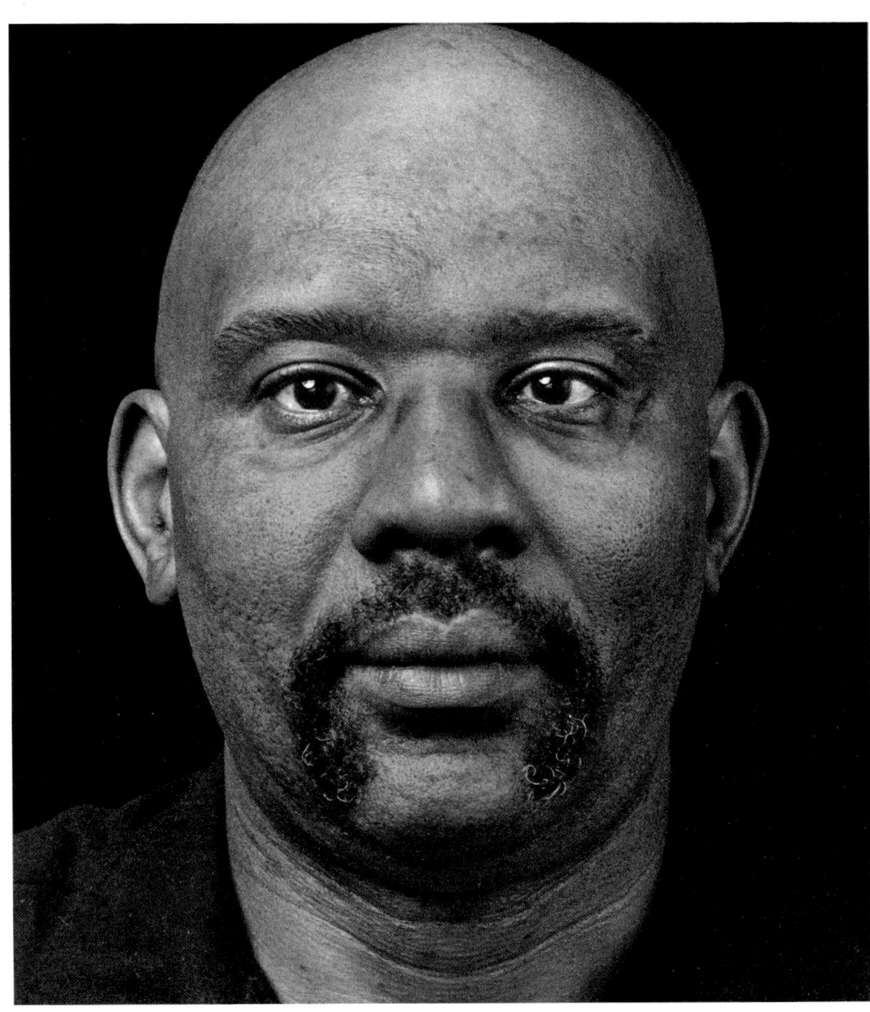

William Nixon, New York City: Western Union security guard (day); ambulance driver (night)

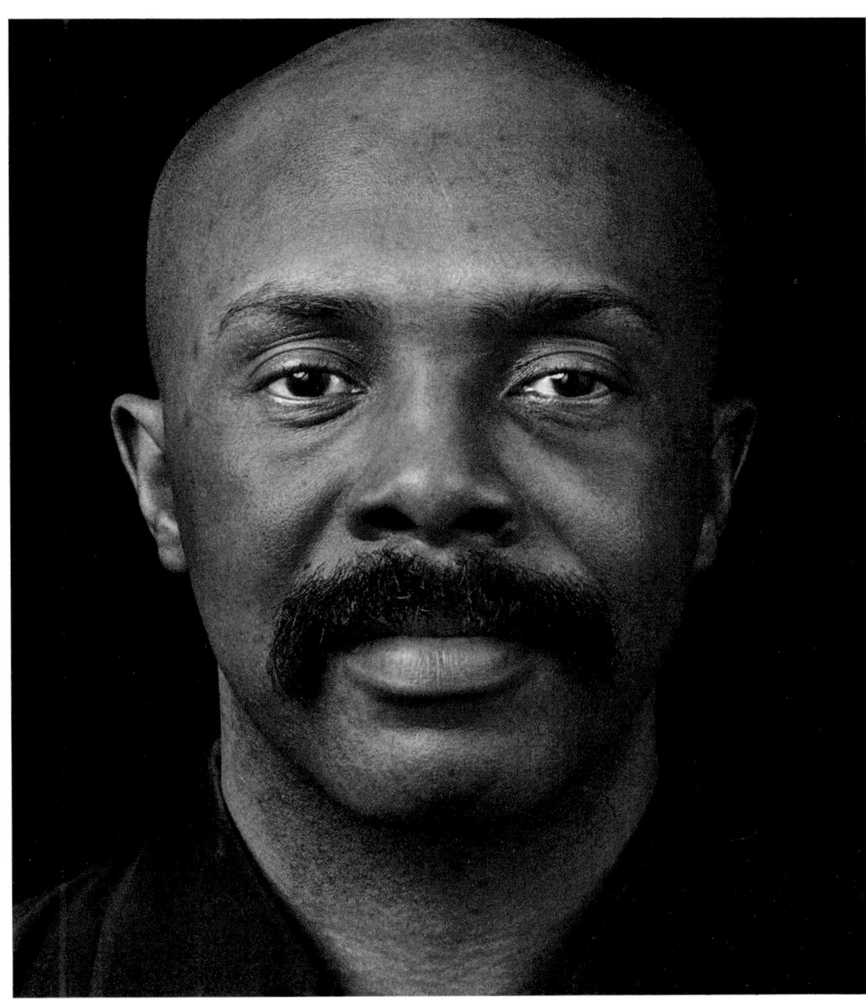

Roscoe Orman, New York City: actor; cast member, "Sesame Street"

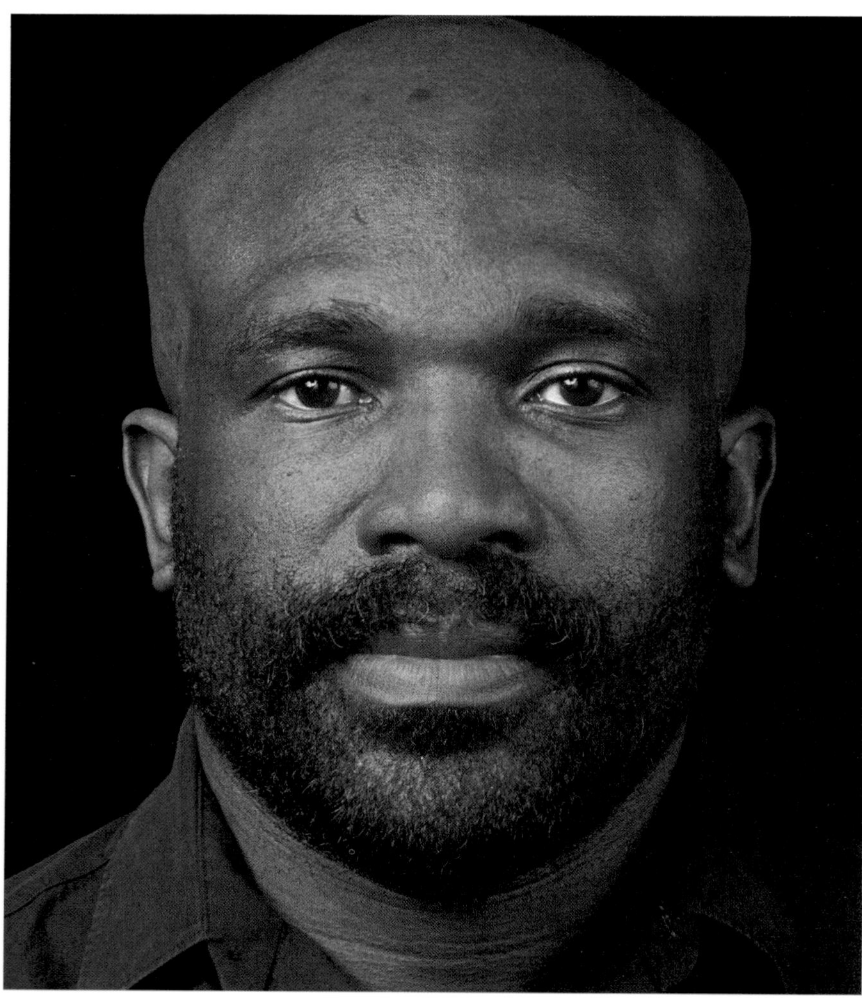

Ossie Bunbury, Brooklyn: president and owner, Heavenly Bodies Health Club

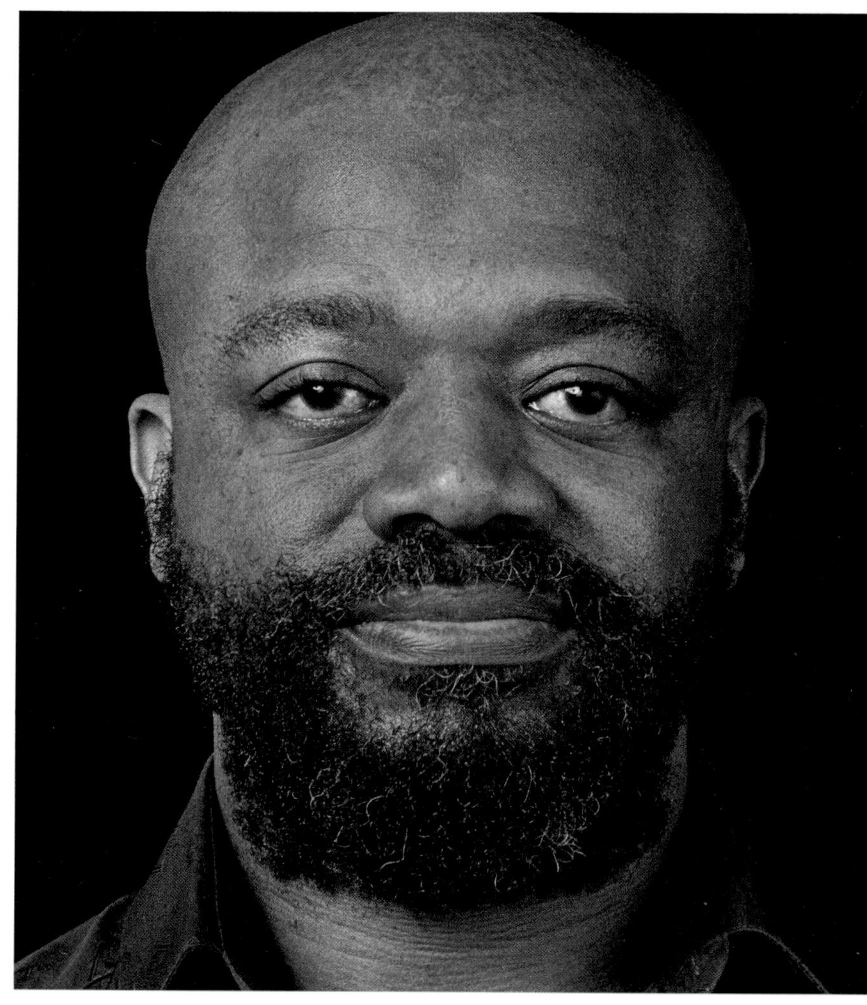

John Jones, New York City: United States Postal Service

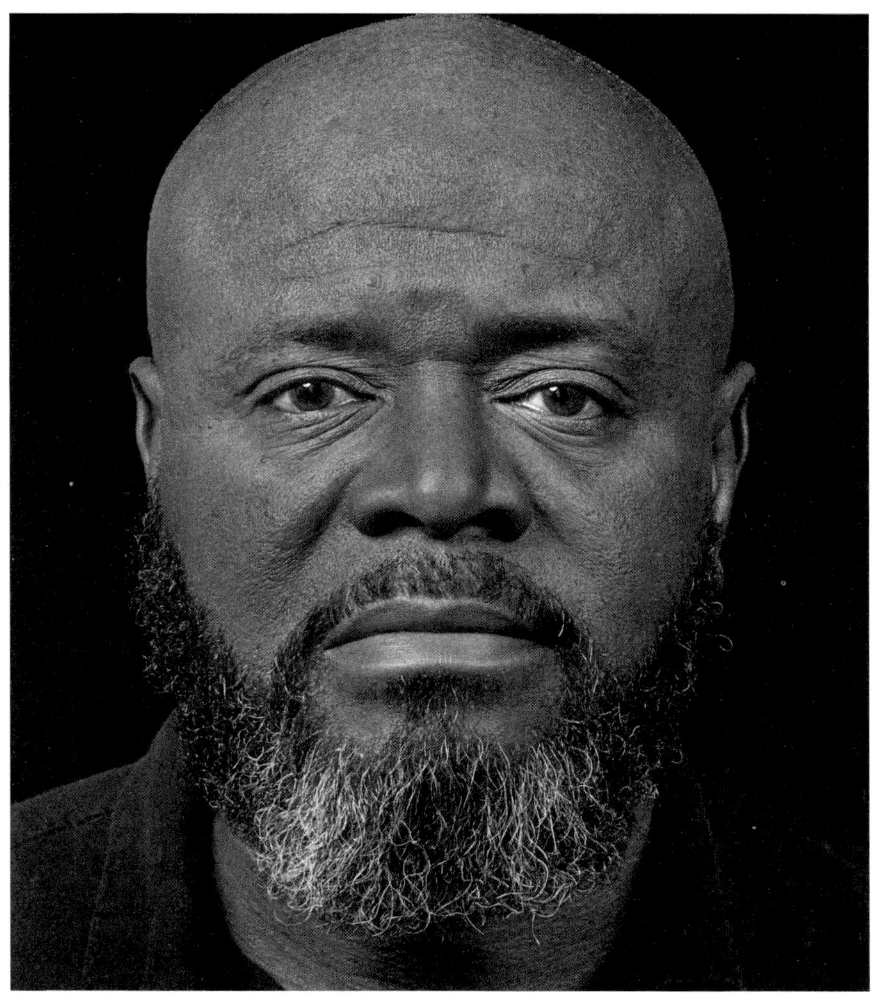

Jerry, New York City

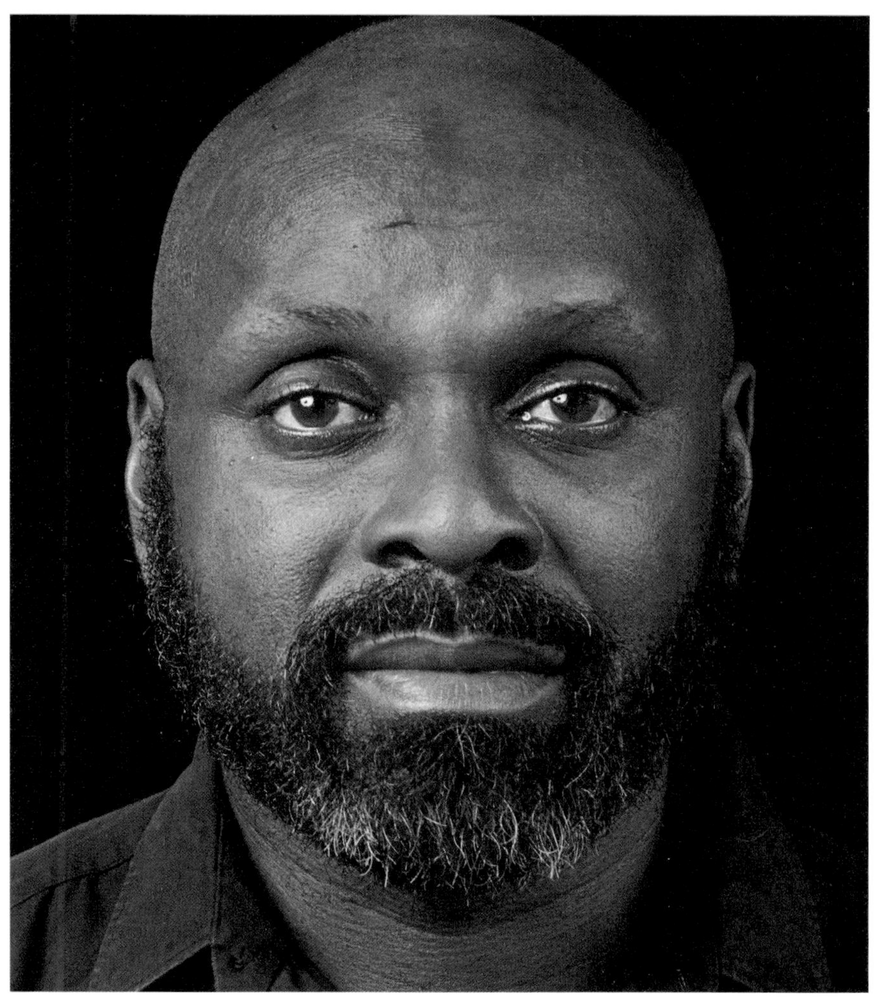

Bob Hamilton, New York City: packer and shipper, D. F. Warehouse

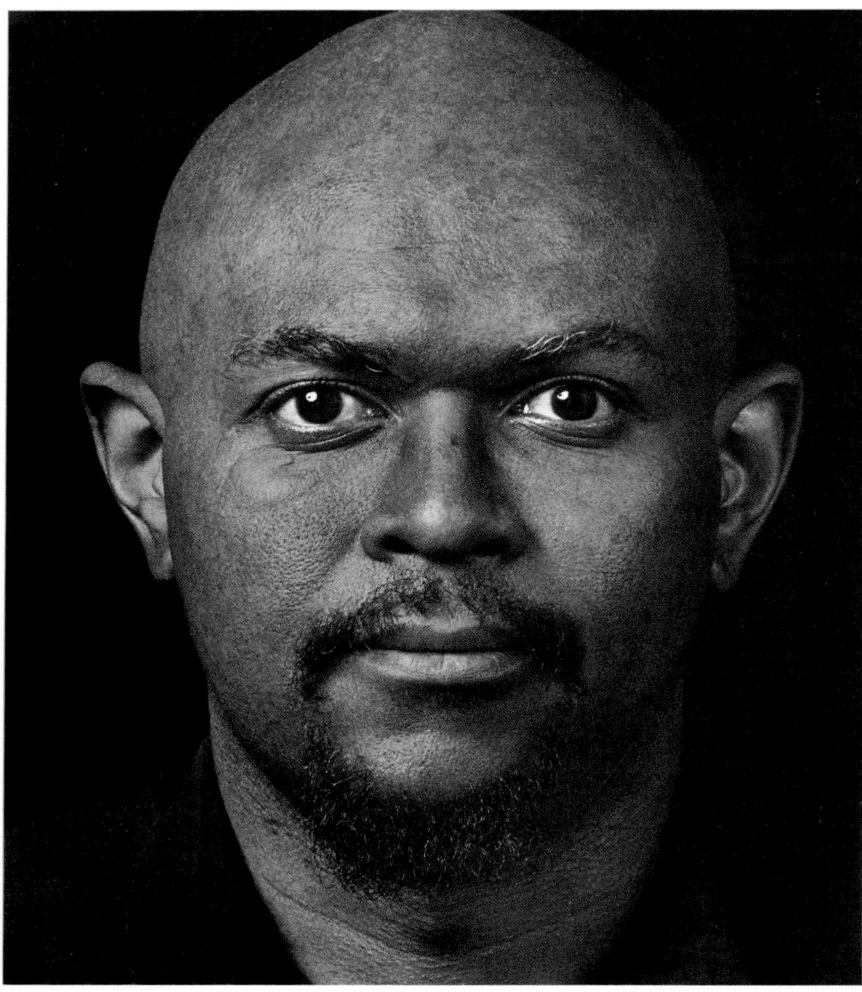

James C. White, New York City: bookkeeping and accounting student

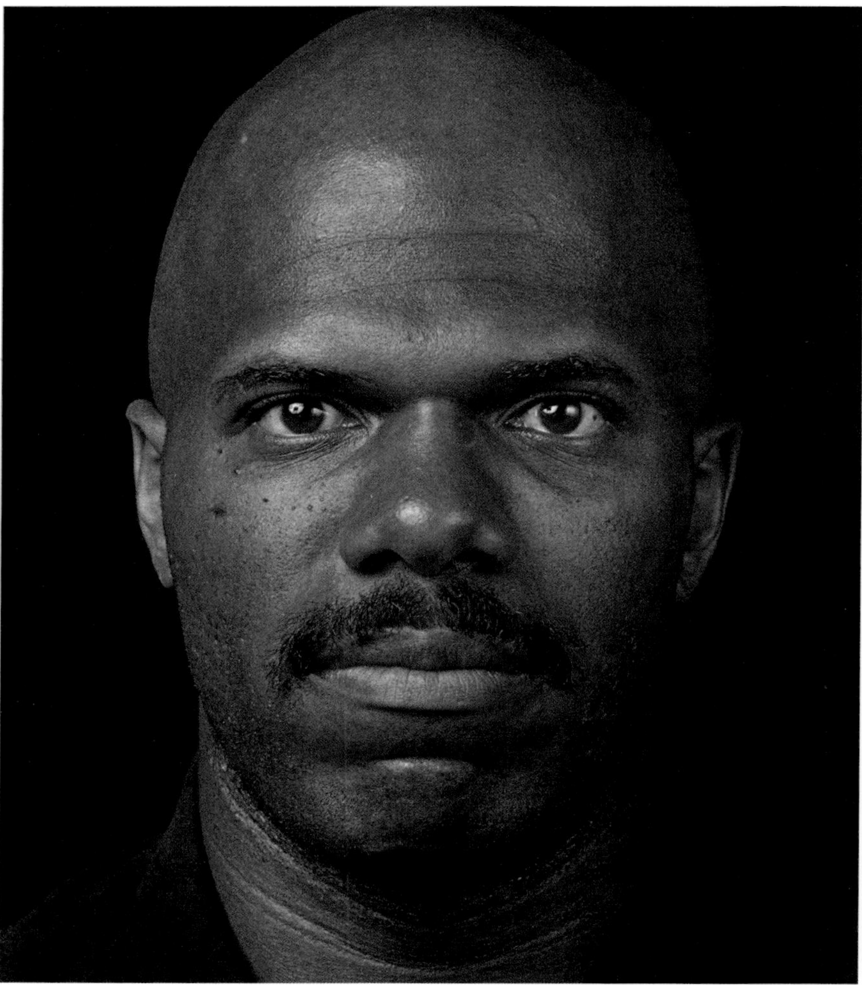

Paul Gilliam, New York City: fireman

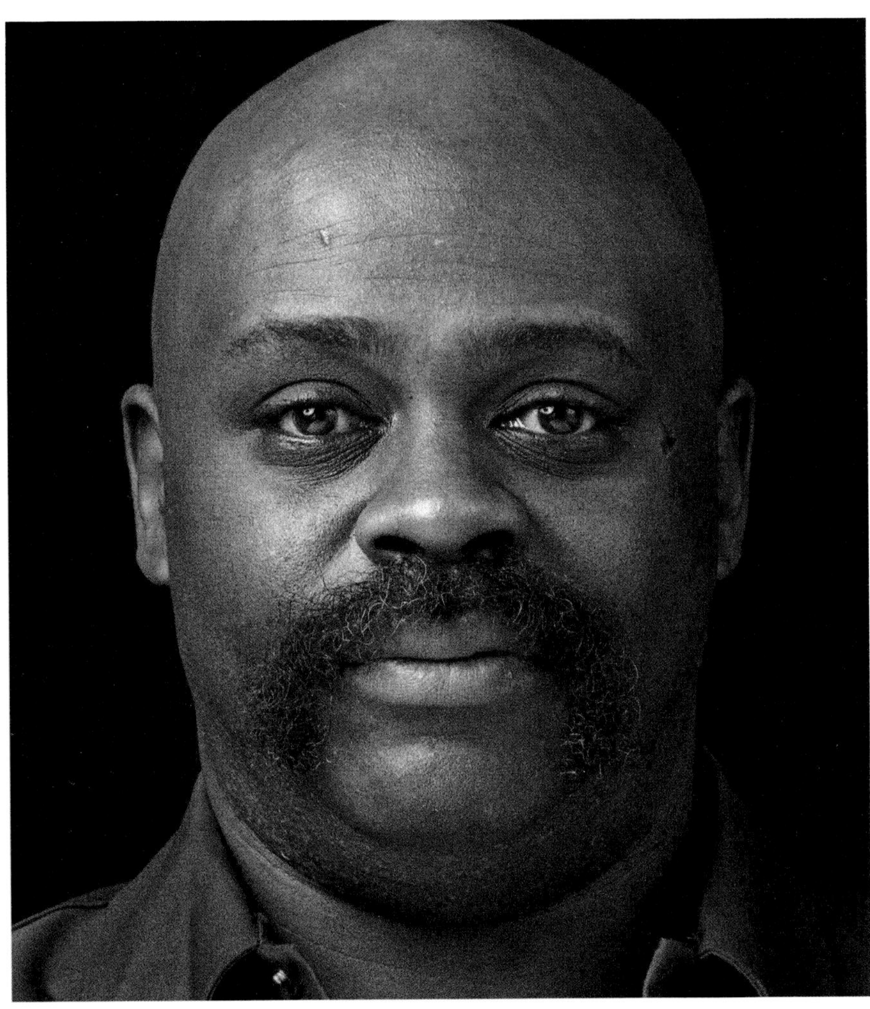

Champion English, New York City: sanitation engineer

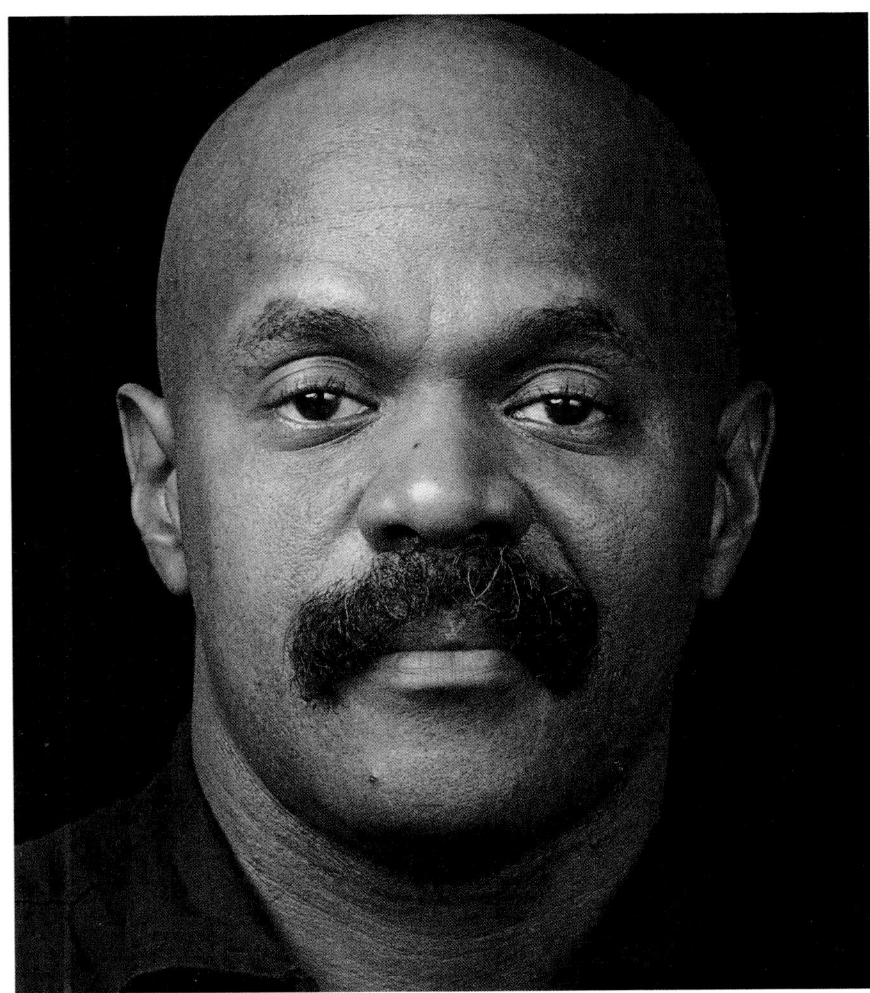

Ron Nelson, New York City: stylist and make-up artist

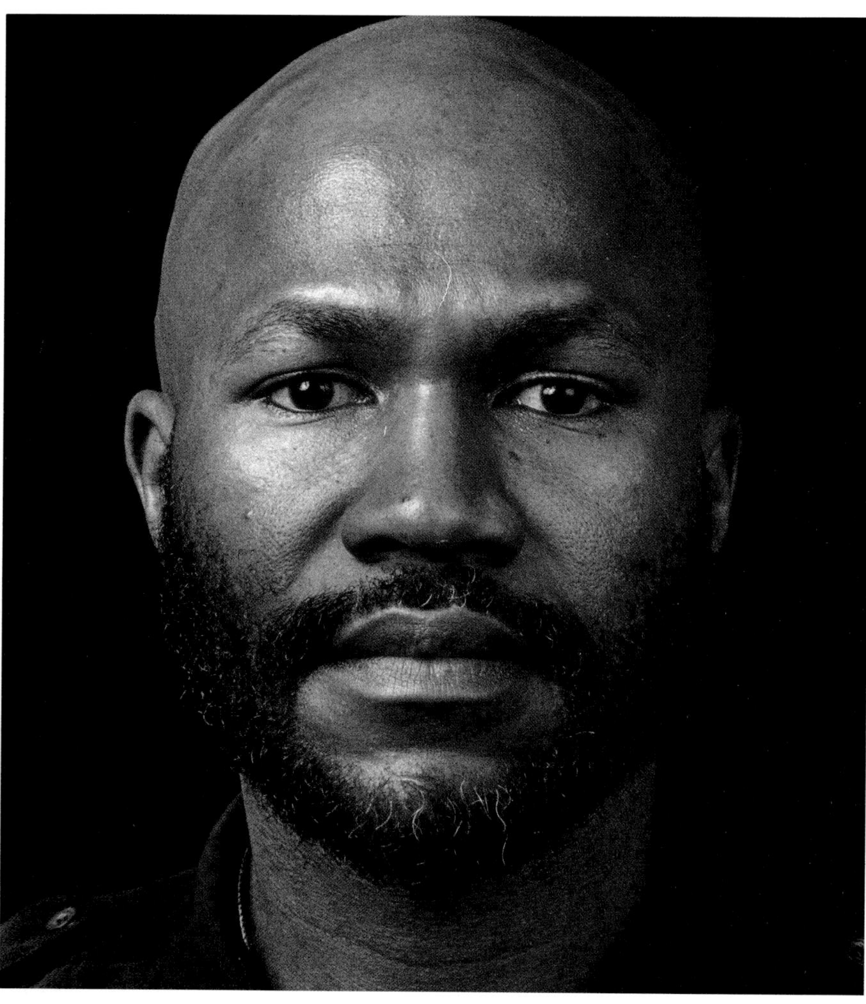

John L. Reids, New York City: administrative supervisor, New York City Department of Social Services

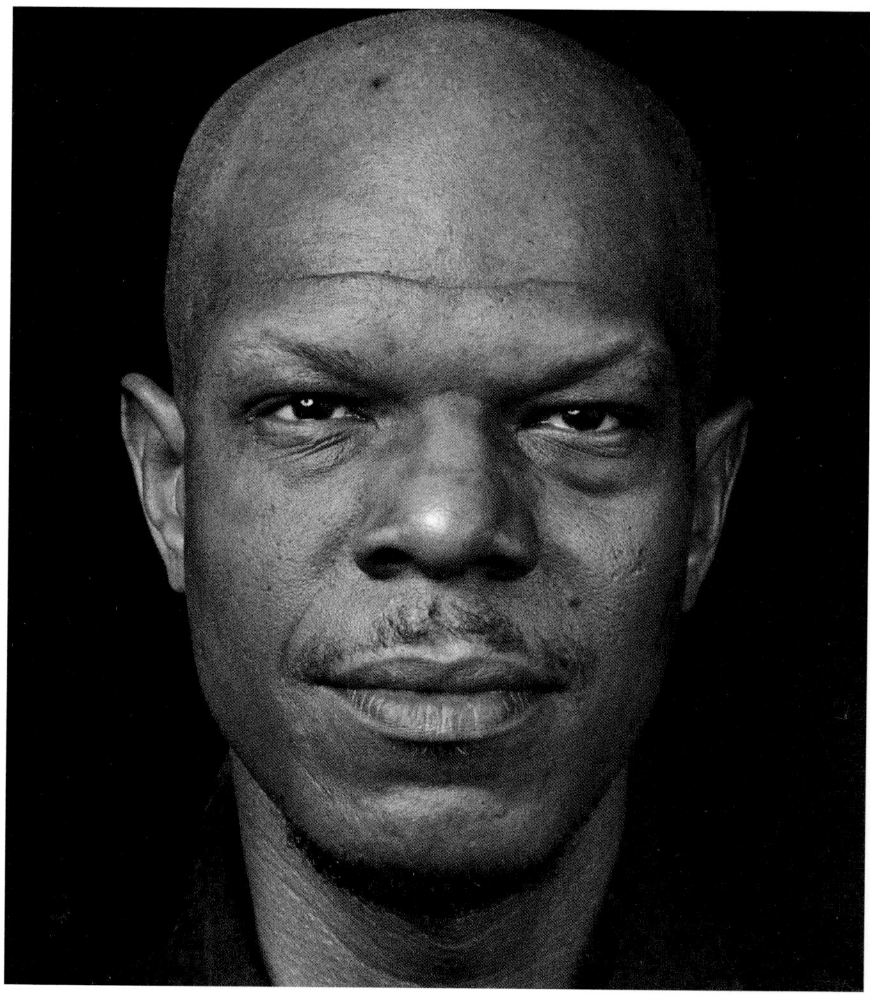

Descott Whitehead, New York City: letter carrier, United States Postal Service

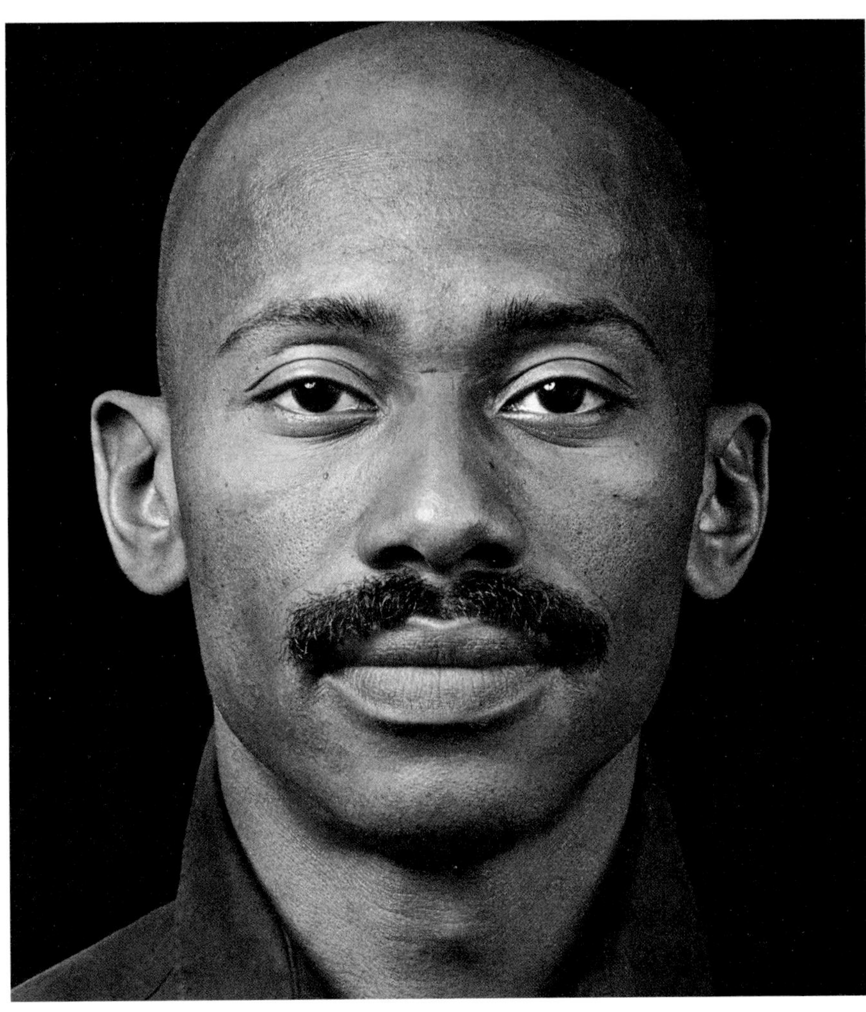

Darnell Young, New York City: assistant meetings coordinator, New York State Society of CPAs

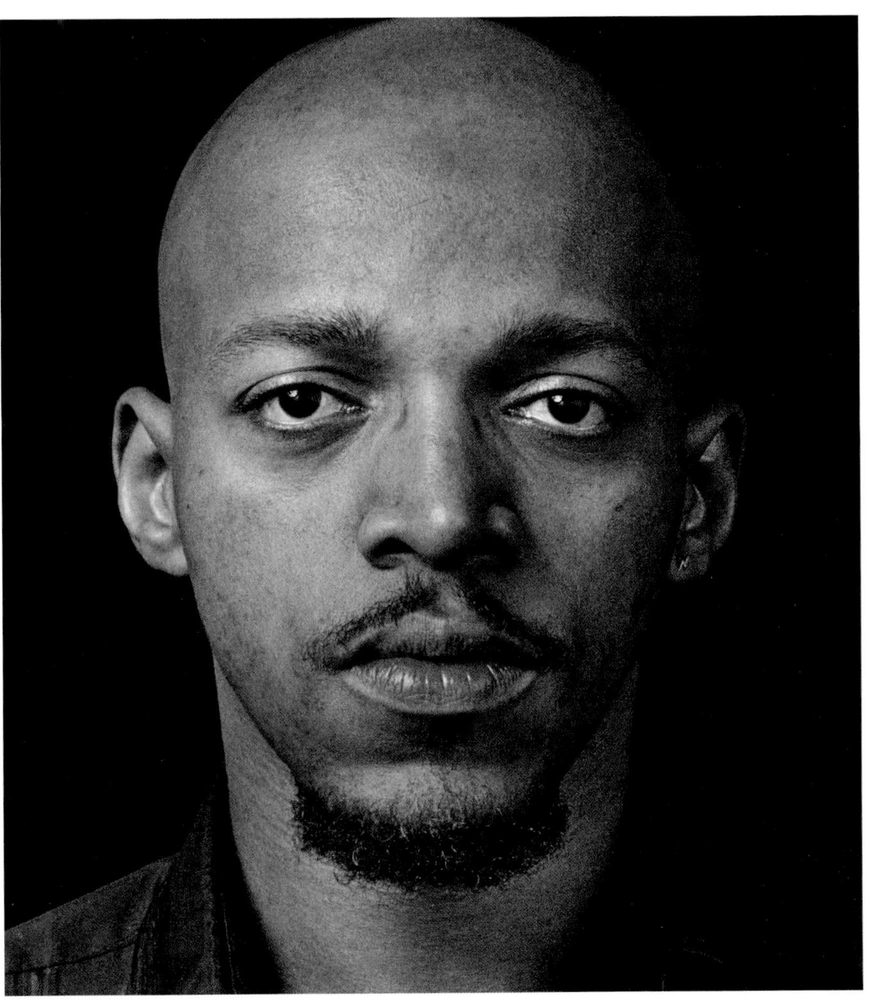

Thomas McNeil, New York City: student of business communications

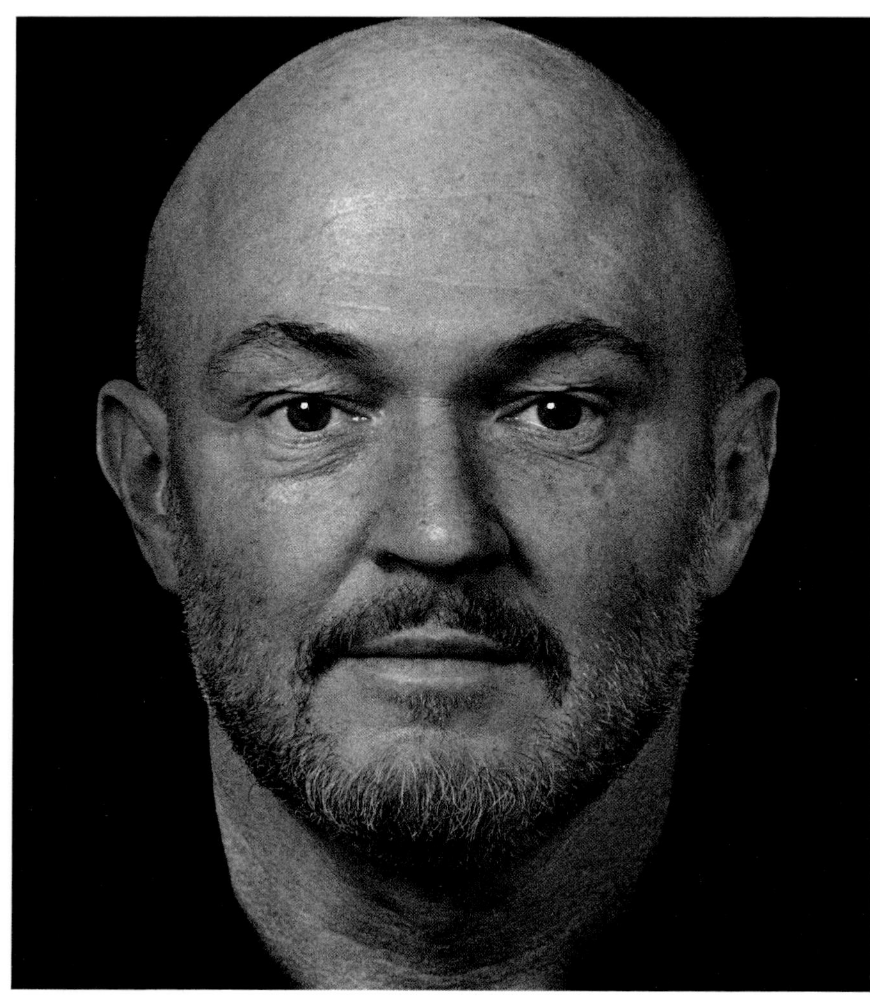

Ronald McNamer, New York City: jewelry designer

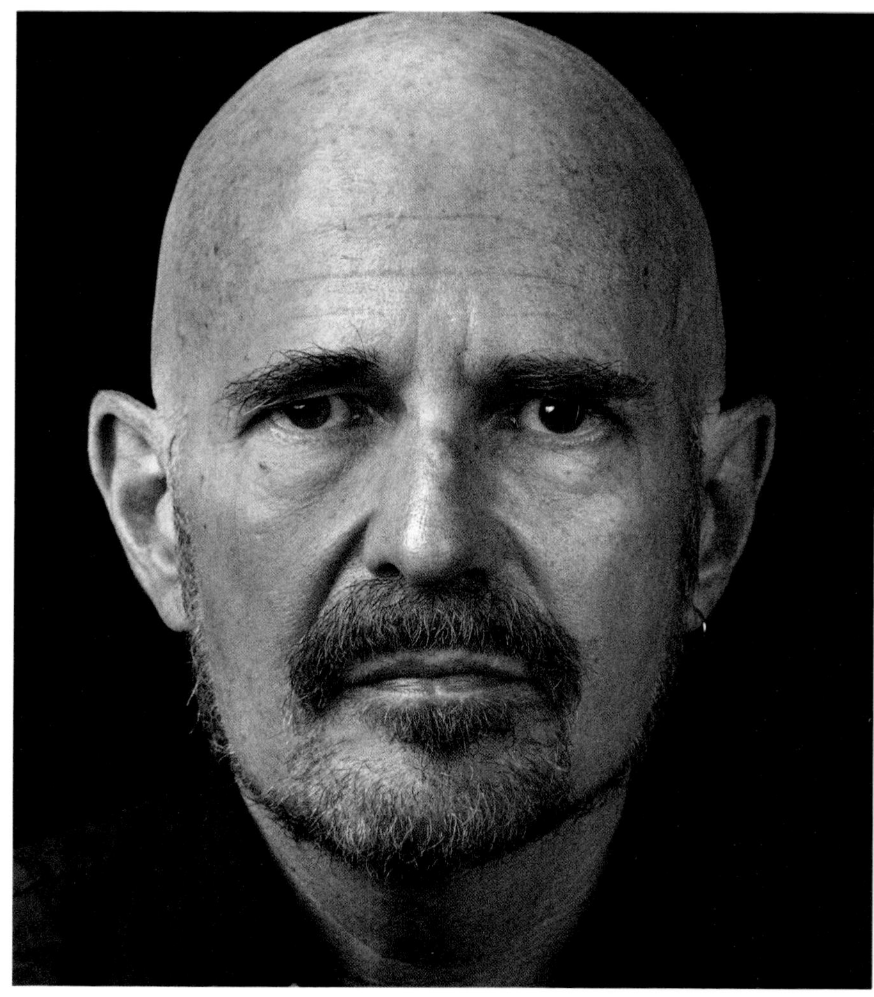

Michael Sonino, New York City: editor and playwright

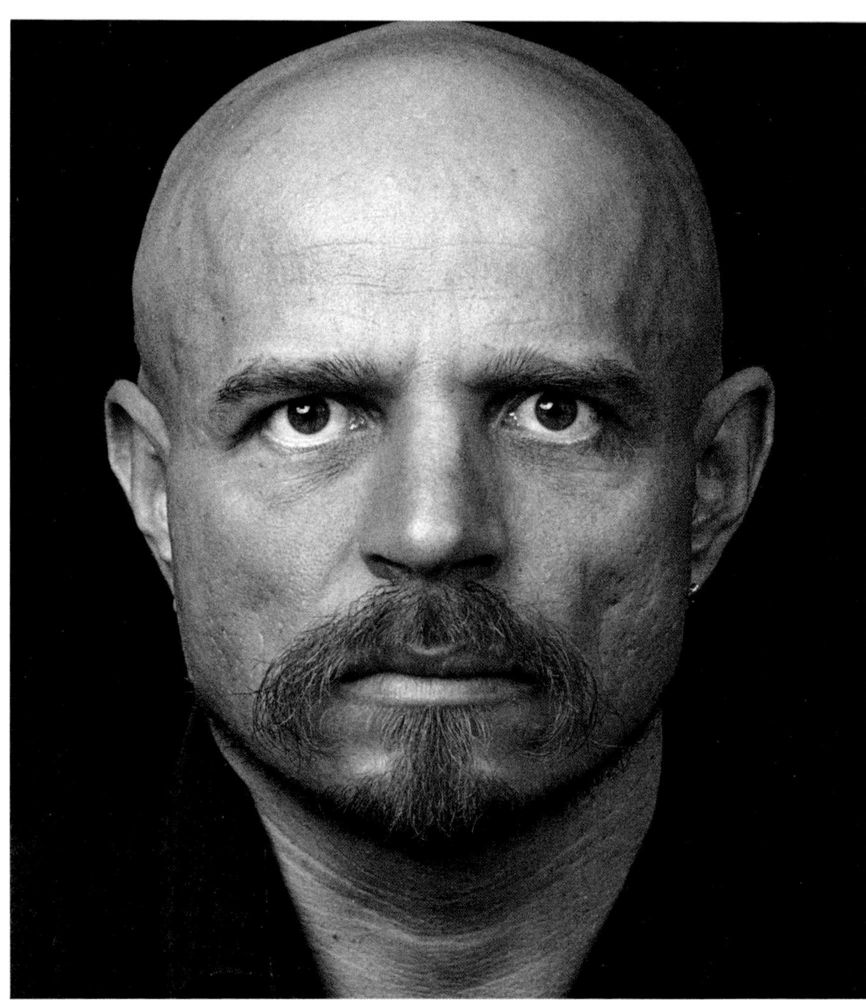

Lenny Romeo, Long Island, New York: senior instructor, the American Combat Karate School; trained by master Rich Barathy in realistic defense techniques, Romeo trains police officers and Secret Service and F.B.I. agents

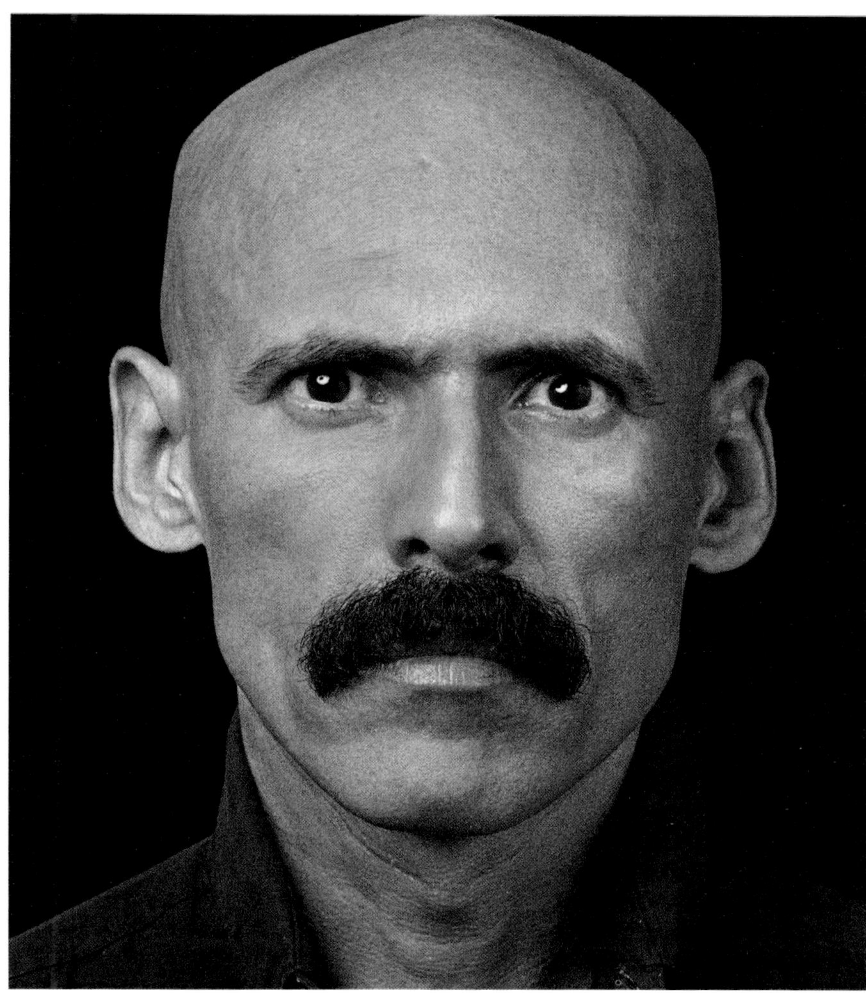

Don Domingo, New York City: paints with his left hand

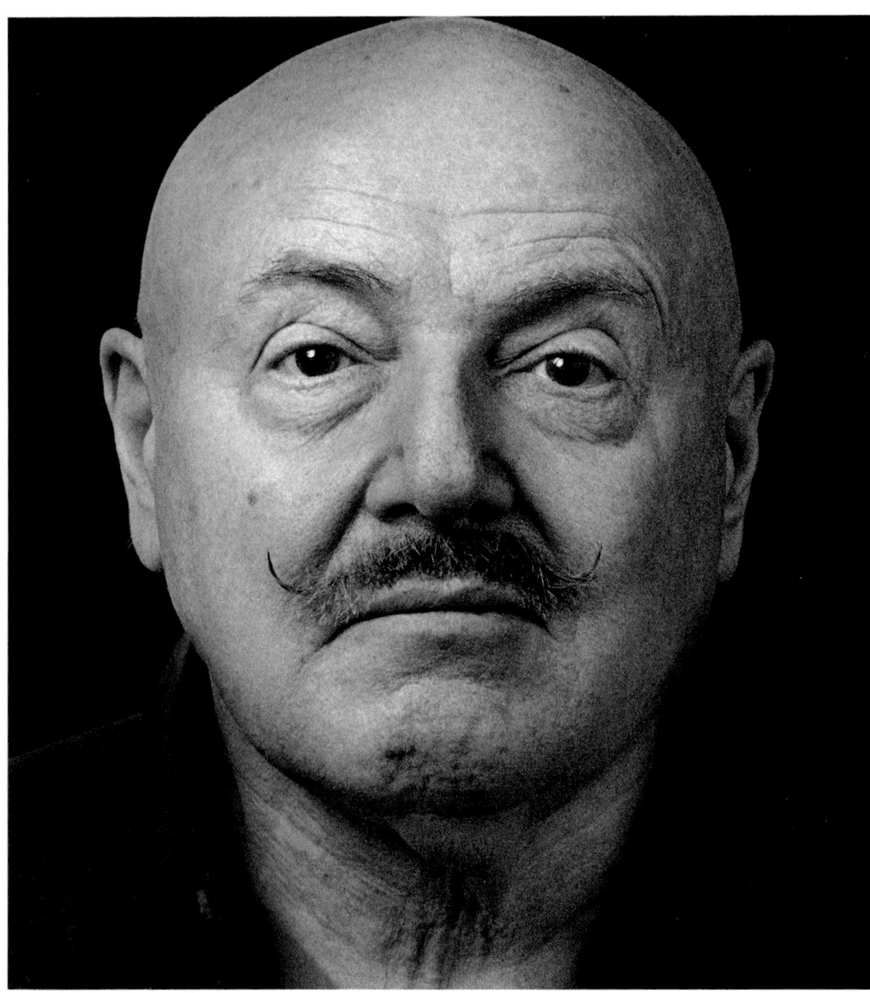

Wade Barnes, New York City: actor and playwright

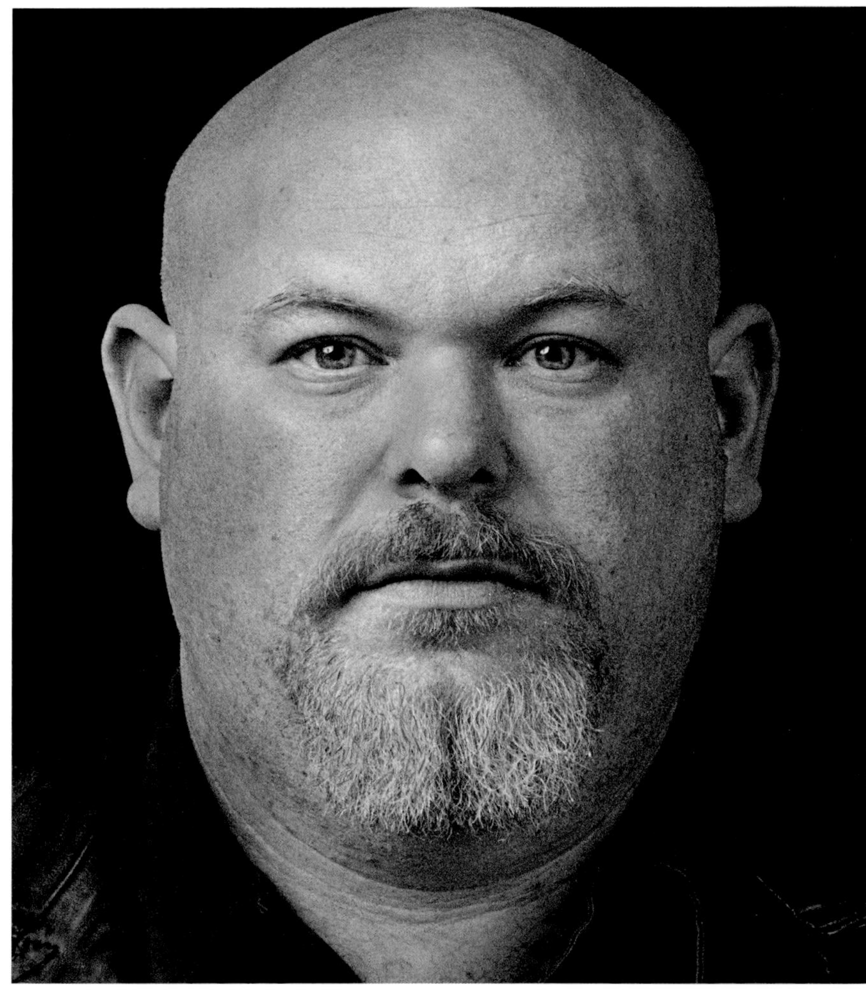

David Bezner, New York City: United States Postal Service employee

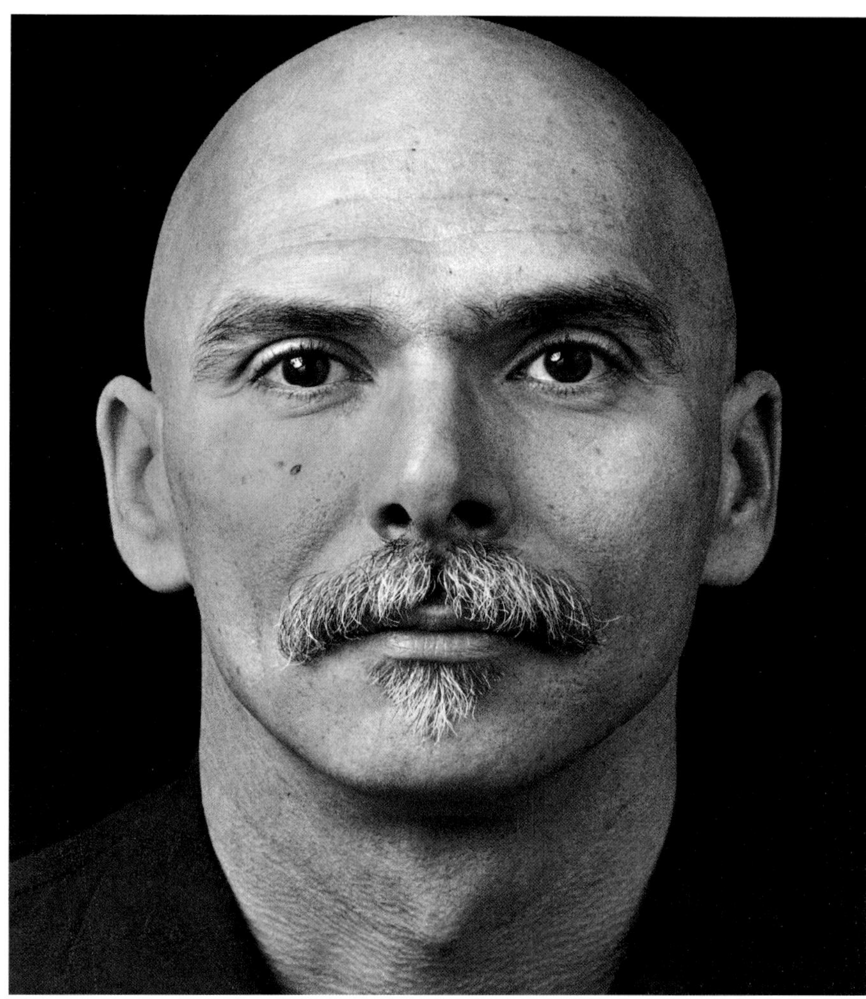

Bartholomew Gianformaggio, New York City: artist and photographer

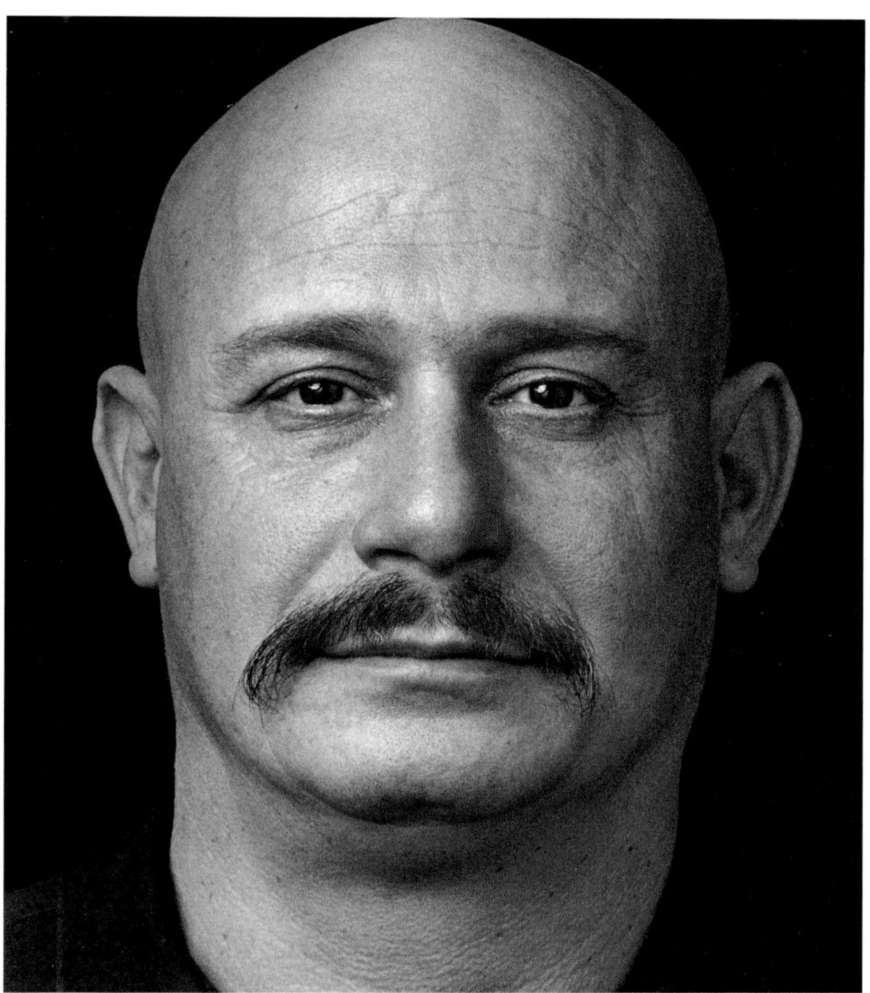

Joe Kipnis, New York City: taxi driver

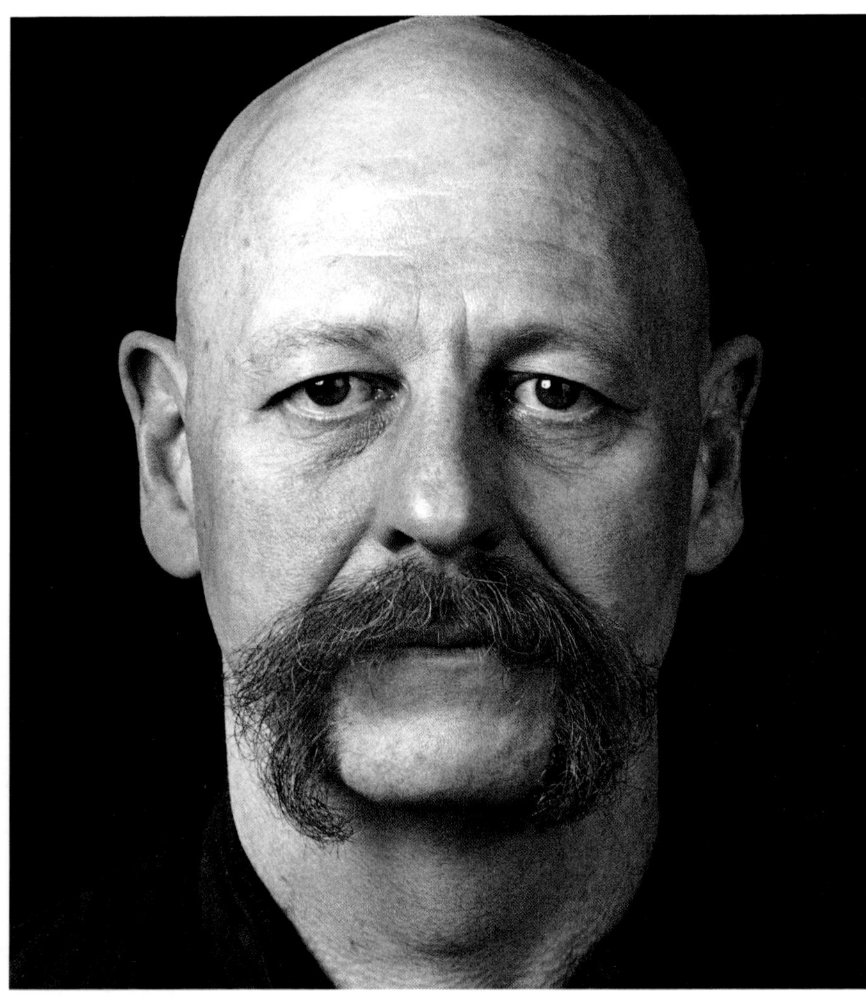

David Hayes, New York City: astrologer

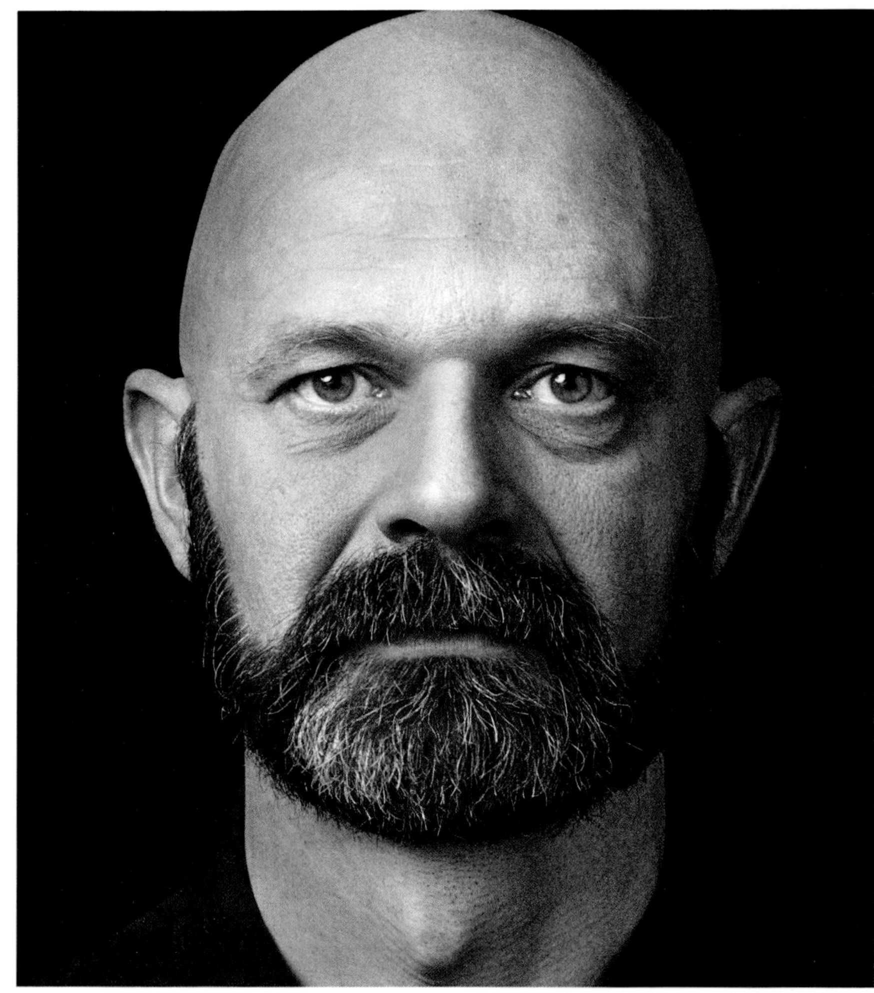

J. F., New York City

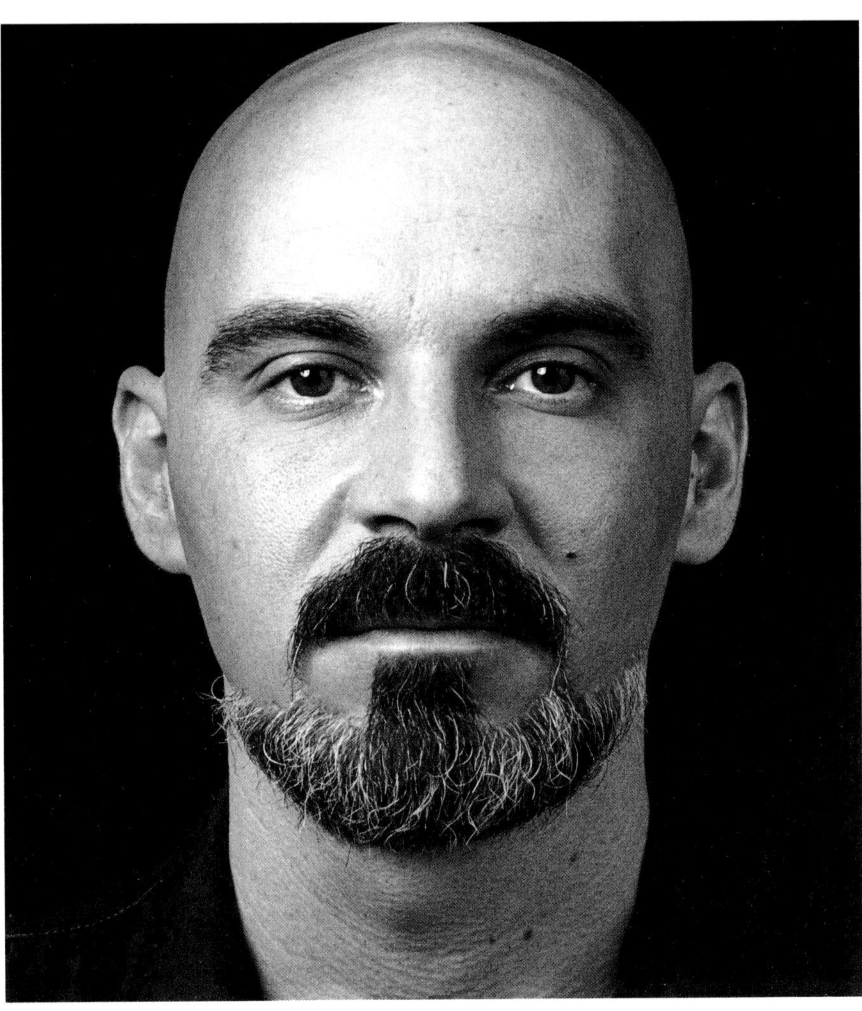

Bill Kellard, New York City: costume designer, "Sesame Street" and television commercials

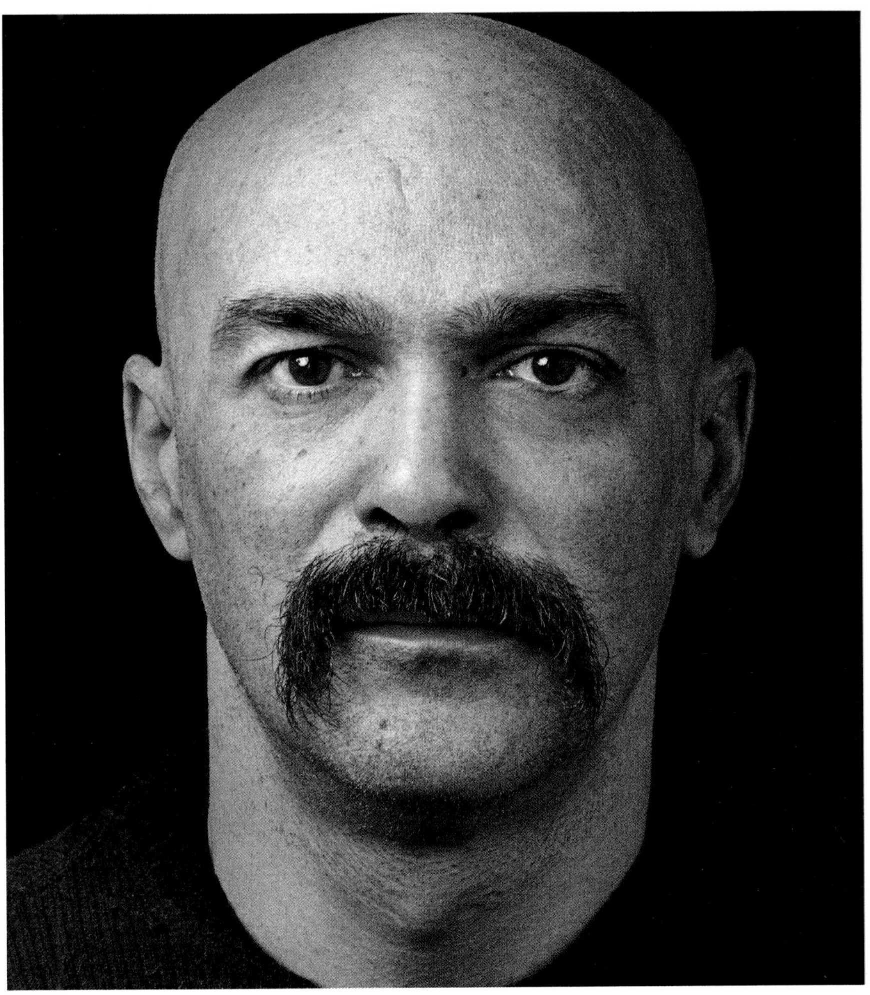

Julio Torres, New York City: founder, director, choreographer, the Latin American Dance Theatre of New York City

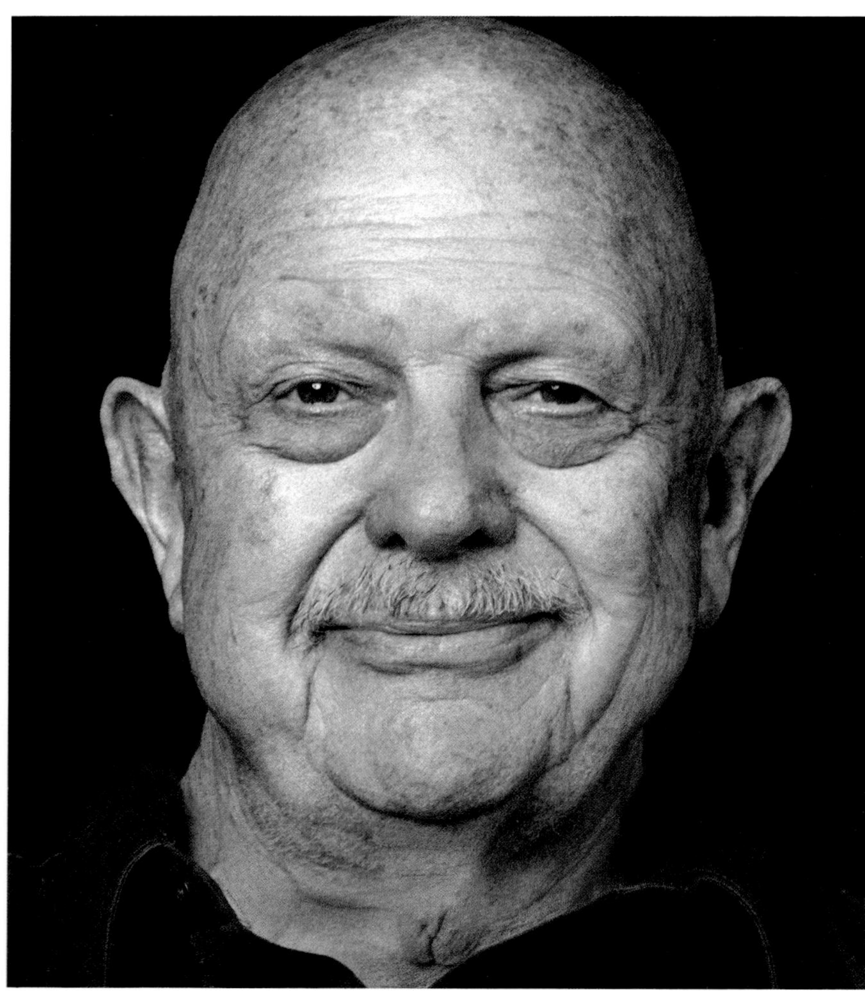

James Beard, New York City: deceased; gourmet chef and author of numerous cookbooks

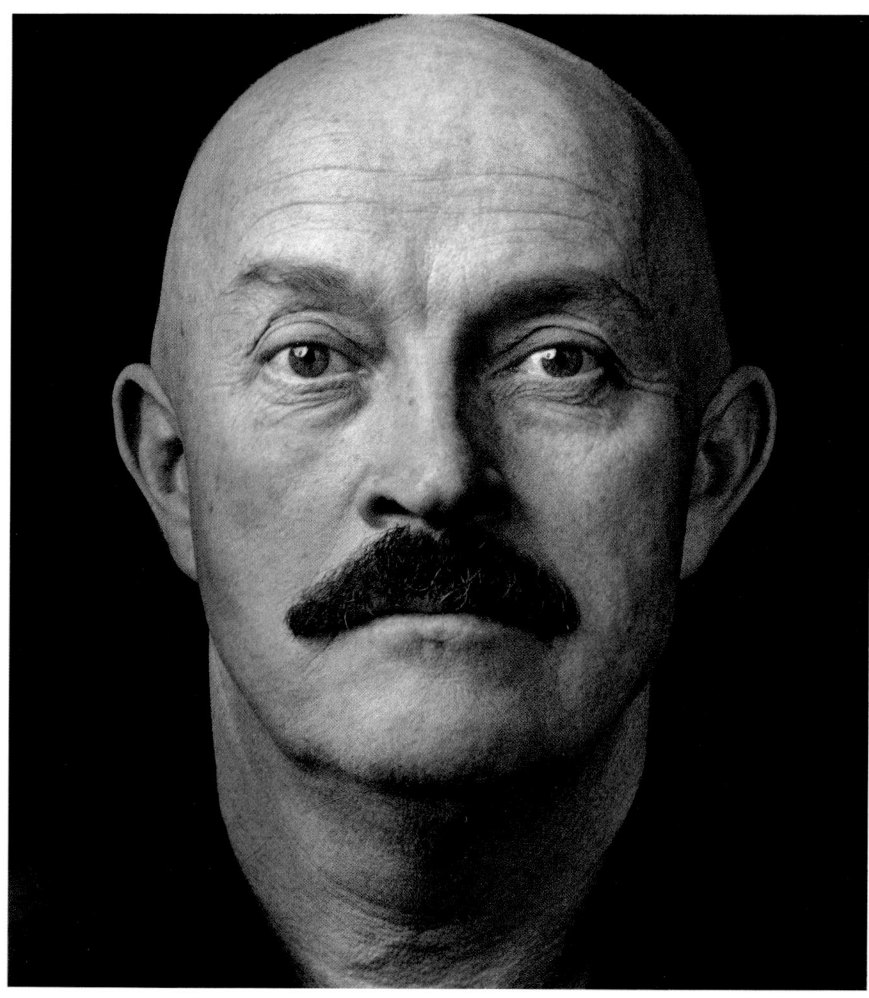

Paul Seaman, New York City: owner, the two Caramba restaurants

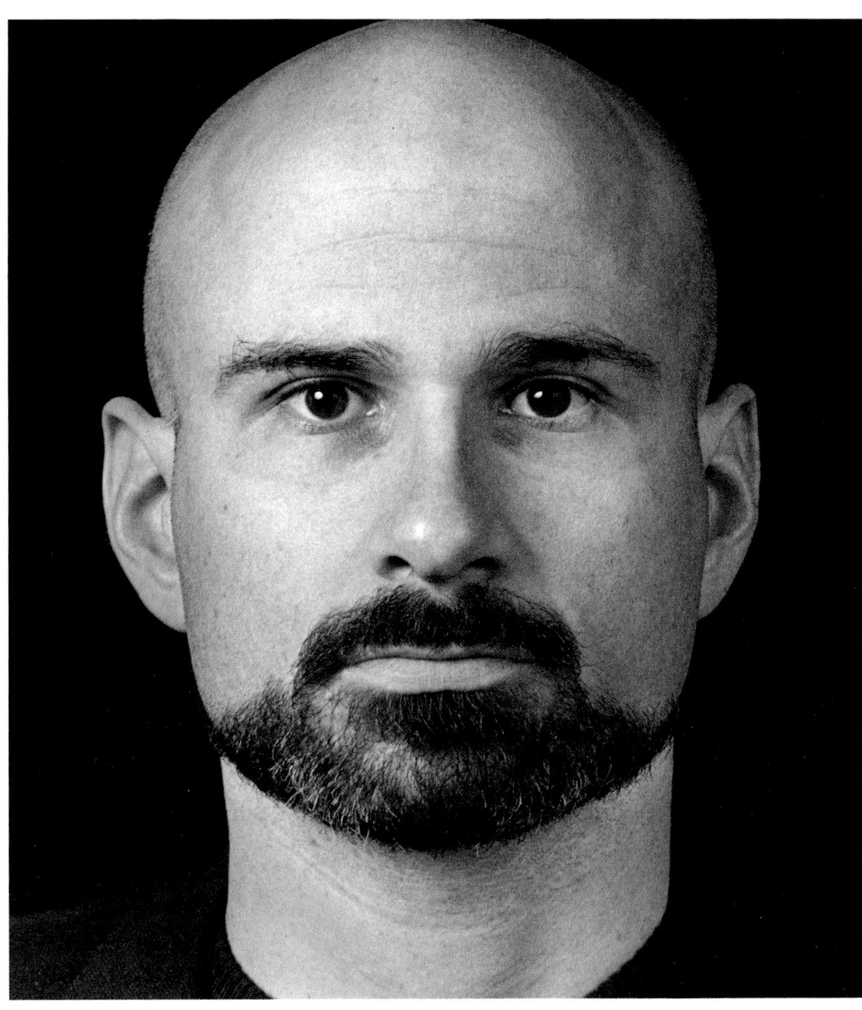

Peter Passel, New York City: journalist; member, *New York Times* editorial board

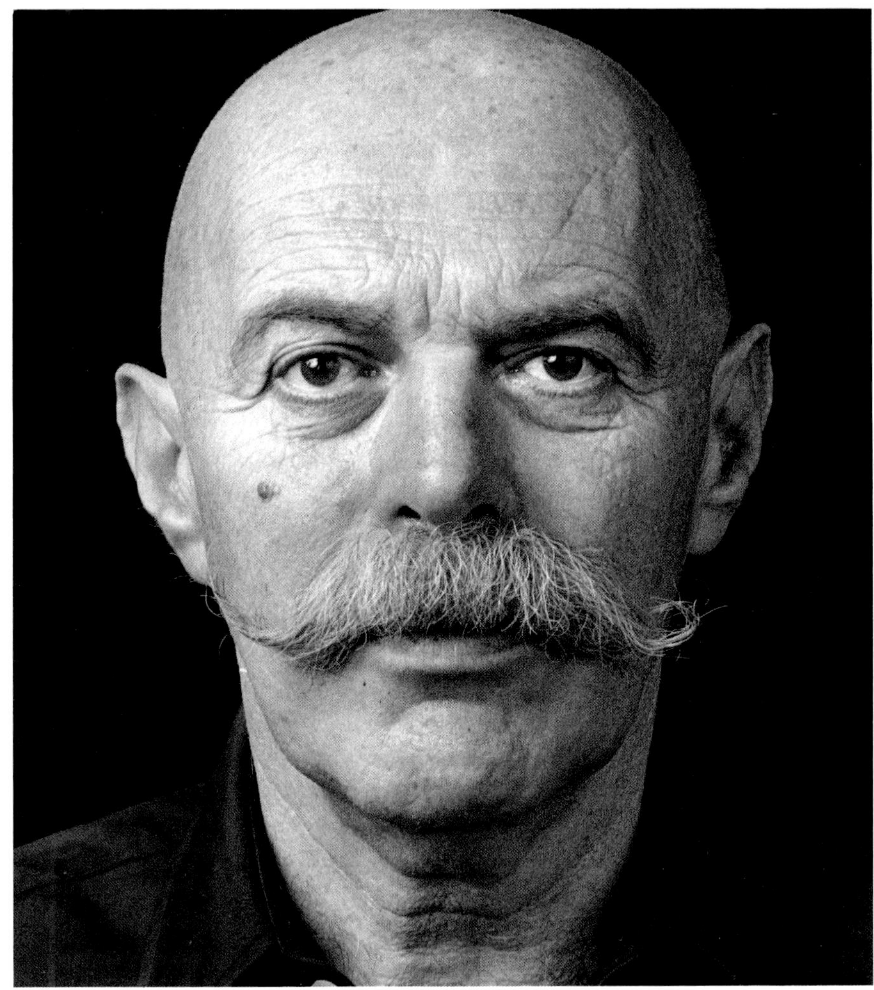

Laszlo Roth, New York City: designer and illustrator; package designer for Helena Rubenstein; contributing illustrator to *The New Yorker*

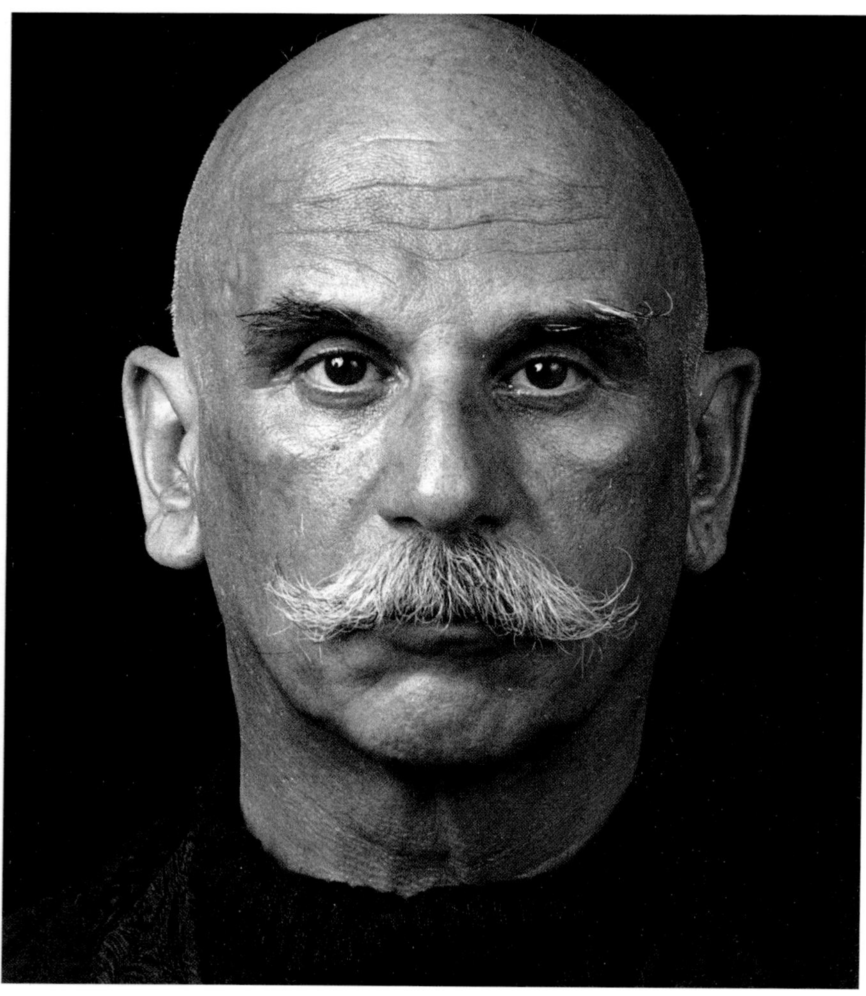

Liboria de Luca, New York City: philosopher, grande chef, grandson of Don Pietro, Barone de Montevago, Sicily

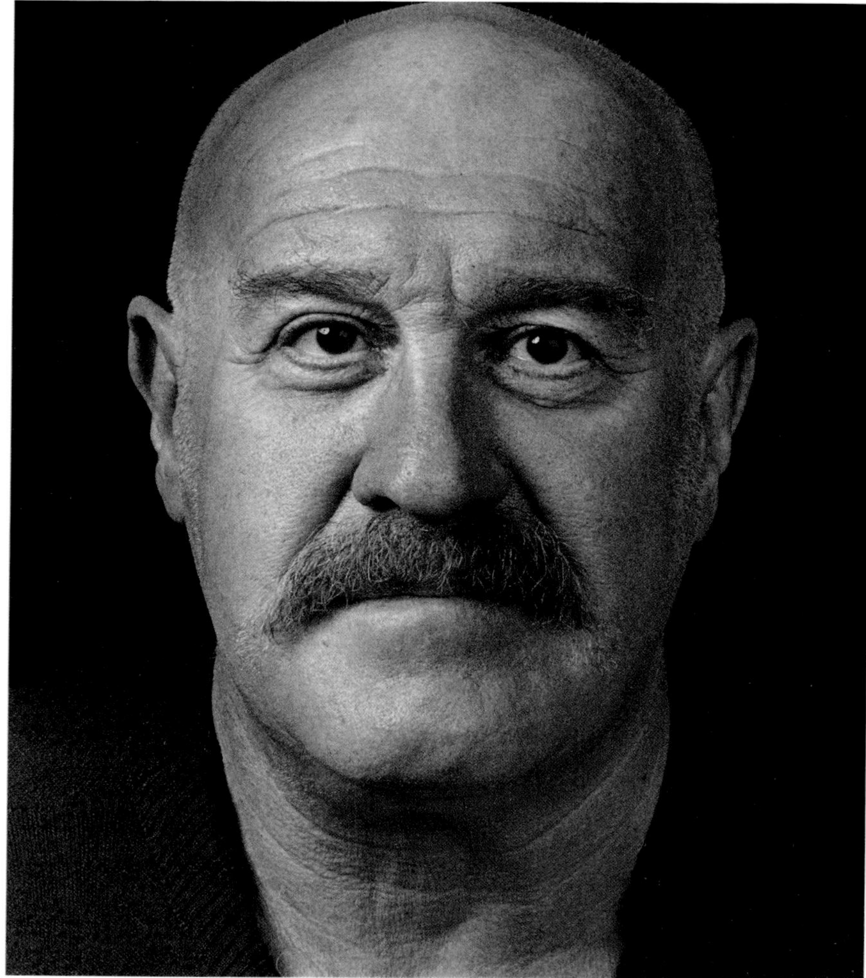

Gordon Ray Press, New York City: photographer; as an actor, appeared on television commercials for Federal Express, Ford Motor Company, and Mr. Goodbar; featured in "As the World Turns," "Another World," and "The Edge of Night"; appeared in *Arthur*

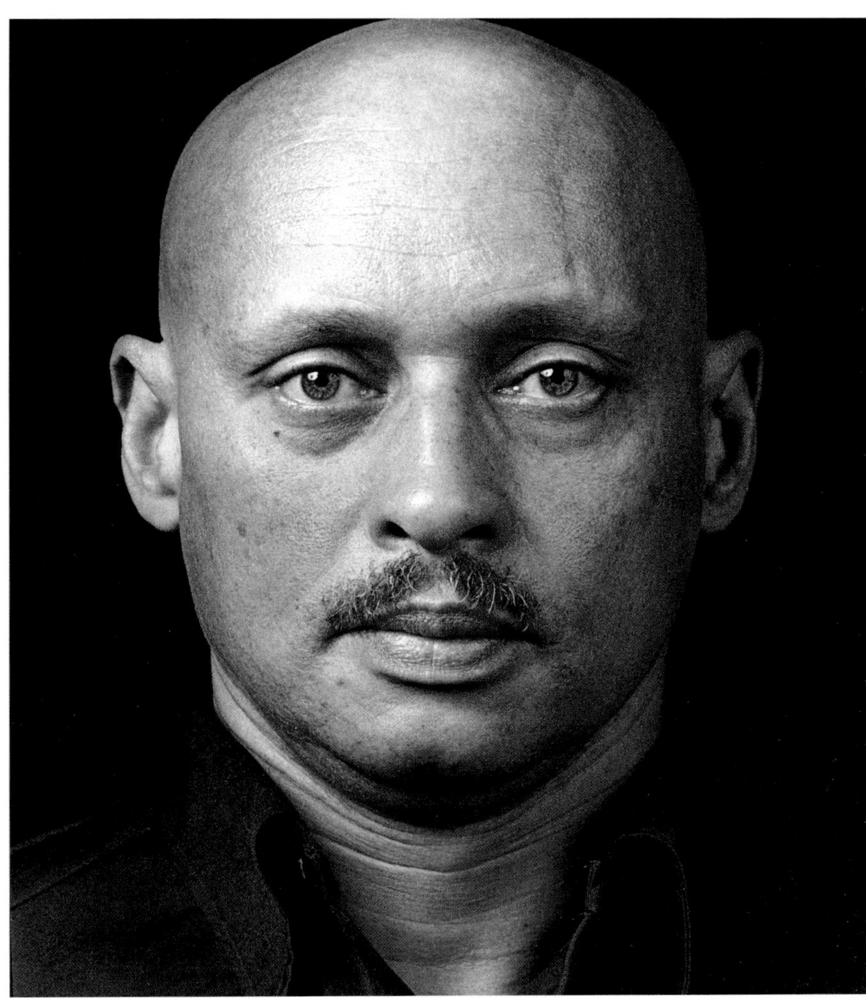

Kenneth Rosa, New York City: chiropractor, jazz pianist, and former contender for Mr. Universe

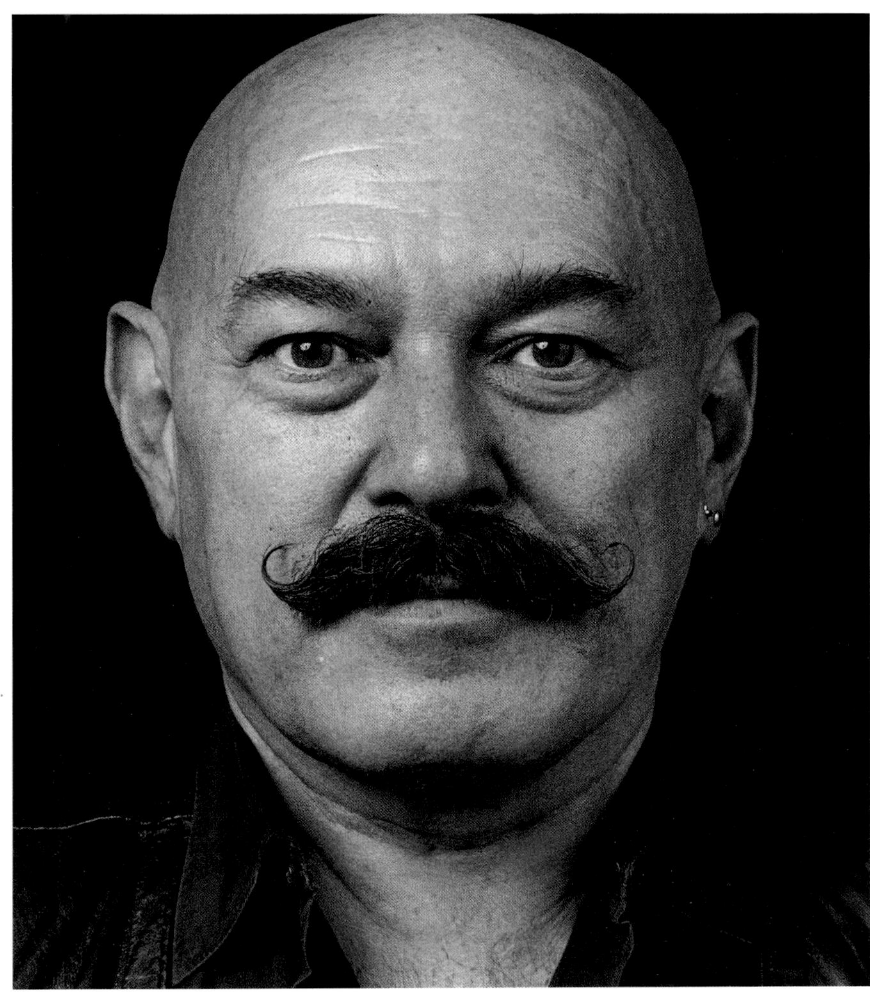

Phil Masnik, New York City: photographer and retired package designer

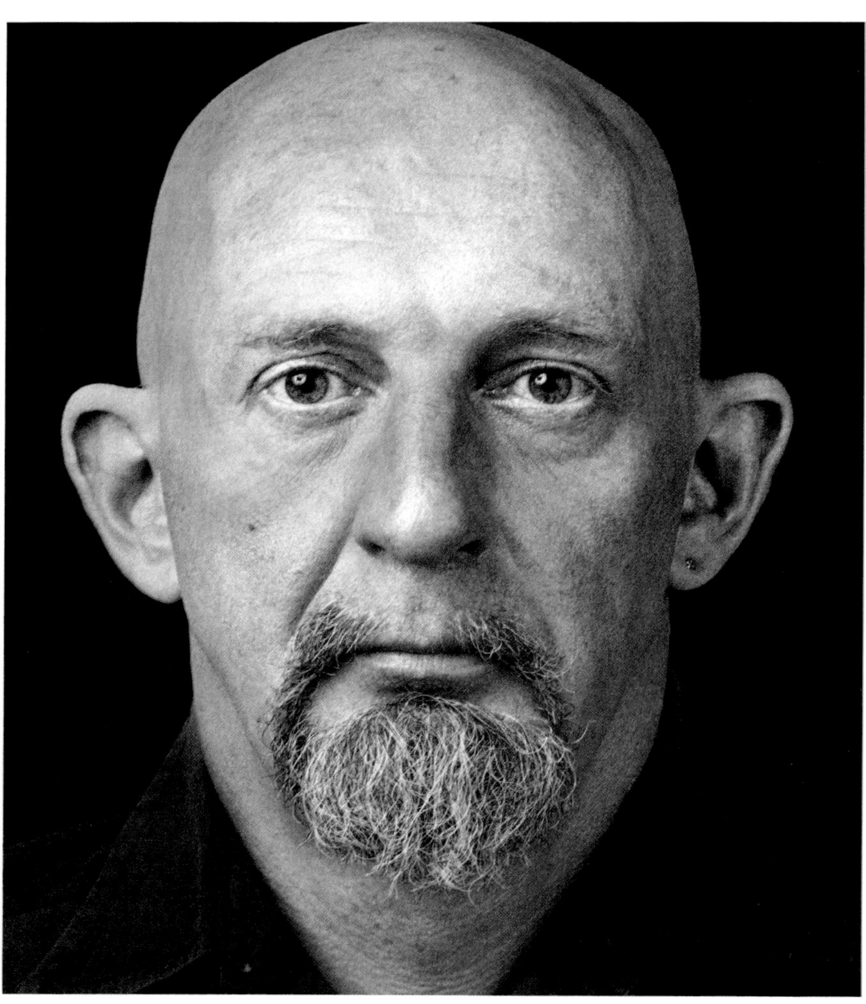

Richard Lancaster, New York City: bank officer

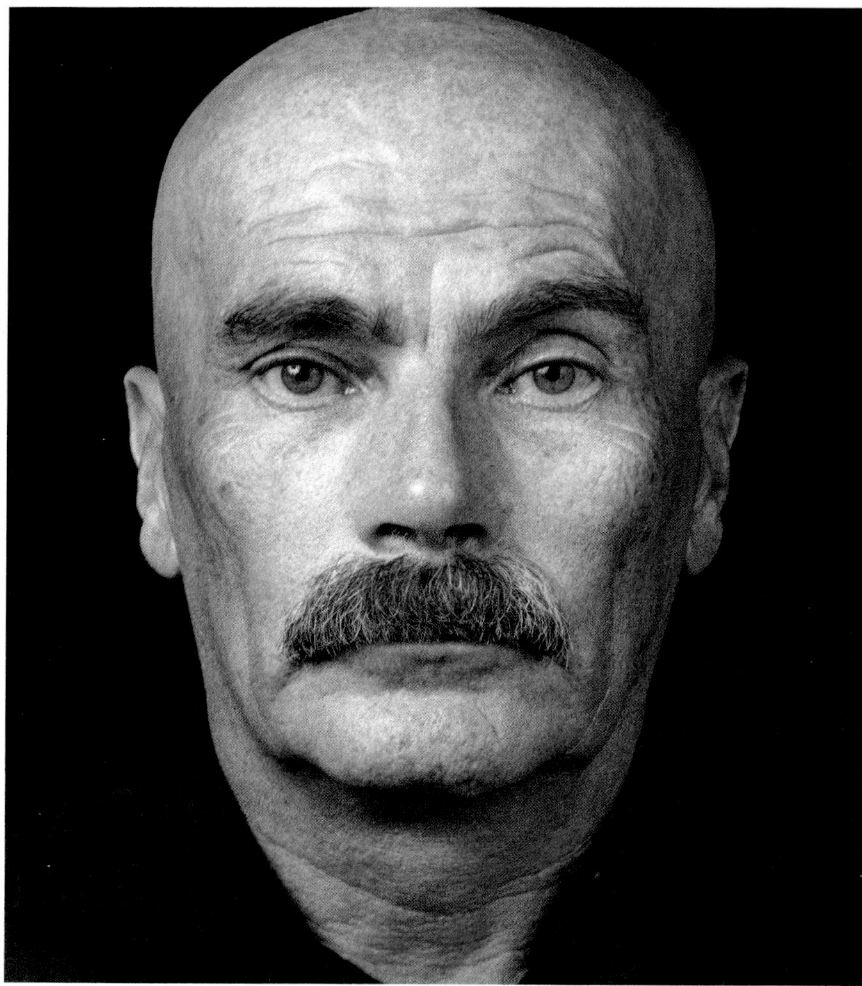

Skee Leeds, New York City: architectural designer; specializes in space analysis; inventor of multilevel carpeted environments

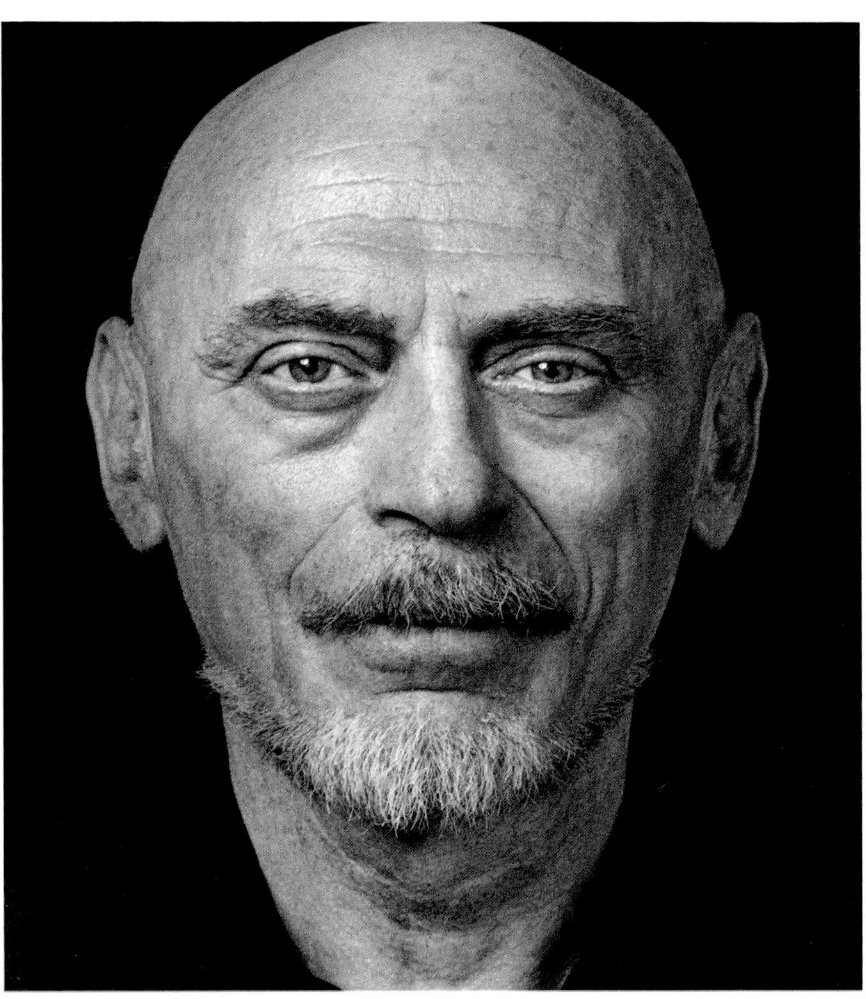

Harold Steinberg, New York City: founder, publisher, and writer, Chelsea House Publishing Co.

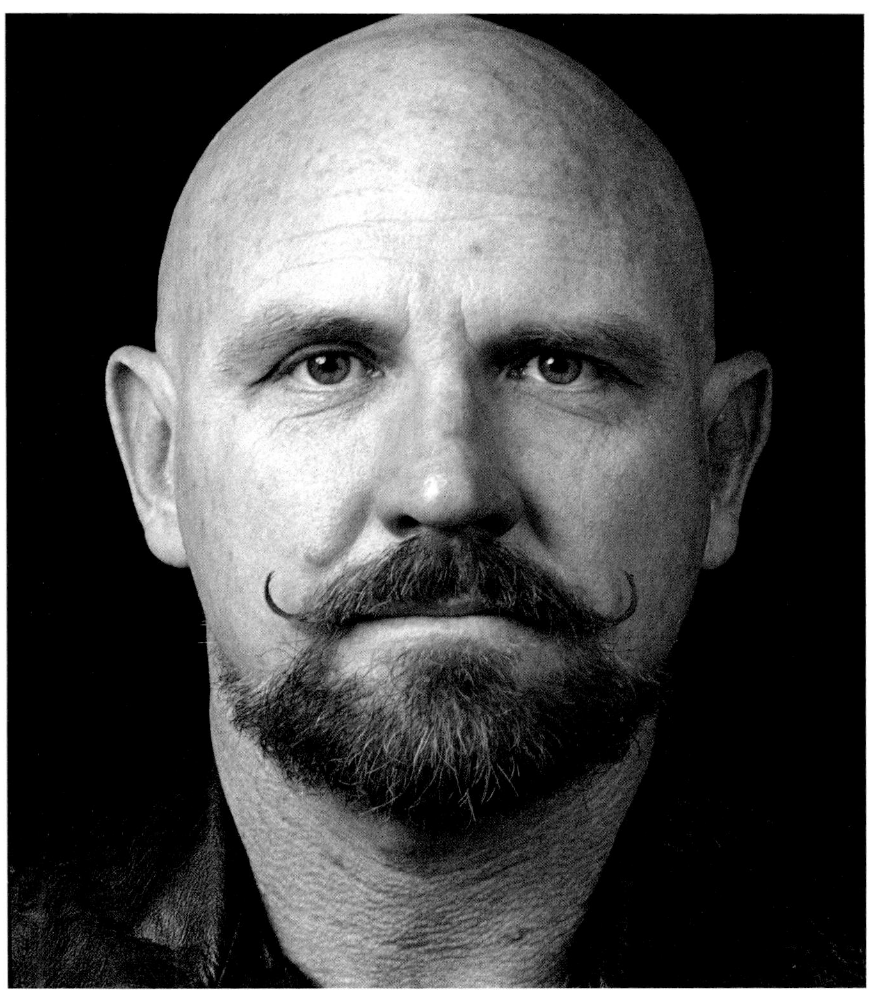

James K. Anderson, New York City: *United Nations Yearbook* editor

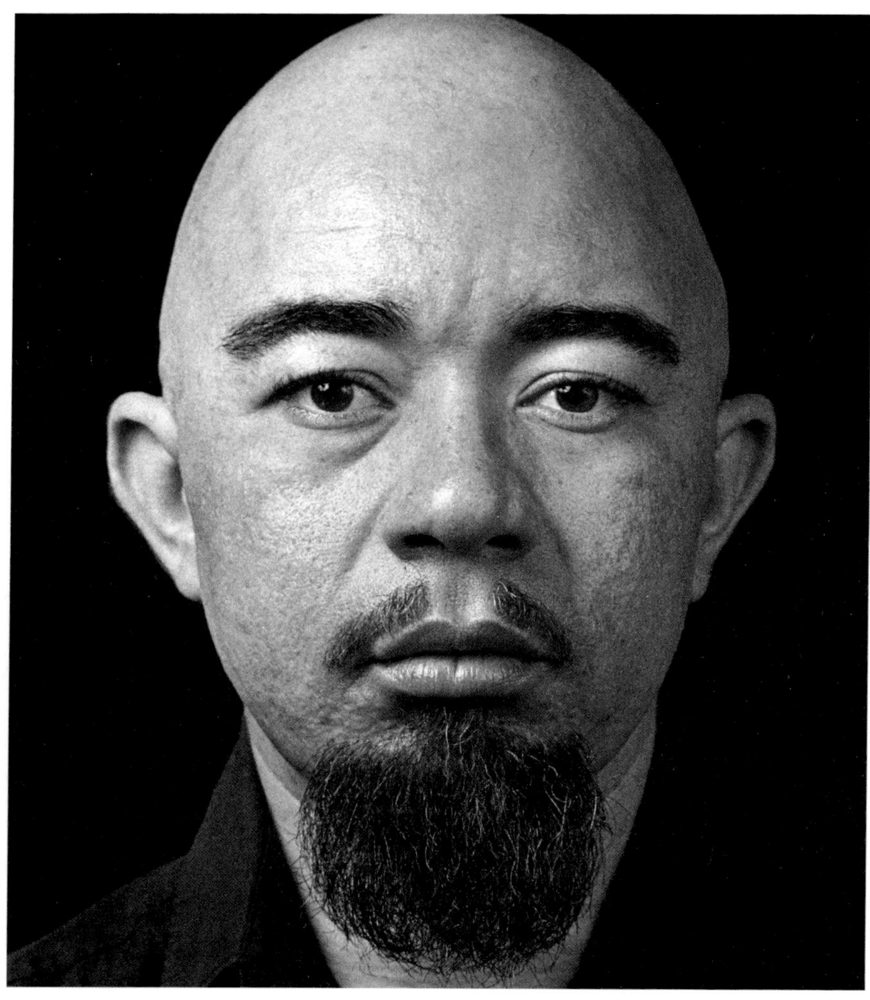

Jerome Shelton, New York City: photographer

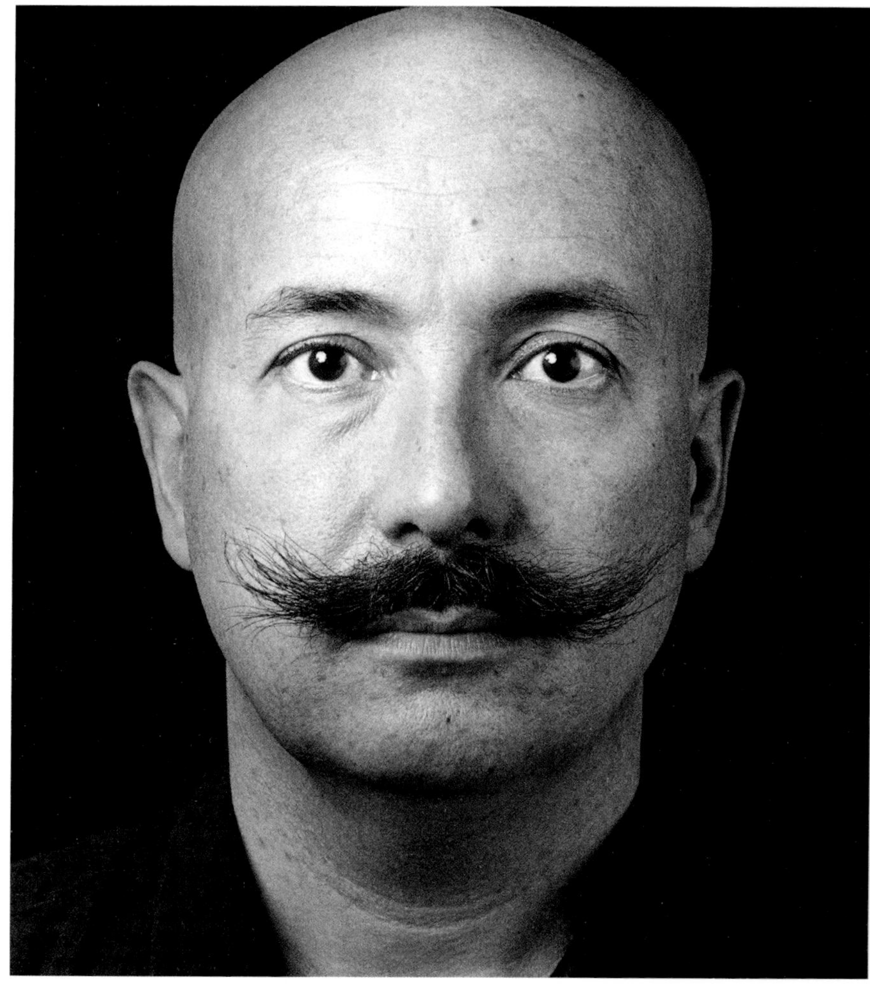

Rico Cardinaz, New York City: vice president of a large steel company

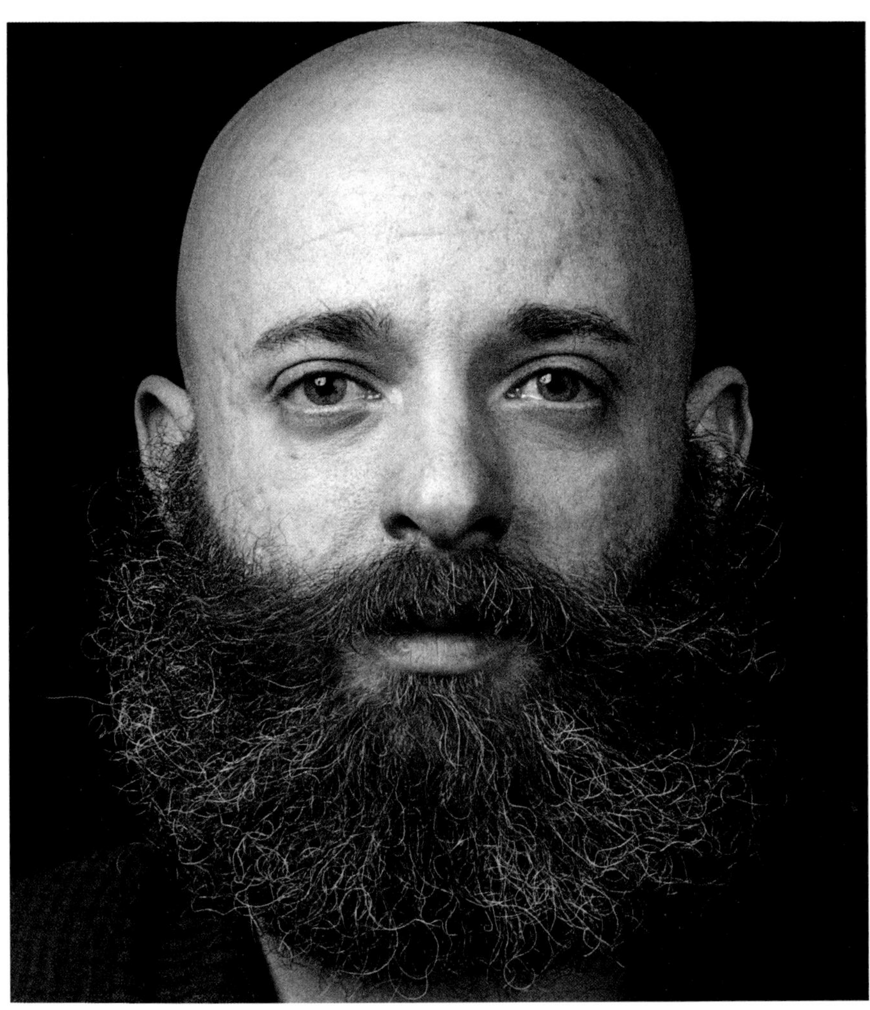

Art Hindin, New York City: antique dealer specializing in art deco and modernism; owner, Retro Modern

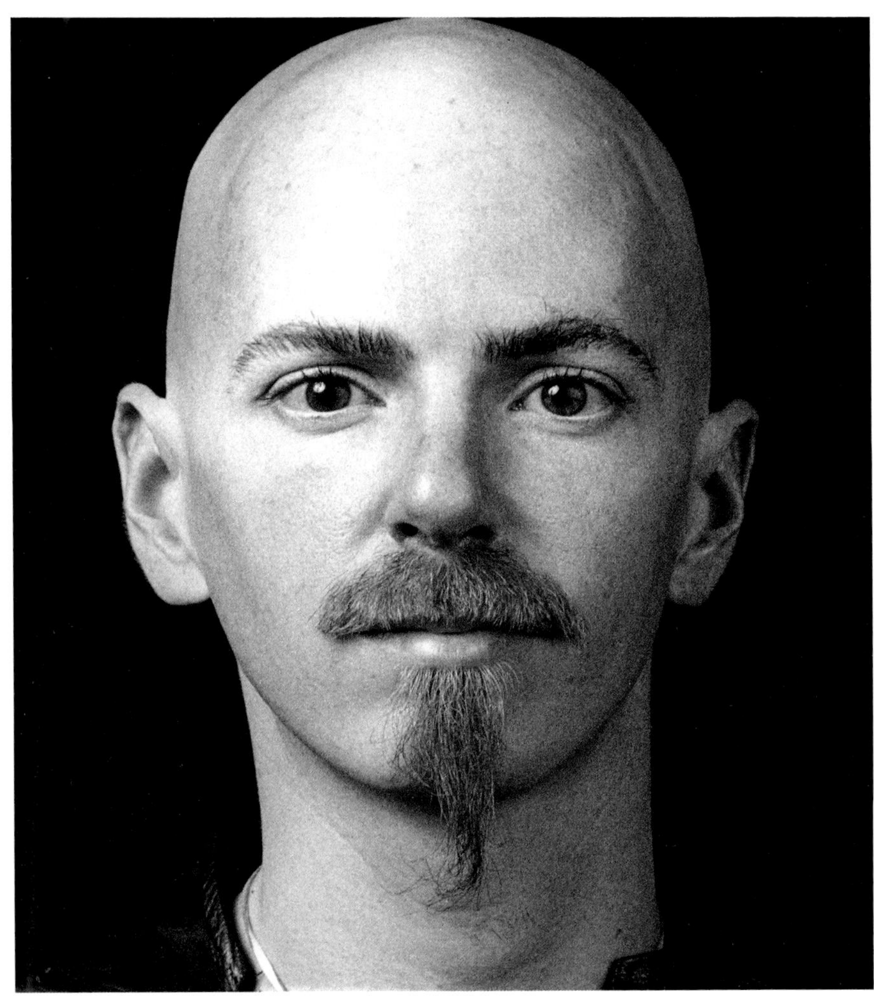

Gary Eller, New York City: mime artist

Afterword by Richard Howard

Nearly two hundred head shots of entirely bald subjects, almost all of them men, posed full face, head on, close up, in the manner of police line-ups, without stipulation as to expression or emotion (no one has said Cheese), the absolute condition of flesh against a featureless outer darkness: the series of photographs Alex Kayser has taken is a meditation upon the responsibility of forms. The form in question here, or rather the form responding, is that impulse of human identity we call the face, the visage, the countenance. In their etymologies, all three words suggest what the photographer's undertaking is to reveal, the made, the seen, the contained. Like so much else about ourselves—like our language, our food, our games—what we had thought was our nature is here revealed to be culture. Here the revelation is principally the effect of series art, which persuades us that each item in a set cannot admit the finality of any one member of that set. It is an art of erasure, in which each object or undertaking is superseded by a different version of itself. It has not arrived at or even acknowledged terminality. And because, by its inconclusive entertainment of the possible, this series of faces refuses narrative (or rather narrativity), because Kayser's photographs are inenarrable, they insist that our transaction with them is not "natural." It has none of the consecrated notions of beginning, middle, and end that are perceived to be the effects of biological life, as of stories. It is not nature here but choice, the assumptions and projections of culture, that produce their effect upon us. These faces are accountable for the way they look, for what they have in them. The beauty of these visages is a devised thing, not merely found but chosen, not merely chosen but invented, like—etymologically again—a poem, a fiction: something made.

But I speak too soon of the effect (the Beautiful) of these hypnotic images. In their formal insistence as Kayser has disposed them, none taking precedence over or leading up to the next (the sequence, although bound in a book, subject to your own progress or regress, shuffle and deal), they seduce us to generalization, they offer anthological proof. In the most abstract sense they *convince*. Indeed, the French call the identifying photographs of criminals produced in evidence or exhibited along with the murder weapon "*pièces à conviction*." Just so. But let me loiter a little by noticing first of all what it is that the invariable absence of hair—these individuals are not so much bald as they are hair-free—constrains us to remark. In English, of course, we have no separate word for hair of the head, no current word, although we have the poetical and archaic *tress*. We have no word that, like *cheveux*, suggests discrimination from body hair and, by its very reluctance to form the singular, proposes something of hair's generic nature. This is a pity, for hair is our physiological myth of gender, of sexuality, of ecstatic growth. The grim assurance that our hair *keeps growing* on our dead skulls betrays something of its separate, elemental, mineral quality (like our nails, our teeth, our bones). Our hair relates us, and not only by analogy, to the movement of water, of fire, of foliage, and of wind, pulsing undulating processes. Take away our hair and we are only human, mortal.

That is what these countenances present: the subtraction of hair, which in Western societies has been the readiest indicator of gender and in the governance of its wearing a clue to social docility or defiance. Without hair to tell us, we do not know much about the class of these persons Kayser has photographed. We cannot follow them into what used to be called their "walks of life." And upon continuous inspection, this inveterate feature—this having-no-hair—is perceived not as a lack but as means and likelihood of recognition. The perfect geometry of the cranial arch over the faces (of every age, of every race) paradoxically releases the countenance from its ordinary obeisances to fashion, to period, and brings us by the strange intensity of series art to a confrontation that must lead us to redefine what it is we mean by beauty.

Consider, as Paul Valéry used to say about a conch, a pebble, a wave-whitened bone, whether, in their absence, it would be possible to image forth—to invent—such faces, particularly in their juxtaposition, their endless *combinatoire*. Speaking as a creator, an artist, a sculptor, say, we might ask: Who could bring forth such things? And yet, speaking as a consumer, say a lover: Who could imagine them as other than they are? Is this not the spectacular beauty to which we are brought down or raised up? Unable to conceive of such things, we yet find them—once regarded—as inconceivable otherwise. It is, I think, the absolute presence of the photographed flesh and its pointed symmetry that accomplishes this for us, and the polarities of black and white camera work. In color, the incidentals would take over; the accidental nature of nature, so to speak, would prevail. But with only the symbolic oppositions of dark and light to work with, the promptings of shadow and the radiance of substance itself, we are lured to acknowledge much more readily the mathematical spell—if not of absolute black and absolute white, then of contrast between pale and dark, between bright and dim—that Renaissance artists and alchemists were always seeking to penetrate. We are lured to acknowledge the arithmetic of interval, the geometry of transition, the algebra of expressive analogy. The wars between singularity and parallelism are fought out on these fields, and the kind of abstraction that Kayser has invoked, has inveigled into his images by refusing to let his subjects *express themselves*, convinces me for the first time that the fascinating analogies of the visage with the genitals that Freud so outrageously proposed are here evident in their simplicity, without distortion, without the willful tugging of a Magritte or a Belmer. A centered singleness, a framing doubleness (regardless of gender) seems to be the bilateral essence of the face and of the reproductive body, the sexual self.

Further, the fact that all these faces are at first glance male (All? Are there not some deceptions, some refusals of our easy contraries? Are there not some women among these men?), male, yet without the signals of masculinity as a class society decrees them—faces without fashion beyond their own devising, jewelry and "facial hair" often of the most excruciating separateness—induces a further rumination on what the laws and license of pure gender might be. Notions of passivity and brutality, images of hardness and softness, of recession and advance are here reversed, flouted, and strangely erased. Surface and symbol exchange their customary positions, and the riddles of sexuality are proposed, proffered in a new way merely because of a simple radical alteration in the way we look at ourselves, time after time, head after head.

Certain correspondences of the exposed cranial arch with the chin, and the varying intervals of the zygomorphic frame around the mouth remind us here of what some news photographs of concentration camps and of shaved-headed collaborationists had hinted: that women look more like men than we had realized and that men look more like women. Or is it that in this artifice of abstraction both sexes approach a new framing of sexuality in which we shall have to reconceive what it is we want from the *other*? Do we want ourselves? Or perhaps the child, the *puer magicus* of the esoteric sciences? And are we ultimately appalled and repelled by precisely the beauty we cite in the transcendence of the accidental? That is, does our desire hang about the corners and crevices of perfection, unable to enter and act where it is displayed so elegantly, so ideally, so accurately? I am not teasingly withholding my solution, for I have none. I am merely prompted to these wonderments by the extraordinary *concordia discors* of all these pure masks, these pale apparitions on a nightmare ground.

And the final question to which Alex Kayser's series of photographs reduces or enlarges us is the matter of identity. (Is it a matter? Is it not, rather, the intersection, the collision, the subsidence of matters?) What is it that lets us, that makes us know a face? What can it be in the human countenance that enables the recognition of one out of a crowd of strangers? There are one or two celebrated visages among those in this book, and like as they are to the rest, we call out their names when we turn to their pages, as on the stairs of an opera house in some foreign city we call out the name when we recognize, among so many likenesses, one that is *unlike*, that is separate, singular—owned. But among these photographs, curiously enough, are so many samenesses, such congruence of form, that we finally wonder, as if by effect of the endless superimposition of transparencies, if the individuality of selfhood is not the greatest myth of all. Kayser's wonderful photographs make us wonder what we know about our looks and our looking. Are we known to each other (are we human) because we approach and fall away from the Beautiful? Are we beautiful because we are human? Or insofar as we are not? Surely the temptation of the total mask has not so much to do with secrecy (What is more accessible than even the most delicate of these lineaments?) as with an archetype of total sexuality, that magical image of the human enclosing and incarnating a self-nourishing desire. Not merely ourselves all over again and not merely the other, but perhaps what Frost meant when he said that what life wants

> Is not its own love back in copy speech
> But counter-love, original response.

Original response! The oxymoron thus reveals what the "facial mask," the face as fetish object, withholds and bestows by "giving itself away" in every sense. Only the camera, as I have suggested, can tell us such things; not our eyes, not the reality of the police line-up, the brothel selection. Consider the very word that governs these images, the word *bald*. When we refer to our National Bird, the bald eagle, we summon up that original sense of brightness, of shining, of "having a white head" that is also at the source of the word *black*. They both proceed from the Indo-European root *bhel*, what is burnt, bleak, and blinds us. That black and the bald, the white and the charred both have their roots in fire, the beginning of all things, as Heraclitus says. No accident then that we must develop a negative in order to have an image, that the blindness and the blaze, the blemish and the blank, all are reworkings of the one primal sound and scene, a blinding flash, a visionary impulse of delight.

Acknowledgments

With great thanks

to everybody who has helped make this project possible:

to all the models, who have given their precious time;

to Caty Monnier, Kate Isler, Alexandra Halász, Isabelle Schnyder, and Felicia Alexander, for their studio assistance;

to Susan Anderson, Felicia, and Barbara, for their printing;

to Lyn Mandelbaum and Alan Axelrod, for the conversation;

to Richard Howard, for the afterword;

to everybody who has brought suggestions and made introductions.